Jacob Mincer

IZA Prize in Labor Economics Series

Since 2002, the Institute for the Study of Labor (IZA) has awarded the annual IZA Prize in Labor Economics for outstanding contributions to policy-relevant labor market research and methodological progress in this sub-discipline of economic science. The IZA Prize is the only international science prize awarded exclusively to labor economists. This special focus acknowledges the global significance of high-quality basic research in labor economics and sound policy advice based on these research findings. As issues of employment and unemployment are among the most urgent challenges of our time, labor economists have an important task and responsibility. The IZA Prize in Labor Economics is today considered one of the most prestigious international awards in the field. It aims to stimulate further research on topics that have enormous implications for our future. All prize-winners contribute a volume to the IZA Prize in Labor Economic Series published by Oxford University Press, which has been established to provide an overview of the laureates' most significant findings.

The IZA Prize in Labor Economics has become an integral part of the institute's manifold activities to promote progress in labor market research. Based on nominations submitted by the IZA Research Fellows, a high-ranking IZA Prize Committee including several Nobel laureates selects the prize-winner. In conjunction with the official award ceremony, which takes place in Berlin each year, the IZA Prize Conference brings together a number of renowned experts to discuss topical labor market issues.

It is not by coincidence that the IZA Prize in Labor Economics Series is published by Oxford University Press. This well-reputed publishing house has shown a great interest in the project from the very beginning as this exclusive series perfectly complements their range of publications. We gratefully acknowledge their excellent cooperation.

Bonn, January 2007

Klaus F. Zimmermann
IZA Director

Winners of the IZA Prize in Labor Economics

2006 David Card, University of California, Berkeley, and Alan Krueger, Princeton University

2005 Dale Mortensen, Northwestern University, and Christopher Pissarides, London School of Economics

2004 Edward Lazear, Stanford University

2003 Orley Ashenfelter, Princeton University

2002 Jacob Mincer, Columbia University

Jacob Mincer 1922–2006

Jacob Mincer

A Founding Father of Modern Labor Economics

Pedro N. Teixeira

OXFORD
UNIVERSITY PRESS

HD
4901
.T45
2007

OXFORD
UNIVERSITY PRESS

Great Clarendon Street, Oxford ox2 6DP

Oxford University Press is a department of the University of Oxford.
It furthers the University's objective of excellence in research, scholarship,
and education by publishing worldwide in

Oxford New York

Auckland Cape Town Dar es Salaam Hong Kong Karachi
Kuala Lumpur Madrid Melbourne Mexico City Nairobi
New Delhi Shanghai Taipei Toronto

With offices in

Argentina Austria Brazil Chile Czech Republic France Greece
Guatemala Hungary Italy Japan Poland Portugal Singapore
South Korea Switzerland Thailand Turkey Ukraine Vietnam

Oxford is a registered trade mark of Oxford University Press
in the UK and in certain other countries

Published in the United States
by Oxford University Press Inc., New York

© IZA, 2007

The moral rights of the author have been asserted
Database right Oxford University Press (maker)

First published 2007

British Library Cataloguing in Publication Data

Data available

Library of Congress Cataloging in Publication Data

Data available

Typeset by SPI Publisher Services, Pondicherry, India
Printed in Great Britain
on acid-free paper by
Biddles Ltd., King's Lynn, Norfolk

ISBN 978–0–19–921131–9

1 3 5 7 9 10 8 6 4 2

Dedicated to the Memory of Jacob Mincer

Foreword

This first volume of the IZA Prize in Labor Economics Series is unique in many respects. It is the first comprehensive account of the lifetime achievement of the great pioneer in labor economics, Jacob Mincer, who won the first IZA Prize in 2002. The volume is authored by the Portuguese economist Pedro T. Teixeira, a veritable expert on Mincer and his work. Remarkably, Jacob Mincer was always available to the author for many enlightening discussions that made this exceptional volume possible. Depicting Mincer's varied research activities against the background of an eventful life, this book is a necessity for everyone interested in the development of what has become the standard toolset of today's labor economists.

After thoroughly preparing this important contribution, we are deeply saddened that Jacob Mincer did not live to see it published. At the age of 84, he passed away in his New York home on August 20, 2006. He will be sorely missed. But his extraordinary lifetime achievement, as described in this volume, will long be remembered.

Bonn, January 2007

Klaus F. Zimmermann
IZA Director

Award Letter

The IZA Prize in Labor Economics 2002 is awarded to one of the most influential labor economists of our time, Jacob Mincer (Professor Emeritus at Columbia University, New York), for his fundamental contributions to the field.

In a series of pioneering studies, Mincer showed the power of price theory in organizing and interpreting bewildering and apparently contradictory empirical evidence on differences in wages across persons and on patterns of female labor supply. His creative use of economic theory applied to interpret data on households and the labor market helped to transform labor economics into one of the major scientific fields in economics. His work is a paragon of empirical science in economics.

Jacob Mincer's scholarly contributions fall into two main categories. Mincer was a leading member of a group of economists at Columbia University and the University of Chicago who systematically developed the empirical foundations of human capital. His 1958 *Journal of Political Economy* article showed the power of the concept of equalizing differences in explaining earnings inequality due to education. His 1962 *Journal of Political Economy* paper presented the first systematic empirical analysis of learning on the job as a determinant of life cycle wage growth. His magisterial *Schooling, Experience and Earnings* (1974) showed the power of the human capital investment concept in accounting for diverse patterns of earnings inequality and wage growth over the life cycle. He demonstrated the empirical importance of complementarity in skill formation—that skill begets—skill and that more educated people do more post-schooling investment in learning. This research established the Mincer earnings function as a widely used and widely replicated cornerstone for interpreting earnings data in many fields of economics. His subsequent work on job turnover, on the measurement of firm specific training, on investment responses to technology change and in accounting for the recent rise in wage inequality within an economic framework, enrich the basic model and show its analytical and empirical power.

Jacob Mincer also pioneered the study of female labor supply and the economics of the household. His seminal 1962 paper on the labor supply of married women showed that accounting for the influence of the price of time on labor—the market wage—explains why female labor supply increased at the same time real wealth of society was increasing. That work, and a subsequent 1963 paper, showed the importance of accounting for the household choices women face in explaining female labor supply and fertility. This research helped to foster the emergence of household economics as a separate independent field. Mincer's insights on labor supply, human capital and fertility helped lay the foundations for understanding how economic development transforms the role of women and the family.

Professor Mincer also played a major role in transforming labor economics into an analytical field through his teaching and his participation in the legendary Labor Workshop at Columbia University. Led and inspired by Jacob Mincer the students and faculty associated with that workshop went on to revolutionize labor economics.

Jacob Mincer is the founding father of modern empirical labor economics. His efforts in developing the scientific instruments and methods used by today's economists to analyze the problems and prospects of the working world are almost unparalleled. The IZA Prize in Labor Economics 2002 honors the life-time achievement of an outstanding scholar and pioneer in labor market research.

George A. Akerlof	University of California, Berkeley
Gary S. Becker	University of Chicago
James J. Heckman	University of Chicago
Gerard Pfann	Maastricht University
Klaus F. Zimmermann	IZA and University of Bonn

Preface

This book originated through a kind offer by IZA to write a book that could provide a general and comprehensive overview of the richness and complexity of Jacob Mincer's lifetime contribution to economic analysis. IZA's generous invitation provided me with a unique opportunity to pursue my long-time interest in Mincer's work. Back in 1997, I became interested in studying the historical roots and development of human capital research (Teixeira 2000) and started to explore the fascinating work of Jacob Mincer. My interest in studying the development of the human capital research program became the central theme of my doctoral dissertation (Teixeira 2003), which I finished in June 2003 at the University of Exeter, under the supervision of Mark Blaug and John Maloney. During my doctoral research I decided that it would be a good idea to talk to some of the leading academics who had launched that research program. When I first contacted Jacob Mincer, he kindly provided me with valuable answers concerning his work and his role in the development of human capital theory. During those interviews I became aware of the conference that was being prepared by several former students and colleagues in honor of Jacob Mincer on the occasion of his 80th birthday and was extremely fortunate to attend the conference and to meet and interview the late Jacob Mincer (for the final result of that interview see Teixeira 2006).

I am sure that this book is an unfinished project that I could still improve in many ways. I would have continued it for many years had it not been for the sake of a deadline (I guess this is the purpose of deadlines). I am sure that I will continue to delve into Mincer's intellectual achievements, and I hope that this book will stimulate others to do the same.

In the preparation of this book I benefited from the help and generosity of many people without whom its successful conclusion would not have been possible.

First and foremost, I would like to honour the memory of the late Jacob Mincer. I had just finished revising the manuscript of the book when I learned the sad news of his passing. Although we have only met a few years ago, I will always keep a vivid recollection of my interaction with him. During the last years, I have learned that Jacob was not only an outstanding economist and scholar, but also a fascinating and kind person. His memory will certainly endure through his important work, but his presence will be sorely missed. I would also like to express my deep gratitude and admiration for Flora Mincer. She has provided me with tremendous help and friendly support. I feel honoured to have interacted with both of them and I sincerely hope that this work does justice to Jacob's intellectual achievements.

I would like to express my gratitude to IZA and especially to its director, Klaus Zimmermann, for having asked me to write this book. Under his leadership, IZA has become a prestigious and dynamic research center and a major platform for the international community of labor researchers. I congratulate them for their initiative in creating the prize in labor economics and especially for awarding it in the first place to Jacob Mincer. I am grateful to several of the staff members of IZA, especially Holger Hinte for his kind and efficient handling of this project.

I would like to thank Barry Chiswick. Barry was one of the first human capital pioneers I interviewed and since then he has often provided me with crucial support in my human capital studies. It was also due to his intervention that I attended the conference in honor of Jacob Mincer. Last but not least, Barry read carefully a draft version of this manuscript and provided me with extensive and most valuable comments that have significantly improved the text.

I am deeply grateful to Roger Backhouse, who for many years has been providing me with his unique generosity and intellectual guidance. Roger was a patient and helpful listener and reader during the many stages of this project and he has provided me with detailed and careful comments and suggestions. It is a privilege to count him as a colleague and friend.

During the gestation of this book, other research commitments provided me with the opportunity to be a visiting scholar at the Center for Studies in Higher Education, University of California, Berkeley (spring 2005) and a visiting professor at the Department of Educational Administration and Policy Studies, the State University of New York, Albany (summer 2006). On both occasions I was welcomed into truly congenial research environments. I am extremely grateful to both institutions for their hospitality and to several people in both universities for generously spending time with me discussing my work. At Berkeley, I would like to thank Brad DeLong, Anne MacLachlan, John Douglass, and Marion Fourcade-Gourinchas. At Albany, I would like to express my gratitude to Alan Wagner and Daniel Levy. A special word of gratitude is due to Rui Pedro Esteves, whose hospitality and friendship made the months spent in Berkeley truly memorable. For my research visit to Berkeley, I was financially supported by CEMPRE the Department of Economics, University of Porto, and the Gulbenkian Foundation. On my stay in Albany, I benefited from being part of the New Century Scholars Program 2005–6 and the enormous generosity of the Fulbright Commission and the Council for International Exchange of Scholars.

Throughout this work, as in all the previous chapters of my academic career, I have been counting on the support and friendship of several colleagues. At my home institution, the Department of Economics of the University of Porto, I am particularly grateful to António Almodovar, Maria de Fátima Brandão, Sofia Castro and Helena Santos. I am also very grateful to CIPES and its director, Alberto Amaral.

I thank Di Davies for her patient and efficient editing of the manuscript. She succeeded in the terrible task of turning my often incomprehensible English style into something clear and readable. I also thank the helpful and kind staff at Oxford University Press.

During the development of this project my life has changed in many ways and once again I felt how generous life has been to me. I thank my family, my friends, and God for being there always, especially when I needed them most.

Contents

Contents

List of Tables

1

Introduction

Although Jacob Mincer is one of the most important economists of the second half of the twentieth century, whose work had tremendous importance for contemporary economics, especially labor economics, little work has been done on his lifetime contribution to economic science.[1] This is surprising because Mincer played a very significant role in shaping contemporary labor economics, not the least by largely determining its research agenda. His work in the sixties and seventies on the determinants of individual earnings (notably human capital) and on labor force supply (especially female participation) as well as more recently with his research on job mobility (cf. Rosen 1992) has had an enormous impact on the way others have approached labor economics.

Fortunately, there are signs that things may be starting to change and there is a growing appreciation of the importance of Mincer's contribution to labor economics. In 2002, IZA decided to create a prize for lifetime achievement in labor economics and awarded it to Mincer. In that same year a conference was held in Mincer's honor on the occasion of his 80th birthday, with the contributions to the conference being recently published (Grossbard 2006). In 2004, the Society of Labor Economists created a career achievement award for lifetime contributions to the field of labor economics and awarded it in its first year to Jacob Mincer and Gary Becker. The prize was later renamed the Mincer Award. Thus, recent years have seen growing efforts to express the discipline's appreciation for Mincer's work.

The main purpose of this book is to contribute to those efforts in promoting a better understanding of Mincer's work and its relevance to the development of contemporary economics. The book aims at providing a comprehensive and detailed presentation of Mincer's lifetime research. This will be done by an analysis of his extensive published work, emphasizing its continuity as a lifetime research program that irreversibly shaped modern labor economics. This analysis will also aim at highlighting the main theoretical and methodological traits that individualize his research. This initial chapter starts by providing a brief biographical sketch of Mincer and then presents an outline of the remaining book.

1.1. A Brief Portrait of Jacob Mincer[2]

Jacob Mincer was born in Tomaszow (Poland) on 15 July 1922 to Dvora and Yitzchak Mincer.[3] He had two sisters: Karolina, two years older, and Fryda, five years younger. The family lived in the house of his paternal grandfather with several other family members. His mother's parents lived a short walk from them. The Mincer and Lederkremer families had settled in Tomaszow before the nineteenth century and both were prominent families in town. At that time Jews represented around 10 percent of the Polish population. Most of them would see their lives tragically disrupted by World War II and the events that preceded it.

From an early age, Jacob gave signs of his thirst for knowledge. He decided to learn to read at 4 years of age. This was stimulated by the fact that his older sister went to public school and he was eager to be able to read those nice books full of beautiful pictures that she brought home. With her help he kept up with her and, before his fifth birthday, he was reading fluently and tried to convince his parents to allow him to start school, though the minimum age of entry was seven. As it happened, the director of the school was a friend of his father's and, impressed by Mincer's ability to read the newspaper, he promised to enroll him as long as his birth certificate stated that his year of birth was 1920 rather than 1922. Thus, Mincer's official papers show him to be two years older than his actual age. The terrible events which occurred some years later proved this to be of tremendous significance. Because he enrolled in school two years earlier, Mincer was able to start university earlier and escape the dreadful fate of most of his family members.

Mincer's fondest recollections of his early school days are the many hours spent at the public library exploring the fascinating world of fairytales. Besides the voracious reading of books, he became addicted to the radio, which stimulated his interest in music and politics. After Jacob finished sixth grade, he applied for high school admission. This required a rather stiff entrance examination. Despite the fact that he applied to a state-run high school, tuition was quite costly, and sending more than one child to high school was a heavy burden on the average family. Both examinations and tuition were a way of rationing high school enrollment, as well as an easy way of imposing a quota limiting the proportion of Jewish students to about 10 percent, the same as their overall representation in Poland. Despite the fact that admission policies restricted the number of Jews in high school, Mincer did not remember encountering anti-Semitism at school, with the exception of sporadic misbehavior by a few pupils. His high school had an emphasis on arts, literature, geography, history, and languages. He was an exceptional student in history and mathematics, to which he owes his lasting interest in reading historical novels and discussing politics with his father.

Throughout his high school years, both the international situation and the domestic Jewish situation kept deteriorating. In 1933, a year after Mincer started high school, Hitler became chancellor of Germany. As fascism spread in Europe, it grew in Poland, and anti-Semitic measures became governmental policy, especially after 1935. All kinds of educational and economic restrictions proliferated. Although Jews could apply for admission to universities, the restrictions were even more severe than for high school admission. Entrance examinations were used as a way of restricting Jewish applicants, so the chances of being accepted were minimal. Knowing this, some Jewish graduates applied to universities abroad, but most countries were not eager to grant visas to Polish Jews, fearing they would not want to return to Poland after they completed their studies. Moreover, it was costly. Mincer's father was willing to finance his studies abroad, thus he applied to the School of Engineering in Lvov (nowadays Ukraine) and to universities in Czechoslovakia (Brno), Italy, and Denmark. Anti-Jewish restrictions were in place in Italy at the time, so he was rejected there. Denmark was not eager, either. He went to Lvov for the entrance examination, but was rejected even though he was sure he had correctly answered virtually all the questions. Hence, he went for the only alternative that accepted him, Brno in Czechoslovakia.

Mincer went to university in Brno in the autumn of 1938 without the slightest notion that he would never see his family again.

The political situation was becoming increasingly complicated and dangerous in Czechoslovakia as well. In the spring of 1938, after Hitler marched into Austria (which became part of Nazi Germany), the Nazis started a campaign against Czechoslovakia. They demanded that the Czech region of Sudeten (where half of the four million inhabitants were Germans) be turned over to Germany. The Czechs refused and hoped for support from their Western allies. The help did not materialize and the Western powers accepted that Nazi Germany took control of the Sudeten. The Czech government resigned and a new government, which accommodated the Germans, was installed in Prague. During the winter a new crisis broke out and Slovak nationalists, with the help of the Nazis, separated from the Czechs by declaring Slovak independence at the beginning of 1939. German propaganda depicted the remaining Czech Republic as a nonviable entity that needed to be protected by the German Reich and, eventually, by March 1939, German troops invaded turning it into a Protectorate under Nazi dominion.

Jacob Mincer's first impulse was to pack up and go home but he followed his father's advice and decided to stay to finish his first academic year provided the situation did not change. However, change it did. In the spring, the Nazis started a campaign of demands on Poland to cede the Polish parts of eastern Prussia, including the city of Danzig (nowadays Gdansk). Some months later, in September, Hitler invaded Poland which precipitated the eruption of World War II as England and France entered the war. Thus, Mincer's attempts to travel home were doomed to fail since now all transportation to Poland was stopped as troops massed on both sides of the border.

By June 1940, Hitler had gained control of most of Western Europe—Norway, Denmark, Belgium, Holland, and France—in less than two months. After the German invasion of Russia, Mincer was not only without protection, but also in mortal danger both as a Jew and as an enemy alien (his hometown had become Russian territory after the partition of Poland between Nazi Germany and Stalin's Russia). Eventually he was arrested in 1941 by the Gestapo, the Nazi secret police, and spent three months in jail. In 1942, the Jewish situation in Brno became critical. Deportations to ghettos or concentration camps in Poland began in earnest and accelerated in the summer. Mincer was again arrested in July 1942 and placed in a large detention center in Brno, enduring severe physical and psychological conditions. By April 1942, he and other prisoners were taken to Wulzburg, a detention camp in south-east Germany. Finally, and after three long years of tremendous suffering, by April 1945, his group was liberated by the Russian army.

Though Mincer was anxious about his family's wellbeing, he wanted to find out what happened to them. As going to Poland would be risky and futile, he decided that the safest move would be to return to Czechoslovakia and find out from people there about the situation in Poland, as well as try to contact his relatives in South Africa and Palestine. The possibility of continuing his studies was also in the back of his mind. In Brno, Mincer found out that, as a student imprisoned during the war, he was entitled to complete his studies at the Czech government's expense. Although he registered at the university in Brno to restart his studies, he was increasingly dissatisfied with his situation and determined to leave Europe.

Eventually, Mincer went to Nurnberg (Germany) and started working for the American army in a special branch of counterintelligence dealing with Nazis and war criminals. During those years of temporary residence in postwar Germany, Mincer was reunited with some relatives and friends each of whom had disturbing stories of survival: Nazi camps, the Gulag, partisans in the forest, being hidden by non-Jewish friends, assuming false nationalities, etc. Although each person's story was different, the experiences they described became increasingly familiar in subsequent years through the Holocaust literature. Some years later, looking back at those tragic times, Mincer recalled that his high school uniforms in Poland included a cap with the Latin inscription *per aspera ad astra* (through hardship to the stars). He thought that this inscription turned out to be mildly prophetic, but *aspera* (hardship) was a huge understatement of things to come, and *astra* (stars), real as they turned out to be, were dimmed by the preceding tragedy.

Very little is known about Mincer's political opinions. Although his family and closest friends knew of his strong, and not always predictable, political views, it is noticeable that throughout his research career, Mincer aimed at keeping a clear separation between his research and his political ideas. One cannot avoid wondering to what extent this was due to the dramatic experience of World War II. He certainly had a good political intuition as shown by his decision, in 1945, to go to Western Europe, and leave Czechoslovakia, despite the immediate lure of economic security and resumption of education in

Brno. This was, in good part, due to his encounters with the Soviets in Brno.

Mincer was determined to leave Europe. Early in 1946 he was able to make contact with some relatives in South Africa about the possibility of joining them, but was turned down by the British High Commissioner for South Africa since only parents, children, or siblings were being admitted. In the meantime, through his boss (who took an interest in his situation), Mincer became aware of the possibility of obtaining a scholarship to study in the USA. These scholarships, available to Jewish students, were a project of the Hillel Foundation (based in New York), and part of a project launched in 1938, after a suggestion by Albert Einstein to the head of the Foundation, Abram Sachar. Mincer attended an interview and a month later received a letter of acceptance from New York, though it took two years until he received a visa. The delay was due to the refusal of the State Department to grant temporary student visas to people who were stateless and who would obviously not want to return to Europe after completion of their studies.

Eventually, in the middle of July, he traveled by ocean liner to the USA. The journey took ten days and Mincer still recalls the excitement when the passengers saw the lights of New York Harbor and the view of the Statue of Liberty in the early hours of 26 July 1946. Although all passengers disembarked after a check by the immigration officials, Mincer was stopped and taken to Ellis Island, which had become a deportation center for illegal aliens. He was told that they had to check the authenticity of his papers, as they had never heard of Emory University. Fortunately, the next day they came with the good news that Emory was 'alive and well', and that, indeed, he was registered there. After instructions from Hillel, he left by train for Atlanta (Georgia).

After all those years of hardship, Mincer was starting a new life in the USA. It would be tempting at this stage to speculate on the impact that those terrible years had on Jacob Mincer's academic career and research interests. Apparently, Mincer did this himself. Some years ago, when asked in a private conversation at a conference how he came up with the important insight regarding the distinction between age and experience, he replied that it was based on his life experience. It was clear to those listening to that conversation that he meant the years he lost during the Holocaust.[4]

Surely, those years left an indelible mark on his personality, though it is impossible to discern how much this affected his research. Since the temptation of intellectual history to perform a psychoanalysis of research careers more often than not ends up in delusion and mistake, we prefer to stop here and leave to the readers to draw their own conclusions.

Before the war, Mincer had started studying engineering due to his special interest in applied mathematics. However, after the war, he did not feel motivated to return to engineering because he thought that the social sciences held more promise for the future. To a certain extent he blamed technology and technological progress for much of the ordeal of World War II and this made him look to the social sciences, which he found not only interesting but even somehow entertaining. Within social sciences he became particularly interested in economics, because of its structured content and because of his idiosyncratic inclination toward mathematics.[5]

At Emory, one of his professors, Ernst Swanson, who had earned a Ph.D. in economics from the University of Chicago, advised him to pursue his graduate studies there, because of the possibility of interacting with Milton Friedman. Swanson told Mincer to apply as well to Columbia, in this case not so much because of the faculty but because of the Department of Economics' strong links with the National Bureau of Economic Research (NBER), and the possibilities that would open for him to do real empirical work.

In fact, Mincer did both after he graduated from Emory in 1950. He went first to Chicago to do graduate work, though Milton Friedman was on sabbatical that year. During this time at Chicago he met his future wife. The main reason Mincer moved to Columbia in 1951 to continue his Ph.D. was that Flora Mincer was offered a job in New York. After he moved to New York City, one of the first things he did was visit the NBER to try to get involved in research there. He was initially hired as a research assistant to Ruth Mack, who was studying business cycles, and this allowed him to meet several other economists. One of them was Bill Greenwald, who taught at the City College, and who, some time later, offered Mincer a teaching position. Mincer became an instructor at the City College during the final years of his doctoral studies (1954–6), thus beginning his long and prolific academic career.

When Mincer arrived at Columbia in the early fifties, the Department of Economics was still largely influenced by institutionalism and, although he tried various courses, the ones that appealed to him most were theoretically based. Of all the members of the department, the people who made a strong impression on him were George Stigler and Arthur Burns, whom he recognized as great teachers. He became closer to Stigler when he was writing his dissertation, though Stigler did not have any direct influence on Mincer's work during that period. Mincer had very limited training in labor economics and, although he attended some of the classes taught by Leo Wolman (who was interested in studying the activities of labor unions), he felt that too much attention was paid to the historical aspects of the labor market and lost interest. In fact, when Mincer decided the topic of his dissertation, he did not think of it as labor economics but as price theory.

It can be argued that Mincer's Ph.D. dissertation was the first systematic contribution to the emergence of human capital theory because of its analysis of the contribution of schooling and training in explaining the current distribution of income and its evolution over time.[6] The study of income distribution was one of the aspects that stimulated economists' interest in education and the use of human capital. By the time Mincer was developing his doctoral work, research on personal income had come a long way since the early debates on Pareto's law. Although there was still some support for the Paretian view that income distribution was highly stable, the significant improvements in the statistics available had created several problems for the Paretian approach and undermined most of its support. It was in this context of growing statistical evidence on income distribution and a stronger appetite for the analysis of causality links between income distribution and socioeconomic characteristics that Mincer developed his doctoral work.

Columbia University occupies a central place in Mincer's academic career, and many of his intellectual affinities are related to this institution. It was at Columbia, as a graduate student, that he developed a lasting admiration for George Stigler (Mincer 1993a) that would influence his research approach and methodological stance. Mincer (1983a) regarded Stigler's work as an attempt at interaction between past achievements and modern attempts of economic theory, based on an idea of continuity and cumulative progress of economic knowledge. Inspired and stimulated by the pioneering efforts of authors like Smith and Marshall, it was the task of the economist to pursue further several of his topics of analysis, correcting and complementing them where necessary with the achievements of modern economic research, notably the development of the modern theory of price and markets and its application to real-life economic problems.

Mincer also admired in Stigler what he would call operationalism in economic analysis. By operationalism Mincer understood the attempt to establish a basic framework of economic theory as a tool of research, defining testable hypotheses, and testing them. This was what Mincer called the 'empirical thrust of the scientific revolution in economics' (1983a: 74), and he considered it to have been pioneered by Stigler in terms of price theory. Underpinning this scientific practice was a philosophical stance not so much concerned with 'the achievement of mathematical precision in modelling or of rigor in the methods of statistical description, each of which is important, but the use of economic theory to produce statistical hypotheses and to test them' (1983a: 74–5).

Several of these aspects are usually presented as important characteristics of Mincer's work as well. On the one hand, there is the application of price theory to labor economics, a field previously dominated by an approach much closer to institutionalism. In that sense Mincer is regarded as a crucial figure in modernizing or *mainstreaming* labor economics. On the other hand, he is recognized by his enduring emphasis on the development of empirically testable theories. This empirical emphasis was reflected in his persistent use of the latest data-sets. Whereas the discipline tended to be seduced by very sophisticated econometric procedures, Mincer tended to distance himself from these developments by considering them as negative by-products of poor and insufficient data (Bloom and Siow 1993). This has led many to admire his work due to the balanced blend of theory and empirical (testable) research.

After finishing his Ph.D. in 1957 at Columbia, Mincer moved back to Chicago to a postdoctoral fellowship, staying there during the 1957/8 academic year. His sponsor at Columbia was Harold Barger who was aware that Schultz, at that time Head of the Economics Department at the University of Chicago, was interested in human capital issues. It was Barger who sent a draft of Mincer's dissertation to Chicago, which led to Mincer being invited to accept a postdoctoral fellowship there. Apparently Mincer was not aware of Schultz's work at that time, mainly because they had different focuses. Schultz's interests were economic growth, development, and agriculture, while Mincer's were inequality and income distribution. However, they soon realized there was a kind of complementarity between analyzing human capital at the macro and micro level.

At Chicago, Mincer was advised to attend the Labor Workshop, which was led by Gregg Lewis. Gregg Lewis told him that what he was doing was labor economics, and Mincer, bearing in mind what he had seen at Columbia, felt very uncomfortable with this. Moreover, labor economics did not have a very high reputation among many mainstream economists because traditionally it had been very eclectic, and many of its practitioners had an apparent disdain for economics. However, at Chicago he attended Gregg Lewis's course and found it very different from the type of labor economics he had encountered thus far. It was particularly appealing to him that Lewis was trying to apply price theory to labor issues, something unusual at that time in labor research. It was at this time he started his research on the labor participation of women. Mincer then returned for another brief spell to the City College of New York, as assistant professor (1958–60), and finally in 1960 he joined the Faculty of Economics at Columbia as an associate professor. He would develop most of his career at Columbia, becoming a full professor in 1962 and Buttenwieser Professor of Economics in 1979; and he has been an emeritus professor since 1991.[7]

It was also at Columbia that Mincer developed a very fruitful professional interaction with Gary Becker who had moved to Columbia in the late fifties (1958). Neither of them regarded themselves, at least initially, as labor economists, but they joined forces and started the Columbia Workshop on Labor Economics. They were aware they were doing something very different from most other labor researchers, but on the other hand they were convinced they were deeply influencing the subject. The two main issues were labor supply and human capital, which they tried to apply to a variety of topics. This interaction between Mincer and Becker would be crucial in shaping the future path of this field, and of human capital in particular, making it sometimes difficult to disentangle the contribution of each to the topic of their common interest. By the late sixties, Becker had left Columbia and moved back to Chicago. Although they remained close friends with very similar intellectual interests, the intensity of their intellectual interaction was certainly more limited.

That the sixties became a crucial period for the development of human capital and modern labor economics is largely due to the close interaction between Gary Becker and Jacob Mincer. They started the Labor Workshop primarily to give students the opportunity to present their work in progress and to stimulate discussion. Many of these students were being supervised by both Mincer and Becker and the workshop became a magnet for many future eminent labor economists. Their meetings at the Labor Workshop continued during most of the week due to their close collaboration also at the NBER. The interaction was so intense that, looking back, Becker reminisced, 'it is hard to know what was his contribution and what was mine. We were engaged together in an exploration, an intellectual venture' (Becker 2006: 23).

Mincer's interaction with Schultz, Gregg Lewis, and Becker also stimulated him to pursue further the role of human capital, especially in determining personal distribution of income. This was apparent in his next contribution to human capital research, presented at the NBER conference of 1961 (Mincer 1962*a*) where he considered the need to avoid placing all the emphasis on formal schooling. Rather, it was important to attach more significance to postschool training and to consider this in a broader perspective (including formal and informal training, and learning from experience). His various estimates of the rates of return to some training activities showed similar results and presented values comparable to those obtained from college education, as well as a positive association between schooling and on-the-job training (Mincer 1962*a*: 73).

Mincer remained at Columbia until his retirement and continued to influence several generations of labor economists through his continued interest in human capital topics. This influence was enhanced by Mincer's ability to develop research work in a collaborative way with his former students or younger colleagues. Several important aspects of his work were the result of close collaboration with his students. In this respect it is worthwhile mentioning his work on income distribution with Barry Chiswick and his research on interruption of labor careers with Solomon Polachek and Haim Ofek.

In the meantime, Mincer also developed a significant part of his research activity at the NBER, in close cooperation with Gary Becker. It should be noted that at that time the NBER had only one office, located in mid-town Manhattan, that drew upon economists from the entire New York metropolitan area. This contributed to make the NBER, during most of the sixties and seventies, the center of a network of researchers interested in human capital topics. This network was nurtured by Becker's and Mincer's graduate students at Columbia, their research assistants at the NBER (who included many graduate students), and several other researchers who came to the NBER due to their interest in developing new applications of the expanding human capital research program. Mincer eventually became the coordinator of the NBER Labor Research Program and, through his activities, left an indelible mark on its activities and on many generations of labor researchers that passed through the NBER.

It was at the NBER that Mincer developed one of his major pieces of research: his book *Schooling, Experience, and Earnings* (1974a). This was a major subsequent contribution to human capital research and to the study of on-the-job training that attempted to update the data developed in his Ph.D. dissertation and to extend the empirical assessment of human capital by measuring the contribution of postschool investments. According to Mincer, these investments had not only an important effect on lifetime earnings but also an important effect on the explanatory power of the model. His lifetime attention to the impact of training activities led him to carry out pioneering work on estimating its rates of return. In the sixties and seventies, because complete data were not available, he did this indirectly and, in the eighties, with the significant improvements in data-sets, he pioneered its direct estimates.

Mincer played no minor role in the theoretical and methodological reshaping of labor research. When Mincer started his academic career, by the end of the fifties, labor economics was becoming a very different subject from what it had previously been. From an earlier heterogeneous field, labor was increasingly connected with (neoclassical) economic theory, though there remained issues as to how much could be achieved along this path. Neoclassical researchers were calling for the use of neoclassical micro theory for analyzing labor markets. By the early sixties, most labor economists opted to endorse a neoclassical approach, and it was neoclassical economics that had taken the reins of the field in terms of its research agenda. Labor economics became much more a part of economics and less heterodox in its approach. This evolution of labor research was very important for the development of human capital theory.

Despite his well-known discretion, Mincer was awarded several honors throughout his career that recognized the relevance of his work to economics and social sciences in general. These included a Distinguished Fellowship of the American Economic Association (AEA) in 1989, an honorary degree from the University of Chicago in 1991, and the first IZA Prize in Labor Economics in 2002. He is a fellow of the American Statistical Association (since 1967) and a member of the National Academy of Education (since 1974), which demonstrate not only his broad interests but also the relevance of his research to a large and multidisciplinary community of scholars. In 2000 he has been elected to the National Academy of Sciences, one of the highest academic honors in the USA. He would pass away on the 20th August 2006, after a long and notable career.

1.2. Structure of the Book

Jacob Mincer is rightly regarded as one of the pioneers of human capital research, and the leading figure of its dissemination in labor research. This book substantiates these claims. Moreover, human capital will be presented as the unifying theme of his research, providing coherence and bringing together his various topics of research. In order to appraise Mincer's work and to identify its novelty, it is necessary to locate his work in its relevant historical context, by seeing it in the debates and patterns of research at the time that Mincer developed his early publications. On the other hand, the book also looks at the impact of Mincer's work on subsequent research in the field. Overall, this book attempts to explain why Jacob Mincer is considered as one of the crucial figures not only in the development of modern labor economics but also in some of its major theoretical and methodological developments during the past forty years.

Jacob Mincer's research tends to be classified as human capital and labor supply studies (he himself appeared to endorse this division in the recent collection of his selected essays). However, if this division is understood as defining clearly independent areas of research, one gets not only an incomplete picture of his work but also a misleading one. Instead, it is better to try to understand Mincer's work as a whole. Doing this helps to illuminate the role of human capital in his research and in modern labor economics. Analyzing the diverse aspects of Mincer's long research career in an integrated way shows that he was crucial not only in the establishment of human capital as a central economic concept, but also as a founder of modern labor economics.

Although the idea that education can provide (economic) benefits had been around for some time, it took economists quite a while to devote significant attention to the analysis of the motivations and effects of more and better education. At least by the late-eighteenth century some people started thinking about skilled individuals as a kind of expensive instrument and machine, a kind of capital whose long-term benefit would compensate the efforts and expenditures of years of early personal and intellectual development. However, only by the late fifties did these metaphors about the economic potential of education and training develop into a research program. The next chapter analyzes the early lack of attention of economists to educational issues and the changes that took place in the mid-twentieth century which contributed to increasing attention being paid to the economic value of education in the postwar period.

It was not only the visibility of education that was changing. Its role in the promotion of personal wealth changed as well. Until the forties and fifties, education was mostly regarded as the result of previous wealth and an instrument for enhancing a cumulative process of wealth inequality. It was believed that, because most of the well-paid jobs required a high level of education and training, education was important. Its importance lay in providing access to exclusive prosperous occupations. And since education and training were costly activities, access to these financially attractive occupations tended to be restricted to wealthy groups that could afford high levels of education. Therefore, education and training were, for these authors, a mechanism of social elite reproduction.

Chapter 3 analyzes Mincer's original work in applying human capital to the analysis of personal income distribution. Until the postwar period, the exploration of the idea of human capital as an explanatory principle for income inequality was very limited and fragmented. Mincer's Ph.D. dissertation became a turning point in this respect, since he proposed to use investment in education and training as a major explanatory principle for the existing distribution of income. The chapter starts with a brief analysis of the debates that marked the development of research in personal income distribution during the first half of the twentieth century. Then Mincer's thesis of 1957 is analyzed by pointing out the way this integrated a broader debate about the purpose and use of research in personal income. The chapter proceeds by covering his subsequent work on human capital and lifetime income and wage patterns, which reached a high point with his 1974 book *Schooling, Experience, and Earnings* and the formulation of the human capital earnings function, which would become a centerpiece of modern labor research.

Despite these fruitful collaborations and developments, human capital analysis faced significant criticism, which became more noticeable in the mid-seventies when the private returns to education started falling rapidly and the contribution of human capital to understanding inequality and labor market outcomes came under severe scrutiny. Thus, in the fourth chapter, the major criticisms of the human capital approach to the labor market and the way human capital dealt with these are examined. Moreover, the chapter assesses Mincer's contribution to these debates and to what extent his research endured those controversies.

In the fifth chapter some of Mincer's main interests regarding the long-term behavior of labor supply are analyzed. When Jacob Mincer started his academic career, labor economics was finishing a long process of change that marked the postwar years, and which was generally characterized by the increasing pervasiveness of neo-classical economic theory. This chapter describes how labor economics changed in the mid-twentieth century in terms of its identity and methodological stance. The growing influence of neoclassical economics in labor research and the stimulus of other prominent labor researchers made Mincer increasingly interested in labor issues, namely in labor supply behavior. Despite initial misgivings, Mincer eventually became comfortable with the label of being a labor economist and indeed it is to labor economics that Mincer devotes essentially his academic career, making several important contributions to this field. This chapter starts by presenting a brief portrait of labor economics in the decades preceding Mincer's work in labor issues in order to highlight the contrast between labor economics until the postwar era and afterward, namely due to the influence of Mincer's and others' work. Then an analysis is made of some of his major pieces of research around the theme of labor supply and lifetime labor income and the way these differed from previous labor research. This work is also closely linked to Mincer's research on human capital.

Jacob Mincer is mostly known for his contribution to the study of income distribution and labor supply, which were both nurtured by his pioneering and persistent work on human capital analysis. However, his intellectual quest led him to explore other multiple aspects of labor research. In Chapter 6, Mincer's work that aimed at better understanding the constantly changing conditions of the labor market, namely workers' mobility and unemployment, is explored. In terms of workers' mobility, Mincer studied the economic motivation of migration and its impact on the labor market and job turnover. With regard to unemployment he explored the link between education and the duration and incidence of unemployment; he analyzed the impact of some labor market regulations and the way these could impair mobility and accumulation of human capital; and eventually he turned his attention to the employment effects of economic growth.

Although Mincer's role in the development of research on these topics was less prominent than the one he played in the aforementioned aspects of income distribution and labor supply, he still made a relevant contribution to various aspects of the labor market. The analysis of this and other pieces of research will provide a better understanding of the major characteristics of Mincer's work, and also assist in grasping his influence on contemporary labor research. Moreover, these topics will also point out that underlying and unifying Mincer's research was his aim at exploring the explanatory power of human capital analysis and its implications for the dynamics of the labor market.

The development of any research program requires the formation of a community of researchers, which needs to be supported intellectually and institutionally. Mincer is certainly a good example of this sociological dimension of the creation of knowledge, and his ability to attract and stimulate students' and colleagues' interest in human capital research was extremely relevant to the development of the human capital research program. In Chapter 7 the aim is to appraise the role played by Jacob Mincer in labor economics. The chapter starts by analyzing the role that Mincer played as a teacher and especially as a mentor to several emerging leading labor economists and the impact that Mincer had on the training of several generations of labor economists. The chapter then examines the impact that this relationship with his students had on the development of the human capital research agenda.

The eighth and final chapter sums up the analysis of Jacob Mincer's prolific and interesting career. This chapter also highlights the hallmarks of Mincer's approach to economic analysis. It points out his major contributions to economic analysis and suggests the topics and features by which his work will continue to influence future generations of (labor) economists.

2

The Changing Role of Education in Economic Analysis

> The revival of the human capital concept in the late fifties was a response to the appearance of a huge residual in growth accounting, as well as to the finding in US data that the largest component of income inequality is the variance of labor incomes. Human capital analysis promised to correct the inadequacies of the old growth theories (Mincer 1997a).

The idea that education can provide benefits, even economic ones, is certainly an old one. At least by the late-eighteenth century some people started thinking about skilled individuals as a kind of expensive instrument and machine, a kind of capital whose long-term benefit would compensate the efforts and expenditures of years of early personal and intellectual development. These metaphors about the economic potential of education and training coalesced in the late fifties, becoming one of the most popular research programs of contemporary economics.

It is nevertheless rather peculiar that it took so much time for economists to pickup on those metaphors and turn them into a full-fledged theoretical framework. Likewise, it is quite interesting to investigate the way prior resistances or lack of attention gave way to subsequent popularity within the discipline. This chapter analyzes the early lack of interest and the increasing attention in the postwar period to the economic value of education.

2.1. Early Debates about the Uses of Human Capital

Since its emergence in the late fifties human capital theory has been frequently presented as a consistent and natural development of some ideas contained in the works of several founding fathers of the discipline, from Smith to Marshall, which would have already provided a simple though clear theoretical basis for the modern developments (Kiker 1968). However, when those authors emphasized the effect of the role of education on human character, they had different purposes in mind. In addition to being obviously intellectually rewarding (consumption perspective) because of its effect on human reason and problem-solving, education was an important subject for classical political economists. When analyzing the benefits of education, classical political economists would concentrate on the political and moral ones.[1] In fact education was valuable mostly because it had a socializing effect on the labor/poor classes, particularly visible in all authors after Smith (West 1964; Blaug 1975). Education was important, and should receive government patronage, because it promoted better human beings and better citizens, hence better workers. But by better workers classical political economists meant more sober, more tractable, and more sexually restrained workers, not necessarily more skilled/efficient ones.

The end of the nineteenth century was characterized by important changes in terms of economic thought, with the decline of the classical school and the emergence of the so-called marginalist revolution. The attention, among marginalism, to education was not very significant.[2] In the more than half a century following the decline of classical political economy, human capital research has hardly made any real progress. The limited use of human capital continued to be metaphorical and the few attempts to make the concept precise fell flat among the discipline, whose mainstream practitioners showed significant resistance to those attempts.

Until the first decades of the twentieth century, the link between education and the labor market, and especially with workers' performance, was almost nonexistent. The few references were limited to a repetition of Adam Smith's compensatory principle. Education was still largely valued for its social benefits or nonmonetary private ones, and very little was mentioned about its potential economic benefits. Even those like Marshall who went further to consider its economic benefits for the country, suggested that individuals would neither realize its importance nor reap the full benefits for that investment.

This lack of interest in the economic value of education persisted and most economists of the early decades of the twentieth century did not seem to care much about education, let alone its economic impact. The published writings from the period indicate that the references to education were not only sparse but also seldom linked with central features of the economic system. Despite some grand rhetorical statements on the importance of education for the individual and society as a whole, the truth was that education was a peripheral issue when it came to the analysis of economic phenomena, notably in terms of the labor market. The attention to human capital was left mostly to authors with other backgrounds and interests.

The importance of human capital emerged in discussions about the value of national wealth and the economic value of the population. A few authors pointed out that, more than its quantity, it was the composition and the quality of the population that contributed to its value.[3] Human capital also played an important role in the debates about the costs of war. For several authors conflicts represented an important loss in terms of human capital through the loss of the skills and knowledge of those workers who died in the conflict. These had an economic value that could be calculated by an analogy with other types of capital, since human capital was also the result of a costly investment (in food, clothing, and education).

Another group of people interested in investigating the role of human capital during the early decades of the twentieth century were the actuaries. For practical reasons life insurance analysis was concerned with the economic value of human life, and the impact that disability, death, and retirement would have on the economic condition of the individual. The development of this type of work led these authors to consider more specific conditions, by exploring the impact on the economic value of life of aspects such as health condition, personal character, and education and training. For each of these categories, and combinations of each, standardized tables were developed that gave the actualized value of their loss in terms of potential future income.[4]

A few academics attempted to address the economic value of education. The most important study in this respect came from Donald Eugene Gorseline (1932) which tried to analyze the probable effect of schooling on individual income by analyzing samples of pairs of blood brothers, one of whom had a different school grade attainment from the other.[5] In another important contribution, the American economist and professor at Harvard J. R. Walsh (1935) poses the question of whether the amount spent in schooling, in particular professional training, 'is, in a strict sense, a capital investment made in a profit-seeking, equalizing market, in response to the same motives which lead to the creation of factories, machinery and the like' (255).

Both Gorseline and Walsh conceded that other factors would affect schooling, such as differences in workplaces, health conditions, chance, and innate ability. Interestingly, both Gorseline and Walsh singled out ability as the most problematic aspect to be dealt with when trying to isolate the effect of education on income, something that modern economists would mostly agree with. Both authors regarded it as practically impossible to isolate completely the effect of education from all the other aforementioned ones, a message that would echo among prominent modern researchers on the topic (cf. Cawley et al. 1996).

However, none of these authors who discussed the economic value of education and used the human capital metaphor was very well known among economists. In fact they had a very restricted impact on their fellow economists and their work would be only rediscovered when the modern analysis of human capital took off from the late fifties onward. None of these attempts to use the human capital metaphor came close to turning it into a central concept of the analysis of the labor market, of personal income success, or of the investigations concerning the wealth of nations.

Human capital remained a problematic expression at various levels. On an immediate basis human capital was problematic because it suggested a cold-blooded approach that regarded people as machines. The idea of putting a value on human life and its productive potential horrified many. Moreover, to talk about the economic value of education seemed to debase the various and high purposes of education, reducing it to a mechanistic approach. The idea of an economic value of education was considered at odds with individual motivations, since the demand for education was not regarded as based on economic or monetary motivations strictly speaking but on social, family, or intellectual ones.

By the forties there are signs of an increasing familiarity with human capital and the economic value of education among academic economists. Economists were starting to pay more attention to the possibility that education had significant economic impacts and that this could be addressed by likening qualified labor to a certain type of capital. However, it was not yet clear to them how this could be done and if it was worthwhile; human capital still meant different things, depending on the author and the topic.

2.2. The Postwar Revival of Growth Analysis

With the exception of some very reactionary minds and a handful of dictators, education and training were always regarded as a positive contribution to any country's progress. Economists were no exception to this favorable evaluation and tended to emphasize the economic, political, and social advantages in promoting the education of large sections of the population. However, until the late fifties the contribution of education was neither very much discussed nor at the core of the debates on the priorities for economic growth and development. Hardly any discussions can be found that go beyond the level of vague generality. The lack of attention to education was part of a broader problem which was the scarce attention devoted to the long-run economic performance of major Western economies. This meant that what is nowadays called growth economics had a loose theoretical corpus and difficulty in giving coherence to several isolated studies as late as the mid-twentieth century.

During the forties and especially the fifties, the situation would change dramatically. The increasing visibility of Keynesianism, by focusing attention on the aggregate level and by promoting the development of national accounts systems, would create a much more favorable context for the development of growth analysis. The wartime experiences of planning and the postwar political context of the cold war would enhance the importance of strengthening the national economic potential and the urgency in analyzing theoretically and empirically the key factors for economic growth.

The reemergence of modern growth theory is arguably associated with Roy Harrod's 'An Essay in Dynamic Theory' (1939). His purpose was basically to propose an outline of a dynamic theory that, based on Keynes' foundations, would explain and predict paths of long-term economic evolution. The other stimulus to the revival of growth analysis came with the work of the Russian émigré Evsey Domar (1946). Domar was influenced by the spread of Keynesianism in the

USA, notably by his former professor, Alvin Hansen.[6] The work of Harrod and Domar contributed to increasing attention being paid by the discipline to growth theory, namely through the development of several planning models using their fixed coefficients approach and its associated emphasis on capital. Their approach nevertheless faced increasing criticism which targeted the lack of a more specific and detailed treatment of labor inputs and the assumption of a fixed relationship between capital and labor. Instead, the use of a production function that abandoned complementarity between factors was proposed, thus expanding the range of possible analytical situations.

By the mid-fifties the use of models allowing for more flexible production functions became more frequent. It is in this line of research that in 1956 the so-called Solow Model emerged, with a similar version published some months later by T. W. Swan (1956). Solow (1957) brought together the theoretical and empirical strands of research on economic growth and highlighted the crude explanation of past growth, notably in terms of the measurement of inputs and their changing quality. The paper was also innovative since it was one of the earliest attempts to incorporate the improvement in the quality of labor over time as a source of increased productivity, and followed T. W. Schultz's remarks about the need to place labor quality at the center of economic growth analysis (see below).

The criticisms on the empirical limitations of growth analysis echoed a long and strong stream of research devoted to the organization, development, and analysis of data on past growth. Arguably the most important part of this empirical work was produced under the framework of the NBER, notably within the research on capital formation and trends led by Simon Kuznets and the research on productivity and employment coordinated by Solomon Fabricant. The NBER research on productivity suggested that there was a significant increase in American productivity during the first half of the twentieth century, for which a convincing explanation was missing. Analyzing this situation, Moses Abramowitz (1956) coined the famous expression of the residual as the 'measure of our ignorance about the causes of economic growth'.

By the early sixties there was an increasing amount of empirical research emphasizing education as a major source of growth. This had been promoted by the postwar revival of growth analysis that stimulated theoretical and empirically rooted answers for the past growth of developed countries. Although in both cases attention had turned initially to the quantity of inputs, especially to physical capital, the subsequent debate and, especially, the empirical difficulties of growth accounting stimulated the search for other sources of growth. As time went by, education and training became one of the best candidates and, despite many limitations, the first empirical exercises contributed to strengthen their case placing them firmly on the research agenda and more importantly in the public and political imagination.

At the same time that many economists were becoming more interested in growth aspects, increasing attention was paid to the performance of less-developed economies. This was regarded as an object of study in itself, with specific conditions and problems, creating a sense of inadequacy of neoclassical economics to explain and to overcome the difficulties faced by those less-developed economies. The context in which development economics emerged, which was also very much dominated by a political orientation and the need to solve policy problems, focused attention on postwar international reconstruction in Europe and the end of colonial empires. Moreover, it was also a time in which trust in the market's capacity to deliver an efficient and effective use of resources was at one of its lowest levels ever. Development economics emerged in a context pervaded by skepticism toward neoclassical economics and its tenets regarding the role of markets, individual choice, and rationality of economic agents.

These iconoclastic developments led to a reaction by neoclassical economists who considered that the idiosyncrasy of development economics was taken too far. They thought that the emphasis on the specificity of less-developed economies was overstated, often as a device for justifying certain kinds of policies and rationales that would be unacceptable in a neoclassical framework. For mainstream economists, the economic agents of less-developed economies/sectors were much more economically rational and responsive to market incentives than how many of the development economists portrayed them. Neoclassical economists considered that this had led to a biased and unsound preference for planning and government intervention that hindered the economic development of those economies. Accordingly, many neoclassical economists voiced the need to reformulate the economic role of government in developing countries, bringing it closer to the standard role in more mature economies. The role of government rather should focus on the removal of those obstacles to privately led economic progress and promote certain services traditionally regarded as public ones that could make a significant contribution to growth such as better education, nutrition, and health. These would raise the skills of the population and speed the diffusion of technical progress. The emphasis on the quality of factors for significant development differences would be a hallmark of the work of these economists.

The emphasis on human capital by neoclassical economists came also via their challenge to the emphasis on capital scarcity, often used as a justification for a much more prominent role of government political intervention on economic development. Many neoclassical economists considered that many developing countries had a traditional preference for physical capital investments as a product of political choice that tended to support investments with strong visibility (and potentially strong electoral impact), instead of more complex, but probably more important, aspects of human development. In fact, those intangibles of technical capacity, flexibility, and innovative skills were increasingly considered as having been at the heart of past Western progress, translated to investments in the form of capital such as education, health, technical skills, and general improvement of the population's productivity.

By the early sixties, when the human capital research program was taking off, the visibility of education and training among economists and policymakers was growing and rapidly becoming a hot topic on the agenda. This was also favored by the new institutional framework emerging in the postwar years with the rise of international agencies. The development of this institutional support created important forums of debate and policymaking that had in many cases a deep and lasting influence on the economic policies of many areas around the globe, and especially in terms of economic priorities. It would be in those debates that education would find its initial way within these organizations' activities and policy advice.

The debates on growth and development economics attracted much attention within and outside the discipline, and the expansion of the government's role in the funding and management of education and science made it a focus of attention. Education was being integrated in growth models, and concentrated much attention in terms of empirical measurement of the sources of growth; it was also becoming a priority for the less-developed parts of the world, especially with the first signs of government withdrawal from direct economic intervention.

The turning point in the attention of growth and development economics to the human capital perspective came with T. W. Schultz's presidential address to the AEA in 1960 (Schultz 1961a). If for many people in the economics discipline this was a first contact with the emergent research on human capital, for Schultz it represented the consolidation of a view that had been emerging in his work for many decades, stressing the role of human capital as a major contribution to the past performance of Western economies. Since his earliest works Schultz emphasized the role of knowledge embodied in technical advances and especially in people's capacities as a powerful instrument for understanding and promoting the development and modernization of agriculture, first, and then of low-income economies. Due to his preoccupation with the maldistribution of resources (especially labor) Schultz emphasized a broad concept of human capital, notably the role of nutrition, health, and migration, which was linked to his focus on modernizing economies. He regarded human capital as something that made people more productive, especially in terms of an activity that made people aware of new and better opportunities and their ability to seize them (Schultz 1974).[7]

2.3. Education and the Debates on Income Distribution

Until the postwar years very limited attention was paid to education and training in the context of income distribution, though things started to change early in the fifties and education and training (or what later became the backbone of the human capital concept) gained increasing visibility. Attention to the potential economic effect of education on income was due to a change of attitude among most economists. Different from many modern economists for whom the externalities of education are a matter of belief (cf. Arrow 1993), most economists prior to World War II regarded the benefits of education as concentrated at the political and moral level rather than at the economic one.

It was not only the visibility of education that was changing, but also its role in the promotion of personal wealth. Until the forties and fifties, education was mostly regarded as the result of previous wealth and an instrument of enhancing a cumulative process of wealth inequality. It was believed that because most of the well-paid jobs required a high level of education and training that education was important. Its importance lay in providing access to exclusive prosperous occupations. And since education and training were costly activities, access to these financially attractive occupations tended to be restricted to those wealthy groups that could afford it. Therefore, education and training were, for these authors, a mechanism of social elite's reproduction.

Nevertheless there were signs that something was fermenting within the profession and that education would gain increasing visibility within income distribution analysis. A major breakthrough came with the study on *Income From Independent Professional Practice* by Milton Friedman and Simon Kuznets (1945). This study was started in 1933 by Kuznets as a by-product of the study of the national income of the USA for 1929–32 (and conducted by the NBER in collaboration with the US Department of Commerce). After some delays Friedman took control of the project in 1937, rewriting much of it, in a way that made it possible for him to submit it as his doctoral dissertation at Columbia University (cf. Hirsch and de Marchi 1990).[8]

Friedman's influence was particularly felt in Section 4.2 of Chapter 4. This part of the study focused on the factors accounting for differences in level of income, with strong emphasis on the role of length of training. Differences in income were regarded as compensation for either longer periods of training or scarcity. This scarcity was due to possible disequilibria caused by restrictions on the free allocation of resources. These disequilibria could be due to unequal access to training due to institutional interferences by government or professional associations. These interferences prevented earnings becoming more equal by restricting occupational decisions.

The analysis of the income of the professions indicated a wide variability of that income, much of it considered to be a compensatory effect of differences in length of training (Friedman and Kuznets 1945: 83). This compensation referred to the direct costs of training and to foregone earnings, though it had to be noted that it was a rough calculus, due to the influence of other elements such as non-pecuniary factors, ability, and social and economic rigidities in the occupational structure (390–1). The role of ability was nevertheless downplayed as a significant explanatory force (237). However, the returns seemed to be well above the extra costs due to the lengthier training, suggesting the existence of access restrictions that were regarded as leading to an underinvestment of professional training. This was due to the peculiarities of capital invested in people, namely the imperfections of the financial markets, since 'the amount invested in professional training will depend less on expected returns than on the number of persons who have or can get the money to finance their training' (391).[9]

The increasing attention that education was receiving during the fifties in terms of income distribution analysis benefited from better and more extensive data. The American census of 1940 for the first time included a classification of incomes by level of education, and the level of detail of the data was significantly expanded in the 1950 census. Although the information presented in the 1940 census was limited, it is nevertheless suggestive that the Bureau of Census decided to promote a detailed and separate analysis of the data on education by Howard Brunsman of the Population and Housing Division (1953).[10]

This pattern of analysis linking socioeconomic characteristics, and especially education, with income was adopted by several other studies. Simon Kuznets (1953) considered that increased opportunities of training had a moderate effect, though the interrelated nature of several of the characteristics of the income recipients, such as in the case of occupation and education, made any conclusions very problematic. However, in his analysis, education was still mostly regarded as an instrument of access to well-paid occupations rather than as an instrument to make people more productive.

Also at that time Margaret Reid (1954) analyzed income by comparing major groups of the population. One of the comparisons was between groups with different years of schooling, finding that the 'median wage or salary income of male workers during 1939 was directly related to additional years of schooling' (103). This result was present for both whites and nonwhites, though less for the latter.[11] Reid also noted that the expensive nature of education restricted accessibility, with negative consequences for both equality of opportunity and productivity. The increase in the average level of education and the reduction of disparities in education would also be expected to increase the level of social accountability of the cost of training, by raising individual awareness of the cost of training and its compensation in income. In contrast to Kuznets (and others), Reid saw education not so much as a consequence of wealth, but as an engine driving it.

Another important study at the time was developed by Herman Miller for the Social Science Research Council in cooperation with the US Department of Commerce and the Bureau of Census (of which the author was a member).[12] The focus of the study was the relationship between those social and economic characteristics reported in the data provided by the 1940 and 1950 censuses, and income as measured in surveys conducted annually since 1944 by the Bureau of Census. Miller concentrated on the common traits from the analysis of the income recipients' data, which was possible due to the improvements in the data available, in order to overcome the traditional dichotomy in terms of inequality theories between those that favored natural factors and those that stressed institutional ones.[13]

According to Miller (1955) education played a significant role in explaining differences between occupations, and in different life income patterns. Low-skilled workers reached their peak earnings at a young age, showing little variation afterward until retirement. In highly skilled groups, workers' earnings increased rapidly between the late twenties and mid-forties, only declining close to retirement. On the other hand there were striking differences in the pattern of variation of income with age among men having different levels of schooling. The dispersion of income within occupational groups tended to increase as educational level and age increased.[14] Although he recognized the existence of those forces of nepotism, unequal financial capacity, and social attrition, Miller considered that increasing access to free higher education and the increase in public education at all levels tended to counterbalance those forces restricting access to certain better-paid occupations.

Thus, throughout the fifties several studies resulted in the view that education and training would be valuable in terms of individual income not because they gave access to well-paid occupations, but because they would enhance the individual's productivity and therefore their prospective lifetime wealth. This was the time when Jacob Mincer was working on his doctoral dissertation that would transform the role of education in personal income by turning this causality link into a generalized explanation for income distribution.

2.4. Education and the Labor Market

It is particularly worthwhile to analyze the view of labor research on skills and training at the time due to its obvious links with human capital theory. Until the late forties there were few studies of patterns of wage differentials (and even fewer studies of skilled workers), and the existing ones were scattered and largely descriptive. These works devoted scarce attention to link wage rates with patterns of socioeconomic characteristics, let alone to educational and training qualifications (see Alderfer 1935; Backman and Gainsbrugh 1949). Moreover, 'the persistence of wage differentials for jobs requiring comparable skills and training was not due to compensating differences in working conditions or in other perquisites' (Alderfer 1935: 251), but rather to noncompetitive practices on both the demand and the supply side (McClaurin and Myers 1942).

Many labor economists devoted very little attention to education and, on the few occasions they did, considered the economic role of education in a rather cursory way and as only one among many other factors that contributed to labor productivity (cf. Lester 1941). Education was regarded less as an instrument of improving directly the productive role of the worker than as a useful instrument in the formation of citizens and responsible social partners. Lloyd Reynolds (1951), one of the most eminent labor economists of the postwar years, considered that there was 'an established belief among employers that skilled workers *ought* to be paid much more than the unskilled. This belief does not seem to be based mainly on competitive reasoning' (239). Reynolds would take a very skeptical stance on the economic effects of education: 'This faith in additional years of education, however, is rarely linked to any concrete notion of how this extra education will enable the child to get into a particular kind of work' (13). Compensation in terms of wages and other employment benefits was not necessarily regarded as the result of productivity performance assessment, as shown by most of the practices in terms of seniority (Harbison 1940). Moreover, the investment perspective of the demand of education did not make much sense due to students' lack of foresight of their future professional careers and the fact that decisions concerning education were founded on other types of motivations.

Education was mostly a mechanism of access to better-paid jobs. Clark Kerr (1954), another leading figure in labor research in the postwar period, regarded the increase in the supply of skilled labor as the result of the advances of public education and of social and class discrimination and not of the economic calculus of the workers and/or their families. Kerr endorsed the view, popular among many labor researchers critical of neoclassical economics, regarding wage differentials being the result of unequal access to educational opportunities, rather than as a result of different types of labor and of productivity (cf. Lester 1941).

In contrast, an emphasis on the importance of education and training to the analysis of wage differences was becoming part of the neoclassical labor canon, notably among Chicago economists. In the early forties, Friedman in his doctoral work had already emphasized the impact of formal training on individual earnings, and throughout the fifties the expression 'human capital' was frequently found in the writings of several Chicago economists. For instance, Becker used it in his doctoral dissertation (submitted in 1955 and supervised by Gregg Lewis). It was also becoming an important concept in the work of people such as T. W. Schultz and Gale Johnson, working on topics other than labor economics.

Melvin Reder, a former Chicago student and then faculty member, was one of the first to analyze the relationship between occupational wage differentials and education. Reder (1954) used education to explain earnings, and not only occupation, finding that median and extreme incomes increased with level of schooling for both sexes and all ages. The advantage of college graduates was very considerable at advanced ages, suggesting that the economic advantages enhanced by education would promote a longer working life, improving the benefits for better-educated laborers. Reder is also one of the few who openly took for granted the impact of training on the quality of workers, and somehow anticipated Becker's later famous dichotomy between general and specific training. These implications would be different to the employer depending on whether the benefits of a better-trained workforce could be reaped: 'employers will not invest in such training unless the prospective net gain (if any) from hiring an untrained instead of a trained worker can be realized very quickly' (Reder 1955: 836).

Also in Chicago, some work had been carried out by doctoral students, mostly supervised by Gregg Lewis, on the effect of education on the labor market. For instance, Morton Zeman (1955) arguably did the earliest systematic study on income differentials between white and nonwhite populations, based on the more extensive socioeconomic characterization provided by the 1940 census. Although he had to restrict most of the analysis to the urban male population, his research covered aspects such as age, occupation, employment, residence, and education. In his results, Zeman noted the importance of educational variables. Income differences increased with age but especially with education. He also found that, although this applied to all groups, the increase in income associated with more education was less for nonwhites, so that racial inequality at similar levels of qualification seemed to increase with education (1955: 87). Moreover, and although nonwhites had benefited from the secular increase in educational attainment, their relative situation seemed to have worsened (1955: 164). T. W. Schultz and Becker would use Zeman's results extensively in the early years of human capital research as a suggestion that education played a very significant role in explaining income differences and performance in the labor market.

A few years later Paul Keat (1959) analyzed long-term changes in occupational wage differentials, paying particular attention to education.[15] In fact, by occupational wage structure he meant the set of skill differentials. His study confirmed previous indications that skill differentials had been falling during the first half of the twentieth century, despite some irregularity within some shorter periods, suggesting that the growth in the average level of schooling had had an important impact on the wages of less-skilled workers. The data indicated also that apprentices' wages had risen significantly in relation to those of unskilled workers, which was understood by Keat as being the result of the substitution of school for training, due to an increase in the average level of schooling that decreased the number of years of training needed. The reduction in the needs of training had reduced its cost, thus having a positive impact on the relative wages of the apprentices.

2.5. Concluding Remarks

Until the mid-twentieth century many economists paid little attention to the economic analysis of education and persistently resisted using human capital as a good analogy for skilled labor. Underpinning these resistances was a belief that education gave access to prestigious and well-paid jobs without really enhancing people's productivity, and because it seemed problematic and not very realistic to regard qualified labor as a type of capital. Moreover, these two strands, the economic analysis of education and the analysis of education in the labor market, were hardly connected, accounting for the lack of relevance of education. Accordingly, the first 150 years or so of economics as (an autonomous) subject of scientific inquiry did not contribute much to the development of human capital research.

In the aftermath of World War II this situation changed prompted by several developments, initially unrelated, that converged to give increasing prominence to the economic effects of education. One of those changes was the postwar revival of growth debates that, alongside the expansion of educational systems in most Western countries, led to an increasing emphasis on the qualification of the labor force as a key factor in explaining differentiated growth performances. The second aspect was the changing possibilities and interests in research on personal income, namely the belief that it was possible to provide causal explanations for the distribution of income, and that education was a good candidate to be included among those potential explanatory factors. Last, and certainly not least, was the growing interest in labor research for skilled human resources.

Seizing the moment, a group of economists frequently connected with Chicago, namely T. W. Schultz, Gary Becker, and Jacob Mincer, managed to turn this metaphor into a whole research program that would spread around many subfields. With different, but largely overlapping interests, these economists regarded this metaphor of human capital as a potential coherent explanation for these various aspects of economic research and in increasingly close collaboration they developed human capital research in a way that would have a major impact on economic analysis and beyond.

3

Placing Human Capital at the Center of Income Distribution

> The facts of income inequality do not speak for themselves in the accumulated statistical frequency distributions. The facts must be recognized in the statistical constructs, and interpreted from them (Jacob Mincer, Ph.D. dissertation, 1957).

Some of Mincer's major contributions to human capital research were carried out in his work on income distribution, starting with his doctoral dissertation. During the first half of the twentieth century, research on personal income had been marked by some important debates about its nature and purpose. In the early decades of the twentieth century the field was dominated by debates about the possibility of redistribution, stimulated by the so-called Pareto's law (cf. Schumpeter 1949). This debate stimulated various reactions. Some researchers decided that to focus on the factors explaining the actual distribution of personal income was a much more fruitful and safe alternative. Others recognized that the data available on income and wealth were particularly scarce and prevented definitive conclusions on the topic. Improvements in data and stronger theoretical emphasis would eventually lead to the emergence of the analysis of the role of education in personal distribution of income.

Until the postwar period, the exploration of the idea of human capital as an explanatory principle for income inequality was very limited and fragmented. Mincer's Ph.D. dissertation became a turning point in this respect. He proposed to use investment in education and training, henceforth widely known as human capital, as a major explanatory principle of the existing distribution of income. In doing this, his work contributed to the modern development of human capital research and helped to significantly shape the subsequent developments of research on income distribution.

This chapter analyzes Mincer's contribution to income distribution research, namely the way he placed human capital at the center of that research. It commences with a brief analysis of the debates that marked the development of research in personal income distribution during the first half of the twentieth century. Then Mincer's thesis of 1957 is analyzed by showing how his work incorporated a broader debate about the purposes and uses of research in personal income. The chapter proceeds by covering Mincer's subsequent work on human capital and lifetime income and wage patterns, which reached a high point with his 1974 book *Schooling, Experience, and Earnings* and the formulation of the human capital earnings function, which would become a centerpiece of modern labor research. The chapter also shows the way Mincer's research has significantly influenced the economic analysis of income distribution.

3.1. Early Debates on Income Distribution Analysis

The topic of personal income distribution gained increasing attention at the turn of the twentieth century due to Pareto and the so-called Pareto's law. Stimulated by his fight against socialism (cf. Cirillo 1979), Pareto devoted a large part of his attention, in the last decade of the nineteenth century, to the analysis of statistical data on personal income distribution. This analysis, in particular its graphical expression, had a serious impact on his work. The plotting of income in relation to a number of families in a double-log framework suggested not only a virtual linearity of the curve for the level of income above tax exemption, but also stability of this distribution in different historical and geographical contexts.

Pareto's conclusions provoked great perplexity because they suggested that the attempts to improve income equality were doomed to fail. This was a timely argument since Europe was facing increased social turbulence due to the so-called social question. Hence, a large part of the subsequent research on personal income focused on testing the applicability of Pareto's law in different geographical and historical contexts. The first results showed that Pareto's theorems tended to perform quite well, in empirical terms, though later work strengthened more skeptical views. Despite the criticism, the persuasive impact of Pareto's analysis persisted well into the thirties, being regarded as an important analytical instrument, representing a significant part of the curve, generally straight, and being an instrument to understand otherwise meaningless data.

However, with time, Pareto's law was increasingly regarded as a mere empirical regularity, without sound theoretical foundations. This view was prominent among many important British economists of the early-twentieth century who had been investigating the factors underlying the distribution of personal income and wealth (Cannan 1905; Dalton 1920). Notable among these was Pigou who considered it unjustifiable to derive any type of law from Pareto's interesting results. He thought there were many circumstances in common that could justify those results and insisted that this distribution could certainly be altered by a change in the laws of inheritance, especially because property incomes seemed to be more unevenly distributed than other types of incomes (e.g. wages). Moreover, if the distribution among individuals of physical, intellectual, and other endowments followed the normal law of error, the curve representing the distribution of wealth would be binomial not hyperbolic, as seemed to be the case.[1]

Despite the strong initial impact of Pareto's work, his ideas on the stability of income distribution generated increasing discomfort. Moreover, several influential authors suggested that not only was it possible to change this distribution, but that through education and training people could gain better qualifications which would give them much better chances to improve their economic conditions. However, these statements were not only lacking quantitative and qualitative support, but were also downplayed vis-à-vis other far more powerful forces such as genetic differences or social arrangements concerning inheritance.

After the initial impact of Pareto's analysis, many authors recognized that, more than anything else, this discussion had highlighted the scarcity and incompleteness of the available statistics on income and wealth. This enhanced quest for improving both the quantity and quality of the available data was felt more in the scientific field which had strong empirical traditions and interests. Accordingly, the calls for better data were frequent, and significant research was carried out on the production of statistical data that could provide a better picture of the situation and of the evolution of personal income distribution. In the USA, with the setting up of the NBER in the early twenties, the statistics on this topic received a significant boost. It is noteworthy that the first study developed by the NBER was devoted to the quantification of American income and its distribution. Another important step to promote empirical research was the establishment by the NBER in 1936 of the Conference on Research in Income and Wealth, which aimed at stimulating cooperative research on these topics in order to contribute to a consensus in terms of concepts, terminology, and methods of exposition.

The growth in empirical studies in personal income also brought some problems. The increasing availability of studies stimulated significant heterogeneity in terms of methods and data, which raised problems of comparability, reliability, and continuity of sources and types of income distribution data. There were also specific problems with the concepts used (especially income), the recipient units, the coverage of income groups, geographic dispersion, class intervals, and accessibility of data. Moreover, the lack of an extensive socioeconomic characterization of the income recipients, in particular the omission of the education factor, was seen as one of the most serious gaps affecting the generality of the studies. It was the scarcity of this information that prevented the discovery of the determinants of the distribution of income (such as education, age, sex, religion, or color) and the assessment of their impact, thus requiring further work.

The persistent emphasis on statistical and quantitative work resulted in reactions from some economists who considered this to have led to a general disregard of a more causal and explanatory perspective. Moreover, these authors regarded the efforts aimed at perfecting the quality of data to be a never-ending task that prevented serious theoretical attempts. Such criticism started to appear more frequently at the beginning of the forties. Maurice Leven's *The Income Structure of the United States* (1938), a study supported by the Brookings Institution, stated that the aim was not to present new data, but to make an analytical contribution by revealing some of the 'truths' provided by the data available. In particular, this study wanted to discuss 'the causes of the wide variation found in the incomes of the American people' (Leven 1938: 1). The significance of this study resided not so much in the results, but mostly in Leven's approach, since it was one of the earliest attempts to adopt an analytical approach toward income size distribution. Moreover, its focus on the socioeconomic characterization of income recipients launched a search for patterns of influence of these factors on income profiles.[2]

A very important contributor to this debate about the analysis of data was Milton Friedman. He criticized what he considered to be an excessive emphasis on estimates and data quality which led to less effort devoted to causal and analytical work, that is, a lack of explanatory focus. For Friedman it was better to have some data rather than none, since it was the purpose of statistics to help researchers in the selection of data and in the development of inference based on them. Besides, there was no such a thing as perfect data.

However, this exploration of a causal link between socioeconomic characteristics (especially education) and income was far from consensual. Simon Kuznets (1953), another leading researcher on the topic at that time, emphasized the effect of the income distribution on the patterns of expenditure and savings, rather than its causes.[3] Kuznets doubted that Friedman's approach exhausted the analysis of the determinants: 'There appear to be persistent, long term differences in real income... only partly reducible by allowances for differences in training, experience, restriction and the like. In other words, mobility of individuals is not sufficient, even in the longer run, to bring about equality of return—though no formal restrictions on mobility exist' (1953: 205). Moreover, and despite allowance for intergroup and intragroup differences, Kuznets believed that a significant part of those differences would remain unexplained, possibly due to differences in ability. Conflicting views about the future of research on income distribution pervaded several volumes of the NBER conference during the late forties and especially in the fifties. These debates surfaced also in the meetings of the AEA after World War II, revealing an increasing visibility of the research on income distribution among the discipline.

The significant improvements in data were regarded by some as creating new possibilities for empirical work and the idea of *modeling* the main forces connected to income distribution gained ground. However, two possibilities still remained: to explore the links between income inequality and macroeconomic variables or focus on the possible factors determining the existing distribution, hence making it possible to change that distribution. Both perspectives had significant contenders and were clearly represented by Friedman and Kuznets. In his quest to identify the forces determining personal income inequality, Friedman emphasized the role of individual decisions (1953). In this he challenged both the exogenous hypothesis of ability and the quasi-exogenous hypothesis of institutional arrangements (such as inheritance rules). He considered that although these factors had some impact, their importance had been overestimated, which overshadowed the role of individual decisions as well as the calculus in terms of monetary and nonmonetary factors. He therefore saw income inequality as largely the product of individual decisions, such as the decisions concerning education and training. In contrast, Kuznets took a more macroeconomic approach as shown in his presidential address at the 1954 meeting of the AEA. There he focused on the relationship between economic growth and income inequality by analyzing the dynamic impact of several major economic and perieconomic variables, such as savings, political regulation, intersector shifts of population, and technology, on aggregated inequality of personal income.

By the late fifties, research on personal income had come a long way since the earlier debates on Pareto's law. The availability of data for the whole distribution, not only for parts of it, resulted in much more extensive empirical knowledge that revealed a less simplistic picture than that portrayed by Pareto's law. It was in this context of burgeoning statistical evidence and stronger theoretical emphasis that education and training gained increasing visibility. However, if the empirical improvements opened significant possibilities for the analysis of the role of education in explaining differences in income, the exploration of this topic was far from certain. The idea of causal analysis not only faced resistance in terms of personal income research, but it also was not understood by everybody in the same way. Moreover, many expressed their skepticism of a perspective that viewed education as a major force affecting the individual's economic potential. This was the time when Jacob Mincer was working on his doctoral dissertation.

3.2. Mincer's Ph.D. Dissertation

To a large extent, Mincer's Ph.D. dissertation (finished in 1957 and published in a revised version in the *Journal of Political Economy* in 1958) can be regarded as the first systematic contribution to the emergence of human capital theory.[4] He started with a highly empirical approach, looking at various characteristics of wage earners such as occupation, education, industry, age, and sex. This tentative work impressed on him the relevance of education and age and led him to search for a general–theoretical approach.

Mincer expressed his views clearly about the relevance and purpose of personal income distribution. Reviewing the past research on the subject, he paid attention to the long and notable list of economists who addressed the issue of income inequality. Among these were Smith and Marshall; the English writers who had reflected on the property hypothesis (namely Cannan, Dalton, and Pigou); and the Americans, Taussig and Fisher. Although he acknowledged the importance of these authors by emphasizing the role of differences of opportunities, namely of training, and transmission of wealth to understand income distribution, Mincer emphasized the general lack of models in the work of most of his predecessors who did not think of income inequality in terms of statistical frequency distribution, but rather in terms of individual income differences.[5]

Mincer's criticism sounded very much like that of Friedman's some years before, namely by emphasizing the previous lack of analysis of empirical results. This had contributed to theoretical analysis lagging behind empirical research to the point that further progress in this field was prevented (Mincer 1957*a*: 2). The enduring view among many economists that personal income basically mirrored factorial distribution of income also contributed to this theoretical underdevelopment. Even recent interest in income distribution, mostly fostered by the so-called Keynesian revolution, had focused on the consequences for macroeconomic variables of a certain income distribution rather than on the investigation of the forces underlying that distribution of income. The emphasis, in most prior research, on forces apparently beyond individual decisions also contributed to this theoretical atrophy (of income distribution research). These included factors such as ability differences and chance, but also included institutional arrangements such as those regarding property and wealth transmission.

Mincer devoted extensive attention to a discussion of the two main streams of previous research on the topic, that is, ability or chance as the major driving force underpinning inequality of personal income. Mincer questioned the loose definition of both the terms 'ability' and 'chance' that made the discussion more difficult (Mincer 1957*a*: 28). He considered ability models, which he traced back to Quetelet and particularly to the idea that abilities were normally distributed, to be more than questionable. He seemed to be particularly uncomfortable with the so-called chance models (1957*a*: 27, 141). Altogether, Mincer considered that there were two main limitations of previous research on chance and ability models. First, he considered these proposed models (with very limited predictability) to be a major criterion for assessing economic models. Secondly, he thought these tended to be single-factor models that could hardly grasp the complexity of forces underlying personal income inequality.

In contrast with previous research on income inequality, Mincer claimed there was a need to explore the implications of rational choice theory. This corresponded to the *endogenization* of the forces underlying income distribution, something he regarded to be a follow-up of the efforts of Marshall (1920) and Fisher (1896, 1897), and especially Friedman (see Friedman and Kuznets 1945). Friedman was clearly a crucial influence, both theoretically and methodologically, on Mincer's doctoral work. In theoretical terms, because Friedman had advocated the analysis of available data searching for a possible role for education. In methodological terms, because their work shared a clear neoclassical framework as well as an emphasis on the construction of models and the assessment of their predictive capacity. In fact, their particular emphasis on empirical work, and its importance for the formulation of concepts and analysis, was encompassed by the preeminence of theory over facts, namely by the construction of explanatory-predictive models (cf. Hirsch and de Marchi 1990). The analyses of both Mincer and Friedman were clearly anchored in the attempt to construct a theoretical explanatory model that could be empirically tested. This followed from their criticism of the lack of theorization in the prior research on this topic.

Despite the strong influence that Friedman's work had on Mincer, some notable differences emerge when their approaches are compared. Whereas Friedman had emphasized the differences in risk taking behavior, Mincer considered it more fruitful to explore Adam Smith's suggestion of the compensation principle (according to which the income distribution was merely compensation for various traits of income receipts). Moreover, Mincer opted to analyze the impact of the differences in training among members of the labor force as a whole, not just of specific skilled groups. Mincer also gave a much more prominent role to education; he extended its focus to include on-the-job training, and tended to downplay, in his analysis, restrictions in terms of occupational choice.

Mincer did not regard the development of human capital as a break with previous research, let alone a revolution in economic theory. At most it was 'a major redirection in labor economics and in related fields' (Mincer 1993a: x). It was only necessary to rediscover the eloquent statements of Smith on human capital, potentiated by the inclusive definition of capital advanced by Fisher at the turn of the century. Smith's contribution had not been previously explored due to fears of criticism of economic reductionism or to stimulating emotional resentment by considering people's capacities as capital (Mincer 1979). Therefore, according to Mincer, the emergence of human capital theory corresponded to two major characteristics of the development of economic theory. On the one hand, it was the idea of continuity and cumulative knowledge, by systematically revising and improving the past legacy. On the other hand, and despite the leading explanatory role of theory, its development was intrinsically linked to its empirical test and a thorough examination of the empirical evidence available.

3.3. Mincer's Initial Model

In his dissertation, Mincer aimed at developing an analytical frame-work, what then became known as the schooling model, which he regarded as a unified explanation for several empirical regularities, more precisely an 'attempt to explore empirical regularities in personal income distribution as analytical consequences of individual differences in investment in human capital, that is in training and experience' (1957a: 1). In fact, one of the aspects Mincer disliked in labor research at those times was the lack of firm theoretical guidance and the resistance to apply neoclassical price theory to labor issues. The more he advanced with his work the more he became convinced that underlying those differences of income was a process of rational choice between alternatives of investment in human capital (Mincer

1957*a*: 30–1). Mincer thought that the empirical evidence provided strong support for the hypothesis that occupational choice was rationally based. This meant that the postponement of earnings to a later stage confirmed Adam Smith's farsighted observations about 'higher annual pay in occupations which require more training' (Mincer 1957*a*: 137).[6]

The emphasis on rational and free choice meant that differences in income were far less the result of chance or natural abilities. Mincer suggested these were, to a large extent, an inevitable compensation for the advantages and disadvantages associated with each occupation, namely in terms of the training demands. This also corresponded to a view that expected a tendency toward equalization of earnings of heterogeneous workers, notably in terms of skills. The equalization tendencies were fostered by the behavior of rational economic agents in a labor market that Mincer believed to be basically competitive (Mincer 1970: 3). This also collided with widespread perceptions in postwar labor research that tended to emphasize the mitigated nature of competition in the labor market.

The model was regarded as a partial and tentative, though unified, explanation of several empirical regularities. Partial and tentative because it corresponded to an abstraction and simplification of reality; and it was an explanation competing with other alternative ones. Despite these limitations, Mincer considered that the model performed fairly well, according to his criteria. These criteria included the conformity of the empirical features with the model's predictions. The powerful character of the human capital model lay, according to Mincer, in its explanatory power of empirical findings. Hence, and despite some carefulness, the positivistic tone 'à la Friedman' emerged in several passages.[7]

According to Mincer, the usefulness of a human capital model to explain income distribution was confirmed by its performance in terms of predictive power. The first main prediction of the model, to which Mincer claimed empirical support, was to understand patterns of occupational choice and the way these related to length of training. Accordingly, Mincer considered that the evidence supported the view of a higher remuneration for occupations requiring more training in order to compensate the individuals not only for the direct costs of training, but especially for the postponement of their earning period.[8] The second main prediction was to understand interoccupational differentials of remuneration. This was illustrated by the impact in terms of the rate of increase of lifetime income as a result of on-the-job training. In fact, human capital, when considered broadly (i.e. to include postschool training), was regarded as a powerful force in terms of promoting a stronger rate of individual economic growth, and by making individuals more productive. This was empirically observable on the steeper slopes of the life-path income curves, and by a greater dispersion of income. Finally, Mincer considered that the various partial examinations had given robustness to the analysis. This was done by analyzing income groups by industry, race, gender, and city size.

He nevertheless presented the results with some caution, due to the limitations of the study. First was the fact that the model could predict reasonably well several empirical regularities, but not their magnitudes. Secondly, the analysis could not assess the relative contribution of each of the factors considered, namely of human capital. This was regarded as a major explanatory force, but its relative importance vis-à-vis other factors remained unknown. Thirdly, it remained to be investigated what the real importance of ability factors and their interaction with human capital was. Fourthly, the analysis had basically assumed equality of opportunity, especially regarding training, though this was hardly tenable in a realistic analysis of income distribution. Finally, Mincer assessed how far the impact of training was either a result of compensatory reward for lengthier and costlier periods of training or the result of restrictive access to longer training, thus to more qualified and better remunerated occupations.

To this were added some important empirical and statistical caveats. The most notable concerned the samples available (only the cross-sectional type). Then Mincer referred to the difficulties in translating concepts into measurable variables, especially the conceptual difficulties associated with training and occupational status. Moreover, he acknowledged some shortcomings in his results which were due to the limited predictive power (mostly on an average basis rather than on an individual one). On the other hand, he faced some difficulties in the translation of the model to 'empirically identifiable, measurable counterparts' (1957a: 291). Therefore, he used age instead of experience as a variable and measured essentially the effects of formal training.

Altogether, and despite those caveats, Mincer thought his results meant that individuals' choices in terms of pre- and postemployment training were decisive for their earning capacity and lifetime income pattern. The differences in terms of training were significant in explaining the differences not only between occupations but also within the same occupation. The importance of the extended concept of training, by including 'experience on the job', was clearly related to the latter aspect. His analysis was focused in terms of identifying patterns of behavior and factors responsible for the present distribution of personal income.

3.4. Exploring the Role of Postschool Investments

A peculiar aspect of Mincer's initial work on human capital was that he developed it largely unaware that other people were interested in turning human capital into an explanatory principle for several economic issues. Mincer and Schultz only became aware of the closeness of their research interests and its unplanned complementarity when Mincer went to Chicago as a postdoctoral fellow (1957–8) after an invitation from Schultz. Mincer's short but intensive period at Chicago would provide him with important stimulus to explore his main areas of research. Foremost among these was to ascertain the relevance of human capital theory (in particular the role of on-the-job training) for lifetime income and income inequality.

This attention to the role of on-the-job training within human capital analysis was apparent in his next contribution to human capital research, which was presented at the 1961 NBER conference organized by T. W. Schultz on 'Investment in Human Beings' and later published as the 1962 supplement of the *Journal of Political Economy*.

This conference owed much to T. W. Schultz's efforts and to his leading role in those early years of 'the human capital revolution'. Schultz (1971) believed that research was not a product of coincidences, but rather the result of a favorable and efficient organizational context.

The 1961 conference and the corresponding volume constituted a landmark in terms of human capital research, because of the wide scope and influential nature of many of the published articles. In a sense the volume became a manifesto for human capital research potential not only in terms of schooling and training but also in terms of migration, health, economic growth, and various aspects of social behavior. Thus, the volume included important pieces such as

Gary Becker's presentation of the analytical framework for his 1964 book *Human Capital*, Jacob Mincer's aforementioned article on the returns to on-the-job training, Burton Weisbrod's piece on the social benefits of human capital, Selma Mushkin's article on health as a human capital investment, Larry Sjastaad's exploration of the migration component of human capital, Edward Denison's paper on the contribution of human capital to economic growth, and an article by George Stigler on the economic value of information seen from a human capital perspective. It is hard to overestimate the importance of this volume for the emergent human capital research program. In a nutshell, this conference and the companion volume identified and advanced the leading topics that would dominate human capital research for many years.

In his contribution to the conference, Mincer (1962*a*) considered the need to avoid placing all the emphasis on formal schooling. Rather, it was important to enhance the significance of postschool training by considering it in a broad perspective (including formal and informal training, and learning from experience). Many workers underwent 'a more specialized and often prolonged process of acquisition of occupational skill, after entry into the labor force' (Mincer 1962*a*: 50). This type of training had been important in Western societies on many occasions in the past, when many skills had been acquired mostly through job experience. Despite the extension of schooling levels to broader groups of society, this type of training is still relevant today. In some cases on-the-job training was complementary to that provided by schooling; in other cases, it was an alternative route to some sections of the labor force.

The main purpose of Mincer's paper was to estimate the magnitude of the investments made in this type of training. Mincer assumed an investment approach that would henceforth characterize the human capital approach to training, that is, that 'an individual takes a job with an initially lower pay than he could otherwise get because he knows that he will benefit from the experience gained in the job taken' (Mincer 1962*a*: 52). Thus, on-the-job training implied an opportunity cost that Mincer tried to assess in his estimation. The estimation of training costs was rather cumbersome because of severe limitations in terms of data.[9]

Despite the limitations in terms of data availability, Mincer considered that one could essentially apply the same framework used before to assess the costs of schooling, considering both direct and indirect, or opportunity costs, borne by individuals in order to increase their future earning potential. These indirect costs, which seemed already to be very significant in the case of schooling, were even more relevant in the case of training, since the direct costs were hardly significant. Training activities were certainly costly, but their direct costs were largely supported by the firms providing the training opportunities.

Mincer tried to circumvent the limitations in terms of data. Inspired by Becker's ongoing work on human capital at the NBER, he compared two average income streams of workers which differed by the amount of training (1962*a*: 54ff.). Given some simplifying assumptions, Mincer first computed the rate of return on the investment of training by which the two groups of workers differed. Then, he calculated the training costs through the comparison of the net earnings streams. For that purpose he used pretax income data on US male workers for the years 1939, 1949, and 1958, classified by age and education. Also, for each year and education group, he calculated annual estimates of the training costs. Accordingly, he obtained approximate estimates of the amount of resources an average male worker was expected to spend on on-the-job training activities during his working life.[10]

The major finding, according to Mincer, was that the opportunity costs of on-the-job activities were often higher than costs of a comparable increment in schooling (1962*a*: 58). However, whereas the amounts of schooling per capita grew at all levels during the period analyzed, the comparable values in on-the-job training increased mostly at the higher levels of education. This meant that empirically there was a positive correlation between schooling and on-the-job training, suggesting that an expansion in schooling would promote further investments in training. At the lower educational levels, some substitutability seemed to exist between schooling and job training, and therefore the expansion of the educational system has led to less emphasis on training at those levels.

Mincer then attempted to calculate the rate of return to some types of training, namely medical specialization and apprenticeships, in order to compare them with the rates of return to investments that included both formal education and on-the-job training. Despite the limitations of the exercise, he concluded that monetary rates of return were similar for schooling and on-the-job training. In some cases, it seemed nevertheless that the private rates of return were higher for total training at the college level than for some types of on-the-job training. The data also suggested that there was some stability in the rate of return to training and some decline in the return to college education, but the weaknesses in the data advised some carefulness in using the data.

Finally, Mincer tried to explore the implications and relevance of those investments in on-the-job training to understand several aspects of labor market behavior. In particular, he used his results to understand differences in income and employment among population groups that differed by levels of education, gender, or ethnicity. Both female and nonwhite workers tended to receive less on-the-job training and this was a major reason in explaining the relative flatness of their age-income profiles. Moreover, and using Becker's distinction between general and specific training, Mincer noted that on-the-job training, where the specific component was likely to be stronger, seemed to be negatively correlated with labor turnover. Hence, the differentials in the amount of on-the-job training received could be extremely relevant in understanding the higher probability of unemployment that affected some groups more, including women and nonwhite workers.

Although some of the differences between groups could be due to discrimination in the labor market, as well as the availability of training opportunities, Mincer considered that his analysis directed at explaining the differences in earnings and employment stability between those groups confirmed not only the validity of the human capital investment approach but also the relevance of differences in the amount of on-the-job training received. It is fascinating how, in an almost impressionistic way, Mincer already highlights some of the more important results that would come from his subsequent work on women's earnings and labor turnover, and the implications of training in both these areas.

His empirical work nevertheless faced important limitations. The main ones were due to the unavailability of direct estimates, and several sources of bias could have led to an underestimation or overestimation of the rates of return to on-the-job training. The latter included cross-sectional income profiles, the misreporting of years of schooling, and the underestimation of the costs of training. The underestimation of costs was most severe on the firms' side. Among those factors leading to an underestimation of the rates of return to training was mainly the omission of survival factors. Finally, there was the possibility of bias in the estimations due to the assumption that differences in income streams of the groups compared were due to differences in training, and the omission of factors such as personal motivation and ability, socioeconomic background, and information.

3.5. Schooling, Experience, and Earnings

The emphasis on on-the-job training would become a hallmark of Mincer's work on human capital. The attention given to this, alongside formal education, was very much visible in his 1974 book *Schooling, Experience, and Earnings* which was a major subsequent contribution to human capital research and to the study of the economic effects of training. In this study, developed within the NBER, Mincer returned to some of the key questions raised in his doctoral dissertation, though now benefiting from the richer data provided by the 1960 census. He therefore attempted to update the analysis developed in his Ph.D. dissertation, which was based on the 1950 census data.

One of the main objectives of the 1974 study was 'to gain some understanding of the observed distributions of earnings from information on the distribution of accumulated net investments in human capital among workers' (Mincer 1974*a*: 2). This was done by introducing the, then to become famous and widely used, human capital earnings function, which related the distributions of earnings and net investments in human capital. This corresponded to Mincer's aim to extend the empirical assessment of human capital by measuring the contribution of postschool investments (especially on-the-job training).

Although the rational allocation of resources implied that most of the human capital investments should be undertaken at an early age, Mincer considered it inadequate to omit other postschool investments. In fact, the differences between these types of human capital investments were consistent with an economic explanation based on the rationality of the agents, since whereas schooling was basically a full-time activity, training was far more a part-time activity and therefore it made sense that the former was largely located at earlier stages of life and the latter at more advanced periods (Mincer 1974*a*: 13).[11]

Despite the continuing limitations in terms of data, Mincer considered that the attempt to measure, even if crudely, postschool investments in human capital was an important contribution toward improving the measurement of lifetime investments in human capital and to understanding the explanatory role of those investments for the analysis of income distribution. This was also part of the effort to attain a better understanding of the links between investments in human capital and earnings. Previous work, mostly due to the availability of data, had placed emphasis on the analysis of schooling investments. However, the empirical results had shown that, despite being positive, the links between educational attainment (measured by years of schooling) and individual earnings were weaker than many had anticipated. Moreover, the empirical analysis had provided limited evidence that fell short of the expectations of the explanatory power of human capital models to define the main features of income distributions. This led to some dismay regarding human capital research.

Mincer recognized the complexity of those links between human capital and earnings. Human capital analysis had to start from schooling analysis but should go much beyond that, promoting a more complete analysis of the nature and type of human capital investments. This included attention to issues concerning schooling such as the quality of schooling (not only quantity) and the analysis of individual differences in learning and in effectively using individuals' stock of human capital.

According to Mincer, even more important was the analysis of postschool investments in human capital. The poor empirical performance of human capital should not be taken as questioning the relevance of human capital analysis but as indicating the inability of the schooling model to capture the complexity of the distribution of earnings. This highlighted the importance of training, largely taking place outside educational institutions, and its relevance for individual earning profiles. It also emphasized the impact of differences in the labor force participation on individual earnings, as pointed out in Mincer's research on labor supply and interlabor force mobility.[12] Mincer expected that the extension of the schooling model to cover postschool investments in human capital would improve the explanatory power of the human capital model and confirm it as a unifying principle for a variety of features of the structure of earnings (Mincer 1974a: 45).

Mincer's book was very well received and would have a major impact, especially due to its contribution in strengthening human capital's empirical case and placing greater emphasis on the role of on-the-job training. This was something that was recognized by critics and supporters alike. It would be regarded by Walter McMahon in the *Journal of Economic Literature* (1975) as a timely antidote to the growing skepticism toward the role of education in explaining different lifetime earnings. Likewise, Robert E. Hall in the *Journal of Political Economy* (1975) praised Mincer's empirical forcefulness and carefulness, namely vis-à-vis more polemical work such as the one spurred by the inequality controversy.

3.6. Extending the Human Capital Model

As previously explained, one of the major motivations of Mincer's 1974 book was to position investments in on-the-job training activities within a human capital analytical framework. Hence, in the second part of the book, Mincer moves decisively to consider the explanatory role of these postschool investments. In particular, he argued that after some years of activity the ability of schooling investments to explain inequality in earnings declined rapidly and that postschool investments became crucial to an understanding of that inequality. Although he accepted that other factors, such as chance, changing market opportunities, and elements of biopsychological development, were important, he nevertheless considered that the evidence available supported the view that work experience was far more important than age in affecting productivity and earnings.

Mincer started with the schooling model and then built-up subsequent investments in human capital. In his model, he pointed out that the two major sets of costs associated with investments in human capital were the direct costs and foregone earnings, that is, the costs associated with the postponement of earnings and the reduction of earning life.[13] However, since many individuals did not stop developing their skills (i.e. investing in human capital), he proceeded to the identification of earning profiles—the variation of earnings with age during the working life.

The consideration of postschool investments in training was nevertheless cumbersome. On the one hand, the information about the quantity of training each worker received was not likely to be available in the near future. On the other hand, even if these data were available they would tend to underestimate the quantity of training the workers actually received, since the data would be based only on formal programs. Faced with the limitations of the data available, Mincer had to make some simplifying assumptions.[14]

A critical concept in human capital analysis introduced by Mincer in this book (and one that would become an essential part of the argumentation about the role of human capital investments for lifetime income) was that of the overtaking age. In fact, the schooling model was far more applicable to the years of working life before the overtaking year than to the subsequent periods, as shown by the continuous decay of the effects of schooling on earnings after the first decade of experience (1974*a*: 54). Mincer analyzed the distribution of earnings at the overtaking age (1974*a*: 52). This aimed to test the schooling model and attempted to assess the contributions of postschool investments to aggregate inequality.

However, Mincer also noted that the inequality estimated at the overtaking age merely reflected differences in schooling. Among those factors was the fact that the distribution of years of schooling only measured in part the differences in schooling investments.[15] Moreover, the overtaking age was not only defined approximately in empirical terms, but could also differ among people with the same amount of schooling, if there were different rates of return to schooling and if their investment profiles were not proportional. These differences in the rates of return to schooling, even for schooling of comparable quality, were rather difficult to measure empirically and were probably due, to a large extent, to unobservable factors.

In the book, Mincer (1974*a*: 73–4) tried to update his pioneering attempts (1962*a*) to estimate the amounts invested in postschool activities by workers per schooling groups.[16] These estimates confirmed his view that monetary values increased with schooling, but that the time-equivalent investments were not strongly related to schooling levels. Hence, the more-schooled workers tended to invest more in postschool activities, but did not spend more time than the less-schooled workers on these activities. The monetary difference was possibly due to complementarities between schooling and postschool activities, differences in abilities, and different opportunities in terms of funding those investments in postschooling (Mincer 1974*a*: 75).

Moreover, these investments in training had an important effect not only on lifetime earnings but also on the explanatory power of the model (Mincer 1974*a*: 44–5). To illustrate further the importance of the postschool investments, Mincer analyzed some studies on promotion practices, which indicated, according to Mincer, that among the important factors in the internal promotion practices, education did not seem to play a very effective role (thus weakening the credentialist argument). According to the same sources, skill and ability were the most important factors among nonseniority ones. Seniority seemed to play an important role for blue-collar workers. Based on these indications, Mincer concluded that the 'postschool productivity growth is causally related not to school but to post-school investments' (1974a: 81).

3.7. The Human Capital Earnings Function

The investment approach that Mincer took to understand age and experience earnings profiles made one of the main contributions of the 1974 book possible—the human capital earnings function. This expanded 'the schooling model to include postschool investments in an econometric analysis of the distribution of earnings' (Mincer 1974a: 83). This was justified by the significant inequality in earnings after two or three decades of work experience, and the apparent contribution that postschool investments gave to explain that inequality. Previous analysis had already pointed out that the inclusion of age, in addition to schooling, in a regression analysis expanded its explanatory power. Moreover, it was also noted that age interacted with schooling in their impact on earnings, and therefore the econometric analysis had to consider the existence of an interactive term. However, whereas age seemed to interact with schooling, this seemed far less the case with experience and schooling.

In defining the functional form of the earnings function, Mincer posed several considerations. First, that the economic theory analyzing optimizing behavior suggested that investment in human capital would decline over the life cycle. Second, that mathematical simplicity and statistical tractability recommended linear and log-linear experience functions. Third, that a functional form that related monetary earnings to years of schooling was a misspecification of the human capital model, since logarithms of earnings presented a better statistical fit.[17] Mincer then applied the human capital earnings function to the cross-sectional distribution of earnings (1974a: 89ff.). This faced some important limitations. Foremost was the fact that although there was individual information on schooling, the equivalent was not available for postschool investments. These differences were obtained mainly through differences in experience.

Although the age-earnings profile was well known among labor and income distribution scholars, Mincer's contribution was in changing the emphasis from age to labor market experience, with major implications for subsequent research (Rosen 1992: 161). It led to the empirical division between general and firm-specific training, reflecting Becker's theoretical insight that became essential to the study of important labor market phenomena such as the gender wage gap or job turnover. Another important feature was to devise a specific quadratical form for the experience terms in order to reflect the implications of the theory of human capital investments over the life cycle.[18] After testing several alternatives, Mincer chose a functional form in which investment was proportional to earnings capacity, with the proportion linearly declining in market experience (Rosen 1992: 162). This choice survived very well the subsequent intense scrutiny.[19]

Thus, the human capital earnings function is neither the result of an ad hoc formulation nor an empirical generalization. It is rather the result of an analysis that combines theoretical considerations with empirical validations. Maybe it is the fact that it is so firmly rooted in Mincer's 'uncommon blend of an insightful data analysis guided by strong conceptual foundations and a thoroughly economic point of view' (Rosen 1992: 157) that explains its enormous and lasting success among labor economists. Thus, it is hard nowadays to find a labor economist who at a certain point of his or her career did not use it. This has even led to the curious expression of 'Mincering the data', that is, fitting the human capital earnings function to the available data (Rosen 1992: 162).

The regression analysis using the human capital earnings function led to the following major findings. First, that despite some functional limitations and restrictions, the schooling and experience variables had a significant explanatory power of aggregate earnings inequality, of around 30 percent. Second, that the partial coefficient of the schooling variable was an estimate of an average rate of return to schooling from which could be obtained, through non-linear formulations, different rates for different levels of schooling. These would tend to decline with years of schooling. Third, that adding the variation in weeks worked would give a very important contribution to the explanatory power of the regression. Moreover, the coefficient associated with that variable suggested a positive correlation between number of weeks worked and weekly earnings with levels of schooling and experience. Fourth, and possibly the most significant conclusion for Mincer, was that adding the experience variable greatly increased the explanatory power of the human capital analysis. This was even more significant for Mincer, since there were clear limitations in the measurement of that variable that suggested its power was significantly understated. Among these limitations he pointed out the lack of direct information on individual postschool investments, leading to the assumption that these were equal for all individuals in the same schooling group.[20]

In his empirical analysis of differences in earnings among schooling groups, Mincer found there were some systematic patterns.[21] First, that at given ages the absolute and relative rates of growth of earnings increased with schooling. Second, that earnings stabilized at earlier ages for those groups with lower schooling levels. Both factors contributed to the explanation that absolute and relative earnings differentials among schooling groups increased with age. This persisted for later ages in the case of weekly earnings. Third, monetary differentials among schooling groups increased with experience, and since the earnings profiles were concave, that increase was more significant with age. Fourth, whereas the experience profiles of log earnings tended to converge with years of experience, age profiles diverged with years of age (Mincer 1974a: 70).

In the model, Mincer also introduced the issue of depreciation of human capital that he had been developing with some of his other research students (see below). Among the factors that contributed to older investments in human capital partially obsolete were the advances in knowledge and the increasing incidence of illness with age. Hence, the depreciation rate was likely to be related to factors such as age, experience, and the size and age of the vintage of human capital.

As far as ability was concerned, Mincer downplayed its effects. On the one hand, he considered that some of the ability measures used to correct the estimation bias included unobserved components of the human capital stock, besides genuine efficient parameters (although he did not substantiate this statement) (Mincer 1974a: 3). On the other hand, and based on other studies, he assumed that the bias, due to the omission of the ability measures in the estimation, was not very significant (maybe some overstatement of the human capital explanatory power). Moreover, he did not seem to be very worried, since his study was not concerned with all the variables explaining earnings, but only with the effects of human capital on earnings. In fact, he had serious doubts regarding the importance given by other authors, especially at that time, to the screening function of education. Although he did not deny education's informational role, he nevertheless considered that the research available indicated that the screening effect was neither dominant nor permanent; otherwise other much cheaper methods of testing would proliferate as an alternative to education (see Mincer 1979).

3.8. Assessing the Explanatory Role of Human Capital in Inequality

The advances in the analytical model and in the availability of data opened new possibilities to assess the role of human capital in explaining income inequality. An earlier attempt to do this was presented in Mincer's article with Barry Chiswick (Chiswick and Mincer 1972), one of his earliest students, on changes in income inequality in post-World War II North America. Accordingly, they used the human capital earnings function, which was an instrument of analysis of time-series changes in income inequality, by relating income inequality to the distribution of age, schooling, employment, and the corelations between these variables. The results indicated that, post-World War II, the changes in aggregate relative income inequality of adult males were due primarily to changes in the distribution of age and employment, with the schooling distribution playing a smaller direct role, though a significant indirect role. In fact, the major role played by changes in employment conditions and the apparent role of schooling on these aspects seemed to support a significant indirect role. In some way this work was also an attempt to cool down the 'excessive' expectations of the egalitarian role of education (cf. Mincer 1979).[22]

The evidence collected in preparation for the 1974 book gave Mincer another major opportunity to assess further the role of human capital in the inequality of personal income. This work pursued further work that people such as Barry Chiswick had been developing on income inequality.[23] In his analysis, Mincer would conclude that together 'schooling and postschooling investments accounted for close to two-thirds of the inequality of earnings of adult, white, urban men in the United States in 1959' (Mincer 1974a: 96).[24]

In his analysis, Mincer adapted the schooling model to a cross section of workers in order to address the distribution analysis (1974a: 24ff.). With regard to the personal distribution of earnings, he noted the following basic implications. First, that the positive skewness traditionally exhibited by distributions of income and earnings could be partly due to the logarithmic transformation that converted absolute differences in earnings into percentage differences in earnings. Second, that the larger the dispersion in the distribution of schooling the larger the relative dispersion and skewness in the distribution of earnings. Finally, that the higher the returns to schooling the greater the inequality in earnings and the skewness of its distribution.

The analysis of distribution of earnings tended to emphasize inequality between groups with different schooling attainment. However, Mincer noted that inequality within groups with the same level of schooling attainment was far from negligible (1974a: 32). First, there were differences in the stock of human capital due to differences in schooling quality and/or rates of return to schooling. Second, there were differences in individual behavior concerning postschool investments in human capital. Finally, there were differences due to the variability in the rates of return to those postschool investments in human capital. In fact, the evidence confirmed that there were marked differences in respect to each of the three factors, though Mincer was particularly concerned with the last two. The analysis of earnings distribution also highlighted the fact that individuals with more schooling seemed to retire later, though still on average presenting a shorter earnings span due to the initial postponement of entry into working life.

Due to the use of cross-sectional data, Mincer paid particular attention to the existence of secular trends in schooling and the extent to which these affected the conclusions concerning inequality (1974a: 107ff.). He concluded that, since schooling seemed to have a negative impact on inequality, the stronger the secular trend toward the expansion of schooling the stronger was the attenuation of aggregate inequality, as larger weights were given to the younger cohorts in which there were smaller relative variances.

Mincer then paid attention to one of the features of personal inequality that had dominated early twentieth-century debates: the clear positive skewness of the distribution. Since Pareto, that positive skewness was consistently treated as a crucial feature of personal income distribution and as a key in explaining the forces underpinning the patterns of inequality. This was particularly the case for the so-called stochastic models that tended to place emphasis on factors beyond the control of individual or society choices in their explanation of personal inequality. Mincer considered that, in terms of skewness, earnings distributions would tend to fit between normal and log-normal distributions.

Mincer was particularly interested in exploring the links between that skewness and schooling. These two aspects seemed to be positively associated (at given levels of experience) more often than was the case between schooling and the log variance of inequality.[25] From a human capital point of view the positive skewness is not defined a priori as an inevitable feature, since it depends on the shape of the distribution of schooling, which is largely exogenous to the model and presents secular changes. Although the schooling distributions of younger age cohorts presented negative skewness, the positive skewness seems to persist overall, due to the positive correlation between monetary means and variances in the age-schooling groups of the earnings structure (Mincer 1974*a*: 111–12). This correlation is explained by patterns of persistence in human capital accumulation, that is, those individuals who accumulate more human capital in early periods (mainly schooling) also tend to accumulate more human capital in subsequent periods of their lives.

The analysis of skewness led Mincer to address one of his major targets of criticism with regard to income distribution analysis, that of stochastic models.[26] Whereas with the so-called ability models Mincer could draw convergence and find some commonalities with the human capital approach, with the stochastic approaches he found less common ground. Although both the human capital and the stochastic approaches share some predictions (e.g. log variances of earnings grew in some schooling groups and during certain phases of the working life), the interpretation given to the same empirical phenomena was very different. Whereas the stochastic approach took temporal variations in income to be the result of variations in chance, the human capital approach regarded variations in earnings to be a systematic and persistent consequence of rational and cumulative investment behavior (Mincer 1974*a*: 116).

In order to compare both approaches, Mincer analyzed panel cor-relations of earnings of individuals belonging to the same cohort in two different time periods. His empirical investigation convinced him that the findings were inconsistent with random shock models and consistent with a human capital model. First, because panel correlations bracketing the overtaking period seem to be relatively weak and stronger afterward. Second, the leveling off the decline in correlations after a seven-year period seems plausible, since the rank-ing of individual earnings will tend to acquire a long-run stability only disturbed by so-called short-run fluctuations.[27]

One of the factors that also helped in understanding the remaining unexplained part of inequality had to do with variations in employ-ment. Mincer recalled Becker's remarks that the variations in weeks of employment were also linked to investments in human capital. On the one hand, the larger the investments in human capital the lower the probability of worker turnover and unemployment. This was particularly the case with specific types of human capital, whose overlap with postschool human capital was significant. On the other hand, the level of investment in human capital was also related to the degree of attachment to labor force participation. Both factors sug-gested that since employment variations were, at least in part, related to human capital investments, then the contribution of employment variation to earnings inequality should also be partially credited to the human capital approach.[28]

This contribution of employment variation to earnings inequality was even more relevant in the case of groups whose attachment to the labor force was weaker. Thus, this is a relevant issue for the comparison between male and female earnings. Whereas the distri-bution of full-time and annual earnings was largely the same for men, those two distributions are very different in the case of women. This contributed to an explanation of why the inequality of earnings of all women was greater than that of all men, with the opposite occurring with the distribution of earnings of full-time workers. The differences in the case of women were significantly linked to labor supply behavior and the more intermittent participation of some women in the labor force, resulting in important interactions with patterns and levels of investment in human capital (see below). Using work that he had developed with some of his students, Mincer noted that women were less likely to invest in more specific types of human capital, namely postschool human capital, which was reflected in their flatter age-earnings profiles in comparison to those of full-time male workers. Mincer also pointed out that the changes in relative inequality with age and schooling that were noted in the earnings structure of male workers were also less pronounced in the earnings structure of full-time female workers, and almost totally absent in the female annual earnings distribution.[29]

The analysis of this variability of earnings within each schooling group was also extremely relevant for the analysis of the complexities of human capital, as well as for the analysis of its contribution vis-à-vis that of other factors related to earnings. The analysis of monetary variances led Mincer to conclude that the observed increases of variances with age and experience were largely influenced by the enormous impact of postschool investments in individuals' earnings and working lives. Mincer also concluded that postschool investments presented significant variability among individuals with the same level of schooling, both in monetary terms and in time allocation (Mincer 1974*a*: 108).[30]

3.9. Concluding Remarks

Until the mid-twentieth century, education played a minor role in the debates about inequality of income. This situation was changing slowly, but received a major contribution with Mincer's doctoral work. In his Ph.D. thesis, Mincer suggested that investment in education and training, henceforth widely known as human capital, was a major explanatory principle for inequality of income. Mincer's doctoral work became a turning point in terms of personal income distribution and the economic role of education and training. Henceforth, education and training became increasingly regarded as powerful forces shaping personal wealth and, for a large part of the subsequent research, an unavoidable element of analysis. His persistent efforts contributed to the acceptance of the human capital view of inequality, alongside the much more established hypothesis of noncompeting groups, ability/genetic factors, and mathematical models based on chance.

Mincer regarded the development of human capital theory as an effective attempt by economists to recapture the intellectual ascendancy on the topic of income distribution, following the path set initially by Smith and then largely ignored until the late fifties. The emphasis of income distribution analysis on human capital was seen by Mincer as an attempt to redress the balance and give proper weight to 'an economic explanation' regarding issues of opportunity, ability, and chance as, basically, constraints on (rational) choices. The proper object of analysis should be those choices and their impact on individuals' lifetime patterns of income. Mincer believed that 'human capital investment lends itself to a more systematic and comprehensive analysis of wage differentials, than those each of the other factors [considered by Smith in his principle of compensatory differences]' (1976: 137).[31] This simple and powerful explanation of human capital should be a hallmark of economic analysis, and attracted Mincer since his earliest research (Mincer 1957a).

In his appraisal of the contribution of several theories to the explanation of inequality of income, Mincer was far more critical of the mathematical/stochastic models. These models tended to adopt a more exclusive and self-sufficient tone damaging to the human capital approach. He therefore considered that these models had received too much attention, without delivering in terms of research. In contrast, human capital, in an inclusive conceptualization that gave proper emphasis to on-the-job training, by underlining the role of individual occupational choice as a powerful and useful instrument of analysis, was able to provide convincing explanations of the skewness of earnings distribution, of the increasing disparity of earnings profiles with age, and of the concentration of investments on training at an early age. Mincer pursued not only the definition of a conceptual framework, in which human capital played a dominant role in income distribution, but also its empirical validation. Moreover, he emphasized the efforts to make this approach compatible with competing ability and chance factors, by integrating them into an enlarged human capital framework.[32]

The relevance of this work to the subsequent development of human capital theory cannot be overestimated. With Mincer's doctoral work, human capital came to be regarded as a powerful force in terms of promoting individuals' earning capacity, by making individuals more productive, as shown by the steeper slopes of the life-path income curves, and by a greater dispersion of incomes. His doctoral dissertation would ensure him a central role in the development of human capital theory. However, by continuing this work further, namely in his major book *Schooling, Experience, and Earnings* (1974a), Mincer provided an updated and more robust defense of the explanatory role of human capital, especially at a time adverse to human capital theory. This book was no small contribution to the revival of human capital analysis in inequality debates after the controversies that characterized the early seventies. Although in recent years economists and policymakers have become more skeptical toward the equalizing potential role of education, the subsequent work of Mincer and others made human capital less vulnerable to criticism to those early and somewhat naive expectations about the explanatory role of education regarding inequality.

4

Appraising the Impact of the Human Capital Research Program

Despite fruitful collaborations and developments, human capital analysis was increasingly challenged. The criticisms became more noticeable in the mid-seventies when the private returns to education started falling rapidly. It was argued that, because earlier estimates of returns to education had been based on cross-sectional data, they had overestimated the returns to education, and with the progressive expansion of educated labor the returns would diminish steadily. The effect of the arrival of the college-educated post-World War II baby boomers on the labor market seemed to fulfill this prophecy (see Freeman 1976). The contribution of human capital in understanding inequality and labor market outcomes came under severe scrutiny from the early seventies onward.

In the following sections, the major criticisms of the human capital approach to the labor market and the way human capital dealt with these will be scrutinized. Moreover, Mincer's contribution to these debates and to what extent his research endured those controversies will be assessed.

4.1. Questioning the Role of Human Capital in Explaining Inequality

From its early days human capital research faced some skepticism regarding its contribution to the explanation of inequality of income, though the criticisms became stronger in the early seventies. The economic situation at the time played no small role. Whereas human capital research had emerged in a period characterized by great hopes in the potential role of education in promoting social mobility, notably in improving the lot of traditionally disadvantaged groups such as women or ethnic minorities, by the end of the decade these hopes had given way to serious skepticism.

Although there were significant expectations that the expansion of education would bring an increasing equality of economic opportunity and income, some authors implied that the empirical evidence, based on an increasing disparity of income, suggested otherwise (Thurow 1970*a*, 1975). Accordingly, factors such as ability, socioeconomic background, or even unidentified variables, seemed to overshadow the previously prominent role given to education. Moreover, education was increasingly regarded as an instrumental variable through which those forces affected earnings capacity. The view among an increasing number of researchers was that education had a role in terms of personal income but this was neither as significant as human capital theory postulated nor the result of individual maximization and intrinsically rational behavior (see Lydall 1976).

Propelled by poor results in terms of social mobility and economic growth, many started to question the real economic effect of schooling. A very controversial debate at the time on the mechanisms of inequality was provided by the so-called Jencks' study (Jencks et al. 1972).[1] Christopher Jencks, supported by a large team of researchers, challenged not simply the equalizing achievements of education, but especially its equalizing potential, thus the strategy of the sixties to promote increasing equality through educational expansion had generally failed, and it could hardly be otherwise (Jencks et al. 1972: 6–8). First, the differences between schools seemed to have rather small long-term effects, despite the fact that there were significant differences in terms of educational expenditures, especially at higher levels of education (37–8). Second, differences in terms of test scores were due to factors that schools did not control (109). Third, the most important determinant of educational attainment seemed to be family background, through (mostly measurable) economic and (more elusive) uneconomic differences (158–9). Fourth, despite significant signs of occupational mobility, there seemed to exist a great deal of variation in occupational status of individuals with similar amounts of education (176, 254). These results led Jencks, and many others, to conclude that economic success was only moderately related to family background, schooling, or ability as measured by standardized tests. Despite the criticisms, Jencks's work contributed nevertheless to instigate a serious amount of skepticism of the role of education in improving one's economic chances, and especially in increasing equality of opportunity.

Part of the criticisms of human capital was related to an increasing dissatisfaction with neoclassical economics and its application to the analysis of the labor market. Leading authors within the radical movement of the seventies, such as Herbert Gintis, Samuel Bowles, and Martin Carnoy, challenged the view that education had a major cognitive role and that earnings were essentially rewarding these enhanced cognitive capacities. Instead, they argued that the educational system was embedded in the social and political system and therefore the educational reward system was made to be consistent with the values of the social system and reflected the structure of social relations in that historical context (Gintis 1971). Accordingly, education was a type of 'cultural imperialism' and its major function was as an instrument of social reproduction transmitting the social and economic structure from one generation to another, through mechanisms of selection, reward, and working practices (Carnoy 1974).

Although schooling could produce some improvement in the economic condition of the lowest stratum, it did not significantly change the overall distribution of income, because it was not suppose to transform the very socioeconomic structure it was supposed to sustain (Carnoy 1974: 362ff.). This perspective rejected the neoclassical assumption that saw tastes and preferences as a given in terms of educational demand. According to the former, the demand for education was endogenously determined, that is, at least partly determined by the level of education attained and by the values transmitted by the educational system (Gintis 1971).[2] In fact, the highest economic stratum would always have more financial capacity to attain higher (and costly) levels of education, and this inequality of educational opportunity contributed to the enduring inequality of income and wealth.

This view of the role of education necessarily emphasized the importance of the socioeconomic background for students' educational achievement, and their economic position. In fact, the socioeconomic background played an important role in terms of lifetime income and professional career indirectly and directly. The indirect effect occurred through students' school achievement, that is, students coming from an economic background with traditionally high levels of qualifications experienced fewer difficulties in adjusting to the reward system of the educational system, thus they tended to be potentially more successful in their schooling attainment. The direct effect was in providing the individual with better financial and living conditions through intergenerational wealth transfers that contributed to perpetuate inequality of wealth (notably in terms of property income).

Even among those accepting a cognitive approach, there was an increasing emphasis on the family background effect on earnings. According to these, the fact that the student had better educated parents, better access to cultural goods, and notably more opportunities to defray the cost of higher levels of education, increased their possibilities of achieving and benefiting from higher levels of education. Some argued from evidence suggesting that parental earnings and characteristics influenced children's test scores and educational achievement, which in turn would affect their earnings (see Corcoran, Jencks, and Olneck 1976). So even if factors such as social discrimination were downplayed, the children of those better off seemed to be at a considerable advantage.

The criticisms came not only from the so-called radical economists but also from mainstream economists. One of the authors who produced some of the most important work in that respect was Paul Taubman, notably through his work on the determinants of income inequality (Taubman 1975). Although Taubman accepted that education had an impact on skills (physical, cognitive, psychological, and affective) and therefore on income potential, this was not only hard to measure, but also should not obscure the importance of other forces accounting for differences in income. These forces acted directly and indirectly (via schooling), and included factors such as ability, health, business assets, and family background (1975: 29ff.).[3] Taubman pointed out that the empirical evidence suggested that several family background variables seemed to be significant, and these included the education and occupation of parents and parents-in-law, home training, the type of school attended, and the type of religious upbringing. Hence, he concluded that, although education and training were important factors in terms of income, those should be regarded as primarily molded by family, religion, and peer groups (1975: 198–9).

The context faced by human capital research throughout the seventies became therefore increasingly more adversarial. The high, and arguably overoptimistic, beliefs in the effect of the role of education on equality of income were left largely unrealized. This had a very damaging effect on the confidence in the economic role of education and on the human capital explanation of income distribution. This situation was further complicated by the debates upon the role of ability and the challenge of the screening theory (see below).

The proponents of human capital research decided to address these challenges on inequality by studying the dual interaction between education and inequality, namely via intergenerational studies.[4] In the late seventies, Becker returned to these topics by focusing on family behavior and its impact on inequality on intra- and inter-generations. In terms of intergenerational mobility he considered the need to de-emphasize the role of chance or luck and to conduct the analysis through stochastic processes (similar to Mincer's approach to distribution of income). In fact, Becker regarded the convergence of human capital research and economic analysis of the family as providing a unified approach to inequality.[5]

It was noted that despite the increase in educational provision (and although the relative inequality of educational provision had declined, the same had not happened in terms of absolute inequality) there was an increase in the median income but not a reduction in the dispersal of income (see Chiswick 1978a). This was relevant not only in socioeconomic terms, but also when comparing different social groups in terms of gender, ethnicity, and region.

Much more attention was paid to the study of returns to education across different population groups, especially in terms of race and gender. Subsequent work on the gender gap tended to support Mincer's original work. It was suggested that the occupational inequality was not so much due to labor market discrimination or unequal opportunities of training and promotion, but to different commitments to the labor market (Goldin and Polachek 1987). These different commitments to the labor market had an impact on the stocks of human capital accumulated by women, though the historical evolution had reduced those differences.

The issue of variability of returns also gave additional visibility to the analysis of the impact of schooling quality. Despite the fact that the evidence of the effect of quality on student achievement has been elusive (Hanushek 1986), quality has been identified as having a significant impact on labor market performance (earnings) and in explaining black–white earnings differences (Card and Krueger 1992*a*). Evidence has been provided on the role played by schooling quality in understanding black–white inequality in earnings and in explaining schooling returns for both groups of workers (Card and Krueger 1992*b*).

Others nevertheless have noted that the effectiveness of discrimination should be taken into account (Heckman and Payner 1989), not only directly but also indirectly, for example, by influencing the patterns of human capital accumulation. This has contributed to the effect of education on black progress being less controversial, though possibly weaker than what was initially supposed (Heckman 1990).

Several decades of research have pointed out the differences in trends regarding gender and race inequalities and the differences in the factors explaining the evolution of those inequalities (Altonji and Blank 1999). The importance of individual attributes, namely in terms of human capital, was highlighted, though this relevance has declined in recent years since the distribution of human capital investments has become more similar across gender and racial groups. Overall, the empirical research confirmed that the role played by education and experience was very important though far more complex than initially suggested, with differentiated effects across socioeconomic, racial, and gender groups.

A significant part of the debate in recent decades about the economic relevance of investment in human capital has concerned the variability of these returns on a long-term basis, especially vis-à-vis the expansion of schooling. With the massive increase in formal qualifications occurring worldwide, many expressed fears that this would produce a significant decline in the returns to education that would eventually question the profitability of higher qualifications. Important research was produced in this respect with most evidence pointing toward a resilience of the high returns to higher formal qualifications (Murphy and Welch 1993), despite the enormous educational upgrading of the working population (Machin 2004). Moreover, the returns have in many instances favored those workers with higher skills.

These trends have reinforced the views of those arguing for the hypothesis of a skill-biased technical change, with some arguing that these effects had become stronger in recent decades (Levy and Murnane 1992).[6] However, evidence points to a long-term trend favoring skilled labor rather than it merely being a short-term trend (Autor, Katz, and Krueger 1998). It has been noted that this skill-bias of technological change was not a historical inevitability, since in the past technological change has moved clearly against skills (Goldin and Katz 1998). Moreover, it was pointed out that the complementarity between technological change and skills could have been promoted by the size of the market, namely by the expansion of skills (Acemoglu 1998), a view supported by theories of induced innovation.

This has reinforced the results at the macro level pointing to a significant role for education and other human capital investments to play in economic growth. However, the same studies have shown that although the contribution of human capital seems to be substantial, it presents significant cross-country variability (Freeman 1987). Moreover, this variability is also present even at the national level. Thus, though the recent wave of empirical work has strengthened the role that human capital may play in economic growth, it has also challenged any mechanistic views that had to a certain extent proliferated in the early years of human capital research by considering that these were not a 'universal panacea' (Rosenzweig 1995). The returns to human capital may be expected to be high in those situations where productive learning opportunities exist and can be exploited. Furthermore, although schooling improves the ability to learn, the existence of high-tech is not enough, since the level of complexity in dealing with those technological improvements is relevant.

Despite the skepticism of the seventies, more recent research has renewed the emphasis on the role of human capital within inequality analysis. Differences in the level and type of investment in human capital have been pointed out as a crucial factor in the understanding of recent changes in the wage structure and earnings inequality in the overall population and between specific population groups (Katz and Autor 1999). Despite the influence of other factors, such as the decline of unionization and labor market regulation, and the acceleration of globalization forces, the key factor in recent inequality changes was the result of supply and demand forces in terms of skills. Although there were specific reasons for the evolution of wages and earnings of certain population groups, human capital became an important part of the explanation of the relative position of each of these groups.

Overall, socioeconomic background was regarded as being over-played, and it was said that education had an independent effect on income, irrespective of family background (Leibowitz 1974). Education was regarded as developing individuals' cognitive capacities, hence their productive potential, and it was more than a mere transmission mechanism of family and societal values. It was not only a legitimizing force, as some had argued, but transferred concrete skills that had an economic value in the labor market. Moreover, what was being considered as the effect of family background could in fact be partly due to the home investments in children's human capital, such as in the time spent and activities done with their parents, especially with the mother (see Leibowitz 1977). Hence, many believed that fidelity to the initially broad classification of types of human capital, with not so much focus on schooling, could produce a stronger case in favor of human capital.

4.2. Qualifications or Credentials?

A significant part of the criticisms faced by human capital throughout the years was related to the neoclassical view of the labor market underpinning it, often echoing earlier debates about the best theoretical and methodological approach to labor economics. Several critics targeted what they regarded the analytical perfectibility of the labor market to be as portrayed by neoclassical researchers, namely by focusing on specific issues such as the marginal return to factors, labor market discrimination, and the level of information available to labor market agents.

One of the main criticisms came via the emergent theory of dual/segmented labor markets. This view was explored in various models of labor market analysis by authors such as Michael Piore, Peter Doeringer, David Gordon, and Michael Reich. Many of these had been influenced by the work of Clark Kerr and other postwar labor researchers on the Balkanization of the labor markets. According to this perspective the labor market was basically divided between qualified and unqualified workers. The former group was able to gain access to the primary labor market, characterized by well-paid jobs, frequent opportunities for training, and stable and attractive careers. For the latter group were reserved the poorly paid and precarious jobs of the secondary market, with high turnover and lack of opportunities of progress and training. Moreover, because the opportunities of on-the-job training were scarce or altogether absent, the possibility that these less-qualified workers would manage to move to better jobs was almost negligible. There seemed to be no redemption for the lack of initial qualifications. According to some of these authors it was this segmentation that explained the failure to significantly improve the condition of traditionally disadvantaged groups such as women and ethnic minorities. If that were the case, human capital would have a potentially minor role in redressing income inequality.

However, the strongest criticism of human capital analysis concerned the way labor market imperfections influenced the returns to schooling through credentialism. The most well known of the early credentialist attacks was authored by Ivar Berg in his *Education and the Jobs: The Great Training Robbery* (1970). According to Berg, the enormous growth of the educational sector had embedded in public opinion a naive and unsubstantiated belief in the potential benefits of education, especially in terms of better job and income opportunities. According to Berg human capital research presented several problems. It gave the impression of a mechanistic impact of education on income that in most cases was too positive and could hardly be fulfilled, leading therefore to frustration and dissatisfaction of workers and job seekers alike.

These claims would start making significant inroads within economics. Around the same time Michael Spence, then working on his doctoral dissertation at Harvard, noted that higher education was a clear example of market signaling.[7] By this he meant that signals were used for observable characteristics that could be manipulated by the individual (as was the case in education), and had costs (signaling costs) that were assumed to be negatively correlated to productivity (Spence 1973: 358). The receivers of the signal read them in light of experience. In general, and despite being productive for the individual, education would not increase the real marginal product at all (if ignoring the external benefits).[8]

This perspective was also being developed by Spence's main thesis supervisor, Kenneth Arrow (then at Harvard), who also wanted to challenge 'the current human capital orthodoxy' (Arrow 1973: 193). Arrow intended to 'formalize views expressed by some sociologists' (Arrow 1973: 193) who had suggested that education had mainly a credentialist effect (referring to the work of Berg). This filtering role of higher education was due to the fact that economic agents had imperfect information, which remained after the hiring process since the individual estimation of workers' productivity was not only difficult but also costly (Arrow 1973: 195, 215). In fact, the social value of education was mostly in its ability to select more productive individuals, and to provide important information to employers.

The screening role of education was part and parcel of increasing attention to the topic of imperfect information in the theory of markets, which also gained momentum in the early seventies. Accordingly, one of its main proponents, Joseph Stiglitz (1975), argued that a world of imperfect information turned the spotlight on education's role as a screening device, since there was an incentive for individuals to signal special abilities. If taken to the extreme, this screening hypothesis asserted that education merely identified students with particular attributes, acquired either at birth or by family background, but did not increase these attributes. This suggested a waste of resources since Stiglitz presented education as having mostly private benefits, not social ones.

The challenge to human capital raised by screening had significant implications for policymaking in general and development policy in particular. On a general basis it questioned the existence of significant productivity effects of education, let alone the externalities normally associated with education. If the productive behavior was hardly influenced by education, it was even less obvious that other secondary effects were significant. Thus the main reason advanced for public funding of education was severely weakened. This was even more critical in those countries still struggling to cover basic government functions, let alone to spend on education which was still considered by many as essentially a social expenditure.

Mincer certainly conceded that initially there could exist a small screening effect but it was neither lasting nor as relevant as most people saw it. He found it hard to accept that people would go to school in order to show employers that they could perform certain work. Since most jobs have a significant degree of specificity why would people prepare for every possible field? Hence, if that were the case he would expect the emergence of widespread testing mechanisms that would replace an educational system that was widely characterized as being general in terms of training. Mincer thought that the fact that people engaged in those general learning processes meant that they were acquiring more than just a credential, and were instead developing their human capital and enhancing their productive skills.

With his focus on long-term analysis, Mincer was able to downplay the controversy raised by screening. He considered that the research available indicated that the screening effect was neither dominant nor permanent, though he did not deny its informational role. Otherwise, other much cheaper methods of testing would proliferate as alternatives to education. It was not attractive for society and for each individual to incur such a great initial cost for training (including foregone income) if there were cheaper and quicker alternatives (see Mincer 1979: 94–5).

Similar to many other human capital researchers, and consistent with his strong attachment to empirical testing, Mincer replied to the screening challenge by calling for an improvement to the empirical side. He considered that significant advances could be made in the measurement of the returns to human capital, by addressing the methodological problems raised and by adopting a more inclusive empirical strategy that attempted to take account of factors such as natural ability and socioeconomic background. In fact, these researchers believed that by producing more accurate measurements they would be strengthening the case in favor of the human capital explanation of earnings, especially given the expected improvements in the measurement of types of human capital that due to data limitations had so far been poorly used in empirical work such as training and home investment in human capital (Becker 1962b). This would come almost notably by improving the evidence about aspects other than schooling such as on-the-job training (Mincer 1976; Ashenfelter 1979).

The attention of many human capital pioneers turned to the empirical front in order to fend off the screening challenge. One of the main strategies for challenging the screening critics was to choose their more extreme version, which stated that education had only a selection role. Although many of the screening theory's main proponents would say that this extreme view was only an explanatory device, it nevertheless became the target of criticisms in a typical 'straw-man' approach.[9]

Some studies focused on the comparison between graduates and nongraduates in an effort to test the screening versus human capital effect of schooling. In some cases the data was split into two groups: one with graduates and the other with dropouts. Joop Hartog (1983: 199) applied this test to a representative sample of the Dutch working population and concluded that the basic and tertiary levels did not dismiss the productivity-augmenting perspective of human capital theory, though the secondary level provided some support for the signaling effect of graduation.

This type of study has attracted interest in the so-called sheepskin effects in the returns to education, that is, the idea that the returns vary according to years of study. Hungerford and Solon (1987), using American data, observed that the returns to education increased discontinuously in diploma years with the largest jump in the returns taking place in the first year of college.[10] More recent research has argued that sheepskin effects existed and mattered (Jaeger and Page 1996). This did not imply that the returns to schooling were limited to diploma years, as had been suggested by the screening approach, but that they were possibly smaller than those for diploma years. The pattern of results indicated that the so-called sheepskin effects appeared to be significant for younger age cohorts but largely nonexistent for older workers (Brown and Sessions 2004). The study of the returns per type of year has provided some additional support for the human capital approach (Groot and Oosterbeek 1994). It was found that dropout years had a positive return, in light of a learning approach; repeating years had a neutral effect, thus not providing a negative signal to employers; and skipping a year had a negative effect, suggesting a less consolidated learning process.

Other studies have developed similar analysis though considering different types of workers. One of these types of studies compared types of occupation, by trying to identify groups of workers that did not have to signal their productivities, hence would not have to spend resources in acquiring the signal. This group of workers was then compared with those groups of workers that were supposed to use education as a signal. The nonprofessional salaried workers tended to be identified as a group of workers potentially strongly affected by screening, while the self-employed were generally identified as less vulnerable. These studies often assumed the absence of self-selection when comparing self-employed and employees (e.g. Grubb 1993), despite the scarce information on whether the decision regarding self-employment was taken prior to, for example, college attendance. Moreover, there was not much information on whether the types of individuals considered in both categories were similar and most of these tests did not control for personal characteristics.

Another of these types of studies developed a similar strategy, by assuming a strong version of the screening hypothesis, namely that education would have only a screening effect. Therefore the ability's signal would have an impact on the hiring process, but, since employers had the opportunity to monitor workers' productivity, they would tend to adjust the remuneration to the marginal productivity level. Accordingly, the sectors analyzed were divided into two groups. The first one, essentially the private sector, was considered less vulnerable to the screening effects over the long term, since the pricing of labor was assumed to converge to its actual marginal productivity level due to competition pressures. The other group, essentially the public sector, was regarded as more persistently vulnerable to the screening effects, lacking ability to significantly adjust to the marginal productivity level. Therefore, in the case of screening, the earnings pattern of similar occupations in both groups would tend to diverge with time.[11]

The comparison of the so-called screened and unscreened sectors supported the human capital approach, though it has been questioned to what extent were these results dependent on the subjectivity of the classifications used in terms of occupations. Is it less controversial to assume that wages are paid at the marginal productivity level in the private sector than the public sector? A consistent pattern was not observable in the comparison between self-employed and employees. Whereas in some cases the comparison suggested that the latter were more affected by screening, in other studies no major difference was detected between both groups in terms of screening. Several problems emerge. It could be that decisions on education are taken prior to decisions regarding work, in which case the test is not effective since one could conclude that the signaling effect is relevant for both cases (or neither). It could be that there is a situation of self-selection, hence a selection bias.

These two types of studies deserve some additional remarks. First, these tests relied on the assumption that screening was to be taken as strong screening, meaning that education had *exclusively* a filtering effect, which was clearly an overstatement of the screening theories. Second, even the authors using this test recognized that a significant degree of subjectivity (with an important impact on the results obtained) was introduced by the classification of the occupations as screened/competitive and unscreened/noncompetitive.[12] Third, those studies that compared different employment sectors assumed that in one of the sectors—the competitive one—the factors were paid at its marginal cost level. However, if that is not exactly the case the test's conclusions became seriously weakened. Finally, the third test assumed parallelism of the age-earning profiles, regardless of differences in terms of on-the-job opportunities between groups with different educational credentials. It could be that there is no postentry in the labor market convergence, because the opportunities of training are unequal and better-educated workers receive more training, which enhances their earnings potential.

Another type of study which focused on siblings (twins or kin groups) assumed that these workers would have a closer socioeconomic background and a genetic proximity, allowing better isolation of the education and ability effects (on the problems of this assumption, see Griliches 1979).[13] One of the first attempts to use this approach was that of Paul Taubman (1976), using the NAS–NRC Twin data. His results indicated that both genetic factors and family environment variables were important in explaining the variance of earnings, and even more important in explaining the variance of schooling (this being also important to the variance of earnings). The effect of genetic and family factors seemed to be less pronounced on earnings when these were influenced by other variables such as on-the-job training and changes in the supply and demand of each specific occupation (Taubman 1976: 866–7).[14] Together with Jere Behrman, Taubman (1989) used this approach with data on eight kin groups provided by the NAS–NRC Twin sample, and concluded that genetic endowments made a large contribution to the amount of schooling received. The same data (the NAS–NRC Twin Offspring) was used by Alan Mathios (1989) who aimed to study the importance of monetary job attributes in total compensation packages. His results suggested that the exclusive use of earnings to assess occupational differences between workers with different educational levels could be inaccurate and misleading.

The interest in twin studies has not ceased, and in recent years several studies pursued this approach further, providing some support for the role of schooling. Some have even suggested that the returns to schooling could be biased downward, possibly due to measurement errors or to a possible negative relationship between ability and schooling (Ashenfelter and Krueger 1994). Others using kin studies have argued that OLS (Ordinary Least Squares) estimates of the schooling effects could have little overall bias, since the effects of measurement errors were counterbalanced by omission regarding family background factors (Ashenfelter and Zimmerman 1997). These studies have also noted that more able individuals were likely to attain more schooling not because of higher marginal benefits, but because of lower marginal costs of schooling (Ashenfelter and Rouse 1998).

Finally, a group of studies have developed so-called natural experiments to assess sorting and human capital effects. These studies have seized the opportunity created by institutional or policy changes in the educational system to perform quasi-natural experiments (Brown and Sessions 2004). Underlying these studies was the idea that one could create instrumental variables that identified the effects of education and ability and overcame the difficulties presented by the endogenization of the former and nonobservability of the latter (Card 2001). Initially, these studies suggested that OLS estimates of the schooling coefficient could be biased downward (Angrist and Krueger 1991). However, more recent work has concluded that the studies using this approach were likely to overestimate the average marginal return to education, possibly even more than OLS estimates.

It is difficult to sum up the main outcomes of this empirical debate, not the least because depending on the type of test chosen the picture obtained from the empirical test also changed. In fact, none of these tests provided a definitive answer to the human capital versus screening debate, and each of the tests presented some flaws that limited its impact. The choice regarding the type of test was not neutral in terms of the results to be obtained and none of the five types of studies provided a consensual approach. It should be noted nonetheless that at the individual level the analysis confirmed that schooling represents a good investment, either due to its productivity or sorting effects (Brown and Sessions 2004).

The extension of the empirical work to countries other than the USA has provided robustness to human capital analysis. Several studies have observed that education was an essential variable in understanding wage differentials (Tachibanaki 1998). Moreover, Mincer's emphasis on training as a major explanatory variable to wage growth was also very important in the application of human capital analysis in this respect. The empirical analysis of both general and specific training was particularly important to some major economies such as Japan and Germany, since German institutions offer apprenticeships and further training and Japanese firms offer firm-based on-the-job training. The importance of different types of training had been highlighted by Mincer's comparative work between the Japanese and American labor markets (see Chapter 6).

Research on unemployment has also contributed to enhance the effects of the role of schooling on labor market analysis. In fact, it has been argued that 'it is widely known that unemployment rates are inversely related to the educational attainment levels of workers' (Ashenfelter and Ham 1979: S99). Schooling seemed to strongly reduce the incidence of unemployment. Educational level, especially university level, seemed to have a strong effect on reducing unemployment periods (Nickell 1979). However, this research has provided less clear evidence about the impact of increased education on the overall level of unemployment.

4.3. Identifying the Effects of Education and Ability on Income

The questions raised by the screening approach provided further impetus to the issue of the effects of ability. Since the development of human capital research, many researchers argued that what was being attributed to formal education could not be mainly due to specific individual abilities that the system was merely identifying. If this were the case, the returns to education would be far more individually specific and should not be generalized, thus the calculus of average returns became misguided in terms of labor market and lifetime income expectations.

Although many researchers agreed that efforts should be concentrated on the empirical side, this was far from straightforward. The problem with the effects of ability was in fact twofold. On the one hand, ability was possibly correlated with schooling achievement, which made it extremely hard to disentangle the effects of each. This led to a very long debate on the real effects of schooling, and resulted in extensive empirical research being carried out on the isolation of both effects. On the other hand, although most people tended to assume that these would be positively correlated, that is, that more able individuals would receive a higher return from similar amounts of schooling, others have pointed out that this might not be the case. Schooling and ability could be negatively correlated, as in the case of the foregone earnings being higher for more able students, thus providing an incentive for them to demand less education than less able students (Weiss 1971). This led to a questioning of the assumption shared by many that a more able individual would invest more in schooling than a less able one.

Several empirical strategies were used to tackle the ability conundrum. Most of the earliest studies developed a straightforward estimation and analysis of the earnings function in order to disentangle the effects of the education and ability variables. One of the most important studies in the ability versus education controversy was that of Zvi Griliches and William Mason (1972). Their results indicated that the introduction of these variables reduced the education coefficient (28%), though the authors considered that this was less than some critics of the human capital theory would expect. Hence, they concluded that, despite the lack of representativeness of their sample, the results 'support the economic and statistical significance of schooling in the explanation of observed differences in income' (1972: S99). Furthermore, Griliches and Mason saw their results as an indication of a 'relatively low independent contribution of measured ability', and as casting doubt 'on the asserted role of genetic forces in the determination of income' (1972: S99).[15]

Other authors followed this attempt to clarify the effects of education and ability on earnings. John Hause (1971, revised in 1972 and 1975) analyzed four different samples: the Rodgers study (1969), Project Talent Data, the NBER–Thorndike sample, and the Husen data on Sweden. His main conclusion was that the variables used to measure cognitive ability did not have an important effect on earnings for those with high levels of schooling, although there was a strong association of measured ability with final school attainment and an increase in the effect of ability on earnings as far as the labor experience was concerned (Hause 1975).

In another important study, Boissiere, Knight, and Sabot (1985) analyzed two developing countries (Kenya and Tanzania) by using one variable for a worker's cognitive skills (literacy and numeracy) and another for reasoning ability (both measures developed specifically for this study by the Princeton Educational Testing Service). The study's main results indicated that the direct returns to reasoning ability were small, those to years of formal schooling were moderate, and those to literacy and numeracy were large. Moreover, it seemed that the main effects of both education and reasoning ability were largely through the development of cognitive skills. The rewards for both numeracy and literacy seemed therefore to be due to their positive effect on workers' productivity.

In general, most studies found a low direct effect of the several ability measures used. However, some have argued that this could be due to factors such as the main effect of ability being indirect, the proxies used, the various dimensions of ability, or even to a correlation between ability and education (see Rosen 1977). In fact, though several scholars recognized this to be a crucial issue and tried to disentangle the effects of ability from those of schooling, the question remained without a satisfying answer. Griliches (1977), in his classic review of the empirical work on the returns to schooling, considered it questionable whether ability had necessarily a positive independent effect on earnings. On the other hand, he noted that the bias due to its omission would be smaller in equations including proxies for 'experience' (Griliches 1977: 4–5). Moreover, he raised the possibility of underestimation of the school coefficient, namely due to errors of measurement of the school variables.

Several approaches have been used to measure the effects of ability. The evidence produced thus far has shown that in the cases aimed at a direct measure of ability, there has been limited impact on the coefficient measuring the effect of education (Rosen 1977; Freeman 1987). Other techniques have been employed, though years of schooling have continued to have a sizable effect on earnings. Among these, the so-called genetic studies have suggested the possible endogeneity of choices regarding schooling, something that has been pursued more systematically in recent years. Most studies have also suggested that background factors seem to have, at most, an indirect effect, though the question remains whether an improvement in measurement will have a major effect on this scene.

The use of panel data has confirmed the productivity-enhancing effect of education, though with a more careful tone than the early human capital empirical studies. More recent work has suggested the existence of a strong correlation between schooling and ability (see Heckman and Vytlacil 2000). This work has also questioned the traditional assumptions regarding the linearity of the effects of age and time on earnings. Other work has argued that despite the issue of measurement errors and the various approaches used to tackle ability (direct measurement, twin studies, and natural experiments), there was still room to believe that OLS estimates were possibly biased upward (Blackburn and Neumark 1993). Moreover, recent work has also suggested that the recent increase in the return to schooling was mostly due to workers with high levels of ability, thus the omission of ability could provide misguided conclusions regarding the individual profitability of schooling (Blackburn and Neumark 1993).

A serious issue raised in recent years regarding the assessment of returns to schooling concerned the option value of schooling. Some researchers have pointed out the need to endogenize decisions concerning schooling, namely by considering decision processes and the effect on choices by changes in the environment, through optimization and dynamic approaches (Keane and Wolpin 1997). This approach was applied to the study of dropout phenomena and the analysis of differences and changes in preferences, skills, and expectations within a sequential model (Eckstein and Wolpin 1999). Research on community colleges has suggested this option value of additional schooling to be significant (Kane and Rouse 1995).

Mincer considered that the empirical advances had provided additional robustness to human capital analysis. On the one hand, he considered that some of the ability measures used to correct the estimation bias included unobserved components of the human capital stock, besides genuinely efficient parameters (Mincer 1974a: 3). On the other hand, and based on other studies, Mincer assumed that the bias due to the omission of the ability in the estimation was not very significant. Thus, he concluded that human capital had refuted not only the screening challenge, but also the skepticism raised by the ability issue about an overemphasis on the role of human capital.

4.4. Concluding Remarks

Despite the advances, human capital research has faced significant criticisms since its outset, especially from the seventies onward. The major criticisms faced by human capital research concerned its contribution to the analysis of inequality and the identification of the factors underpinning the returns normally awarded to schooling. Mincer played no minor role in these debates, not the least by stimulating further investments in the empirical side. He, as well as others, considered that significant advances could be made in the measurement of the returns to human capital, by addressing the role of factors such as natural ability and socioeconomic background.

It is not easy to summarize the complexity and richness of these efforts which attempted to clarify the link between education and earnings. It has been observed that a degree was more significant for earnings than years of schooling, though doubts have remained about whether this difference was due to a credentialist effect or to the additional years of schooling. Although there is a positive relationship between years of education and earnings, it has been clarified that this is not linear and its effects are very unequal among different socioeconomic, racial, and gender groups. Moreover, in several studies a large part of the variance of earnings remained unexplained, even when considering factors other than education.

Despite the shortcomings there were important advances, though these were possibly less definitive than some scholars had hoped. The improvements were not restricted to the theoretical level, but included the empirical as well. Namely, there were improvements in terms of better specification of the models, better measurement of the variables, the range of statistical techniques used, and the type of samples used (Blaug 1976a). Moreover, the depth of ignorance was greatly reduced by the significant number of questions raised, in part, as a by-product of this empirical research. The effect of schooling (and other human capital variables) on earnings has received general support under certain market and informational conditions (Card 1999). However, the analysis of this effect, and of its interaction with other variables, proved to be much more complex than most authors had anticipated.

The impact of Mincer's work on labor economics endured not only through the development of the human capital research program, namely via his influence on many labor economists with whom he interacted closely, but also in shaping the interests and views of many economists. Mincer's influence on contemporary economics surfaced throughout the debates in recent decades on the role of human capital in explaining inequality of income and the labor market's earning power and performance. These debates have shown that, despite the controversy, Mincer's views had a major impact in shaping the views of the discipline about those topics, even among several less congenial to human capital research.

5

Human Capital and the Long-Term View of the Labor Market

When Jacob Mincer started his academic career, labor economics was finishing a long process of change that marked the postwar years. This transformation, crucial for understanding the emergence of human capital theory, was generally characterized by the increasing pervasiveness of neoclassical economic theory in a field traditionally more attached to an empirical or institutionalist research agenda. In fact, this traditional prominence of institutional economics was something that made Mincer uncomfortable with labor economics. As a graduate student in economics at Columbia University he had attended some classes in labor economics and disliked what he considered the lack of analytical focus and theoretical guidance. These early memories led him to stay away from labor economics in his early career.

However, the growing influence of neoclassical economics in labor research drew his attention. Under the stimulus of some labor researchers such as Gregg Lewis, Melvin Reder, and Albert Rees, he became increasingly interested in labor issues, namely in labor supply behavior. This would become a permanent feature of his work and a large part of his career would be devoted to labor research, with a special emphasis on the long-term behavior of labor market agents, that would significantly shape the research agenda of labor economists from the 1960s onward. Through this work, Mincer would actually make a significant contribution to the contemporary dominance of neoclassical economics in labor research.

In this chapter, a brief portrait of labor economics in the decades preceding Mincer's work in labor issues will be presented. Then an analysis will be made of some of his major pieces of research around the theme of labor supply and lifetime labor income and the way these differed from previous labor research. This work is also presented in a way that shows the close links between Mincer's research on human capital and the long-term behavior of labor supply.

5.1. The Transformation of Labor Economics: From Early Twentieth-century Pluralism to Postwar Neoclassical Ascendancy

In the early decades of the twentieth century, labor research was quite different from what we presently regard as labor economics. It was very broadly and loosely defined as labor problems and labor issues. It had much more fragile links with the economic discipline, both theoretically and institutionally. It hardly used neoclassical theory, let alone price theory. It preferred interdisciplinary approaches, historical and industry studies (notably on the role and development of union and employer organizations). The heterogeneity of researchers in terms of interests and approaches was reflected in a lack of cohesion of the field. Most labor researchers were sympathetic toward institutionalism, particularly with the work being inspired by John R. Commons and his group at Wisconsin (McNulty 1986).[1]

The presence of neoclassical economics in labor research during the early decades of the twentieth century was not very apparent due to disciplinary and methodological reasons. On the one hand, labor issues were hardly at the forefront of microeconomic research. If there was some attention, it was via unemployment matters, and, particularly from the thirties onward, this would be analyzed from a macroeconomic perspective. On the other hand, if the labor market was to be regarded as analogous to any market for goods and services, there was hardly any significant advance in microeconomic theory that justified renewed attention to its functioning. Any standard economics principles text would do. Neoclassicists/general theorists considered that the institutionalists' critical perspective was due to their poor mastery of the basic price/economic theory. Moreover, the neoclassicists claimed that the institutionalists' alternative approach was not based on a sound theoretical framework, but rather was a poorly disguised attempt to find an apparent economic justification for trade unions and government regulation.

The most important exception to this lack of visibility of neoclassical analysis of labor markets was John Hicks's influential book *The Theory of Wages* (1932). Hicks aimed to tackle the emerging realities of trade unionism and state regulation of the labor markets by building on the familiar framework of market regulation and supply–demand competition. The neoclassical competitive model was for him 'a good simplified model of the labor market' (1932: 5), since it represented the main traits and tendencies of the real market, though he felt that some complications should be introduced to make it more realistic, notably to cope with some of the rigidities and some of the dynamic character of economic life and to take into consideration the institutional context and its effect on the functioning of markets (e.g. unions and business organizations). However, even in these respects the general economic theory was useful for understanding the rationale and motivations of those institutional forces (cf. Hicks 1932: 136ff.), since these could distort, but not change, the nature of the market and economic labor relations.[2]

It would be misleading to reduce interwar labor economics to a debate between institutionalists and neoclassicists, since one of the major characteristics of the authors of this period was their significant degree of eclecticism. Several of the most important authors combined a basic adherence to the neoclassical perspective with a strong emphasis on empirical research, in order to improve the former and to provide a better view on actual labor market behavior. This is illustrated by three leading figures in labor research and economics in the interwar period (all of them would become president of the AEA). Paul Douglas (1934) considered that economic science should pay more attention to the contribution that the inductive statistical method could make, since this would be an effective way to overcome the sterile disputes between empirically empty theoretical economics and the theoretically blind institutional approach. Douglas considered that the standard theory represented a fairly good account of the reality of labor markets that needed to be improved through inductive research (1934: 97ff.) and pursued this view in his important work on wages (1930, 1934). Sumner Slichter (1941), whose work was characterized by a pervading interest in the application of economic principles to specific problems, had a major interest in the analysis of unionism and its impact on shaping industrial relations. Thus, in his analysis, Slichter emphasized the economic rationale underlying union behavior in contrast to the institutional approach that emphasized political motivations (cf. Slichter 1939, 1941). In his work, Harry Millis (1873–1948) did not consider the several noncompetitive elements existing in the labor markets as reason enough to discard orthodox wage theory, since this should be regarded as a portrait of general tendencies (see Brown et al. 1949).

These elements suggest that during the interwar period labor research shared the pluralism that characterized economics as a discipline, especially in the USA (Morgan and Rutherford 1998). The end of World War II saw a redefinition of labor economics research, namely with a progressive closeness to economics, and especially neoclassical economics. This was certainly related to the emergence of a new generation of labor (economist) researchers that included most of the researchers who would dominate the field during the following two decades such as John Dunlop, Clark Kerr, Richard Lester, Gregg Lewis, Melvin Reder, Albert Rees, Lloyd Reynolds, and Arthur Ross. Although this new generation still presented signs of eclecticism, they shared a much stronger economics background than most of their predecessors in the field and had more extensive knowledge of neoclassical standard theory. This would be a key factor in making labor research much more focused on the analysis of economic motivations and in popularizing among labor research a whole set of concepts, assumptions, and instruments from economic theory. However, they were also exposed to other influences, and in particular there were still important remaining links with the institutionalists and with inductive labor research from the prewar period. Their frequent eclecticism in terms of affiliations and influences was somehow synthesized by making the basic (neoclassical) framework more realistic and more robust in terms of and through the empirical evidence.

The historical context and professional careers of these researchers would also make a contribution to some of the remaining eclecticism, since this was a generation that came of age at the time of the Great Depression. This nurtured the view among those labor economists that the market mechanism did not always operate as effectively and automatically as the standard theory predicted, namely in terms of unemployment, and led many of them to support some auxiliary government regulation. Moreover, this generation of labor economists had also observed the ascendancy of unionism and collective bargaining and the way these had shaped the operation of market forces. These perceptions were strengthened by their experience during World War II of wage stabilization and industrial arbitration within several American governmental agencies, especially the War Labor Board (WLB) (Kaufman 1993: 87). Altogether, it seems that it promoted among many of those researchers the aim to develop an economic theory able to cope with the more complex and somehow distinct reality of the labor markets.

During this transitional generation many authors believed that it was possible to synthesize the two leading alternative schools of research in the field.[3] They believed that by developing a sort of middle ground they could not only overcome the tensions that frequently dominated the field, but by building on the strengths of each side they would create a synthesis that regarded neoclassical and institutional economics as potentially complementary. A large proportion of the research in labor economics from the late forties until the late fifties is part of this attempt of creating a synthesis. However, the idea of synthesis was not necessarily the same for all of them, and the degree of reexamination required by neoclassical economics varied during the period and among authors, from minor aspects to major criticisms. These differences would coalesce during the fifties around a set of major theoretical and methodological debates, eventually leading to a theoretical and methodological clarification within labor research.

The idea that the labor market was a peculiar type was very much embedded in the debates of this period. On the one hand, there were those who believed that the neoclassical model of the market had to be adjusted in order to account for the specificities of this commodity and the institutional framework affecting labor relations. On the other hand, there were those who considered that this institutional dimension and the uneconomical character of the so-called labor supply and demand posed major limitations to the use of (neoclassical) economic theory and its explanatory effectiveness. Hence they called for a new, interdisciplinary approach that would live up to the complexities of this peculiar type of market. In fact, one aspect that concentrated many of the research energies of those labor economists was the development of empirical work on local labor markets. This corresponded to the attempt to improve the neoclassical framework, notably by giving it a (stronger) empirical basis. Altogether, this work strengthened the idea among those revisionists that the actual operation of the labor market was significantly different from the standard model, and hence that empirical evidence had to be used to reformulate it.

However, some neoclassicists considered that the works of Clark Kerr and others had taken the institutional dimension too far (Kerr 1954). Despite acknowledging the institutional dimension of labor markets, they considered that the approach by Kerr and his colleagues, of putting too much emphasis on certain minor aspects, overlooked the pervasiveness of market factors in labor contexts. Labor markets had some specific characteristics, but their overall functioning could be represented by competitive market forces (see Goldner 1955). These differences in emphasis would develop into a major clarification about the methodological essence of labor research.

An important debate of this period concerned the neoclassical assumptions of the employers' behavior, in particular the idea they would pay labor at its marginal productivity level, itself part of the so-called 'full-cost' controversy of the 1940–50s (see Mongin 1992). This came to the forefront in the controversy over marginalism initiated by Lester's analysis (1946) of the relationship between wages and employment. Based on a survey of business managers, Lester's analysis found major shortcomings in the marginal analysis, since his results suggested that employment decisions were mostly based on market demand rather than prospects of wages and profits, making employment a function of output rather than of wage rates. The results also suggested to him that most managers lacked marginal calculus, since they regarded it as either unnecessary or impractical.

This was fiercely attacked by Fritz Machlup (1946), who considered that Lester's criticisms resulted from a careless analysis of the survey and a poor understanding of the implications of marginal analysis. For Machlup, the fact that business managers sometimes made routine decisions, that the decisions were largely subjective, or that other nonpecuniary aspects were taken into consideration, did not represent a failure of the theory, but rather a narrow view of marginal theory. He also challenged the idea that an individual had to understand the fundamentals of the process to use it, considering this a basic flaw in the understanding of social sciences. For Machlup, this critical literature on marginal productivity theory failed to perceive that underpinning common nontechnical language was a basic rationale of maximization by individual business people. Lester (1947a) replied that Machlup had rephrased marginal analysis in a subtle way, which he regarded as a retraction due to criticisms and the conflicting evidence.

Another aspect of the labor market that attracted vast attention at the time was workers' behavior, notably in the role of unions, which was not surprising having in mind the significant rise in unionization in the USA during the first half of the forties. As this important debate surfaced, more differences emerged between neoclassicists and revisionists, and even among revisionists. Some like Dunlop (1944) regarded unions mostly as wage maximizing units, within a basic neoclassical framework. Others like Ross (1948) among the new generation would place the emphasis on the political side. Following the Wisconsin tradition, these authors emphasized the secondary role of economic theory when it came to the analysis of unionism, hence the misleading nature of taking it as a monopoly (Ross 1948), and regarded unions as institutionalized bureaucracies mostly determined by internal forces such as matters of distribution of power. Among the new generation, the large majority would emphasize a mix of economic and political dimensions, both illustrating the shortcomings of neoclassical tradition and the need to integrate the institutional dimension, in order to provide a more realistic picture (Shister 1946; Lester 1947*b*; Ulman 1951).

The different views of the labor market and its protagonists had necessarily to shape the way labor economists would see the wage determination process. Many of the new labor researchers frequently expressed doubts about the competitive assumption on wage pricing. For the neoclassicists who regarded labor markets as analogous to other types of competitive markets, the process of wage determination was not very different from the one defined by competitive market theory. Although some forces could delay or limit to a minor extent the impact of competitive markets, by no means was this to be considered a central aspect in terms of wage determination. Those authors closer to the neoclassical approach also attempted to show that collective bargaining did not have as much impact on wage determination as many had stated, and kept regarding the competitive market as the benchmark for wage determination, and hence for labor research. It was crucial to maintain a general theoretical analysis, especially given the burgeoning amount of statistical evidence and data on wages. Otherwise labor economics and especially wage determination risked falling into a casuistic analysis (Dunlop 1957).

By the end of the mid-fifties labor economics was becoming a very different subject. From a previously heterogeneous field, labor was increasingly connected to economic theory, though there remained issues as to how much could be achieved along this path. The aforementioned debates contributed very much to this change, and at the same time led to a crystallization of positions. Instead of attempts to develop a revisionist type of neoclassicism that paid particular attention to the empirical results of labor research (and following the prewar traditions), neoclassical researchers were calling for unequivocal support for the use of neoclassical micro theory in analyzing labor markets. Labor analysis should overcome its hesitations in using the supply–demand–price framework to analyze labor behavior. For people such as Stigler, Machlup, Rottenberg, and Gregg Lewis, among others, the criticisms undermined labor analysis instead of improving it. It destroyed a theoretical framework without providing an alternative. For these authors the middle ground aimed for by the revisionists would become a muddled ground. Their criticisms were supported in a renewed confidence in the capacity of neoclassical theory to explain various patterns of social behavior.

This evolution of labor research would be very important for the development of post-fifties labor research, notably the topic that arguably dominated labor economics in the following decades— human capital theory. The main idea was that, despite some imperfections, labor markets are essentially competitive. By competitive it was not meant that labor markets verified precisely all the conditions of the competitive model, but that the so-called imperfections of real labor markets were not crucial for the determination of the general picture of the labor market, that is, they did not challenge the main predictions of the competitive labor model.

There was also a methodological shift that placed emphasis on general models of individual decision, quantification and econometric testing, and the assessment of models through their predictive power rather than by their realism. This methodological shift that switched emphasis away from realism to predictive power, under the influence of Friedman and Stigler, was also important to labor research, through their Chicago connections. It would be in this context that Mincer would develop most of his research. Although initially ambivalent with the label of labor economist, Mincer would become increasingly comfortable with it to eventually became of one of the leading researchers in the field.

5.2. Mincer's First Forays into Labor Economics

Mincer's short but intensive period at Chicago would provide him with an important stimulus to explore two of his main areas of research—the role of on-the-job training and labor supply, both closely connected to his human capital interests. Stimulated by Gregg Lewis and others at Chicago, throughout the sixties Mincer devoted significant attention to reevaluating the evolution of the labor force, especially where the participation of women was concerned.

Apparently, his initial interest was largely motivated by personal reasons:

I was interested in labor force participation of women, because of my wife. I knew (...) she would not simply become a housewife, that was our start. That was an example of the role of wages in labor force participation. From the very start I believed that wages have a positive, not a negative, impact over labor force participation. The negative effect came of course because of the residual. If you just relate wages to participation, at that time you would get a negative effect (I'm talking about women), but once you take income as a separate variable, you will see that the wage has a positive effect that in fact is stronger than the income effect. (Mincer quoted in Teixeira 2006: 13–14)

The first foray by Mincer into the analysis of labor force participation was presented at the 1959 meeting of the AEA (Mincer 1960*b*) where he tried to link labor supply, family income, and consumption. From the outset, Mincer noted the importance of focusing on the family. In his introductory remarks, Mincer pointed out the traditional sharp division in income distribution analysis between the study of factors explaining the size of income and the study of the effects of a certain income distribution on economic behavior such as consumption patterns. However, he noted that, despite the recognition of inter-dependence between family status, personal income, and size of the consumer unit, 'little effort had gone into investigating the manner in which individual incomes are pooled into a consumer unit total, and even less into exploring the consequences of this pooling on observed consumption behavior' (Mincer 1960*b*: 574).

Hence, he tried to explore 'the effects of family income composition on income levels, income dispersion, and saving behavior of consumer units' (Mincer 1960*b*: 574–5), by using data from the

1950 Survey of Consumer Expenditures provided by the Bureau of Labor Statistics. In his analysis he built on his previous analysis of the explanatory role of education to income distribution. Thus, he pointed out that both absolute and relative income dispersion increased with age and with educational and occupational level of adult male income recipients, and this was explained in part by the differences in the slopes and curvatures of the age-income profiles by education. Overall, he found that the measures of inequality based on family income did not differ significantly from those obtained from the income dispersion of the family's head.

The interaction between income and wives' labor force participation seemed to be very significant in the case of certain groups. For the analysis, Mincer used the then novel distinction between permanent and transitory income proposed by Milton Friedman among others. In groups where the head was not fully employed there was a strong negative correlation between the husband's earnings and the wife's labor rates. Thus, even a transitory negative development in the income of the family's main earner would stimulate an expansion of the labor force participation of the wife. The relevance of transitory income variations in explaining labor force behavior was apparent in all age-education groups, with the exception of the highest group.

Although the evidence was still very limited and fragmented, the results led Mincer to conclude that family income formation, consumption, and labor force behavior were interrelated through simultaneous choices within the household. Thus, one needed to explore one aspect in conjunction with the others in order to fully understand each of these three economic phenomenon.[4]

5.3. Paradoxes in Labor Supply

The relevance of the family perspective was crucial to Mincer when it came to the analysis of labor force participation. The early work on this topic had been very much shaped by Lionel Robbins's classic article (1934). However, Robbins's analysis is focused on the individual, and the family is basically absent. Moreover, in Robbins's framework the dichotomies income/wages and income/prices were the same. According to Mincer, that created an empirical problem: 'If you wanted to apply this theory to empirical data, you couldn't get a separate fully-fledged supply curve. All you would get is the net differential resulting from the coexistence of these two variables' (Mincer quoted in Teixeira 2006: 13). Subsequent authors who looked at this topic, such as Paul Douglas (1934) and Clarence Long (1958), had looked at wages and found a negative effect on labor force activity. According to Mincer their conclusions were due to the fact that income and price variables were not separate. Hence, he decided to address the issue of labor supply within the family and differentiate between income and wage, namely because if the family pooled its income, there would be one income variable, and then each individual would have a wage, which is the price variable.

The results that Mincer presented at the 1959 AEA meeting were part of a larger venture which aimed at understanding the labor force participation of family members. When Mincer went to Chicago as a postdoctoral fellow he started writing the article based on his dissertation for the *Journal of Political Economy* (1958). This provided him with the opportunity to interact more closely with Gregg Lewis and Albert Rees. In attending their courses Mincer realized that both Gregg Lewis and Albert Rees were at that time very interested in the labor force participation of women. The visibility of the topic had been further enhanced by the recent publication of Clarence Long's book *The Labor Force under Changing Income and Employment* (1958), to which he had dedicated many years of work and that summed up the state-of-the-art on the topic.

Interest in this topic seems to have been suggested by the empirically paradoxical behavior of women, reflected in an apparent contradiction between the cross-sectional and time-series data. The basic question was, according to Mincer: 'Why was it that while in cross-sections in families where husbands were doing well, wives don't work; over time wages have been rising and instead of women dropping out of the labor force, their participation in the labor force increased?' Neither Lewis nor Rees had an answer to that. They tried all kinds of approaches: '. . . but it occurred to me that a simple price-theoretical approach could do. I still don't know why they didn't think of that before me' (Mincer quoted in Teixeira 2006: 11). Gregg Lewis became very interested in his approach and invited Mincer to a conference on labor economics that he was organizing for the NBER.

The main result of these early years of research on labor topics was the paper presented at the famous 1960 NBER Conference on Labor Economics (Mincer 1962*b*). Mincer attempted to show that cross-sectional and time-series data presented a similar picture in terms of the labor force participation of married women. The apparent contradiction was due to the analysis of cross-sectional data in terms of gross relations between the income of husbands and the labor participation of wives, which produced results sensitive to both transitory income and the covariation of wives' earning power with husbands' income. Since transitory income is not relevant to secular trends, and the female wage rate has risen at least as fast as the male rate, the cross-sectional negative income relation became a positive secular relation.

Mincer (1962b) proposed to solve this paradox through a conceptual reevaluation of the work–leisure choices. His view was to consider leisure not merely as a consumption activity, but also as including factors, such as education, that had a productive element. Moreover, he thought it important to expand the concept of leisure by considering the hours of work at home, in nonmarket activities. The issue of leisure was therefore insufficient to understand the labor force participation of married women, since change in hours of leisure could have a very different effect on hours of work in the market depending on the causal factors on hours of work at home (Mincer 1962b: 65).

Using data from the Bureau of Labor Statistics' 1950 Survey of Consumer Expenditures, Mincer related the employment status of wives to income and experience of husbands, roughly standardized by age, education, and family type (1962b: 76). For all but one of the age groups the positive effect of the female wage rate was stronger than the negative effect of the family head's. As expected, the youngest group with small children presented a strong negative income effect or a weak positive wage rate effect, or even both, due to the choices regarding the allocation of time between the market and the household.

Mincer then tried to assess to what extent his analysis could help in understanding some secular patterns, by using data from census surveys (Mincer 1962b: 85ff.). The empirical results seemed to be consistent with the data. Among the patterns observed, Mincer emphasized that the gross relation between participation rates and earning power (measured by education) of wives was positive and strong. He noted as well that the increase in participation with increasing wage rates of wives was stronger when the income of husbands was held constant than when it was not. Finally, he noted that the data also reflected the fact that higher education and occupational level presented greater relative importance of transitory components in the income variance.

The analysis also suggested that the negative income elasticity had been decreasing over time or that the positive wage rate elasticity had been growing over time. Both developments were predictable since the degree of substitutability between home production and wage goods had been increasing over time (Mincer 1962b: 94). Moreover, the increase in labor productivity verified in market activities was likely to be reflected also in home production, thus reducing the amount of hours required for home production and allowing additional hours for market activities.

In his comments on the paper at the conference, Clarence Long (1958), a long-time researcher in labor force participation, considered that Mincer had not only introduced some important elements to the analysis, but also had been convincing in his analysis. He noted nevertheless that some work remained to be done, namely that the equation proposed by Mincer did not fully explain the rise in women's participation, nor did it predict the decennial movements accurately. Long suggested that the study should be expanded to include the labor behavior of nonwhite women, which seemed to challenge some of Mincer's conclusions. Finally, Long suggested the use of annual data to test year-to-year changes. These caveats led Clarence Long to take a more skeptical stance, despite acknowledging Mincer's fertile, stimulating, and resourceful analysis.

Mincer continued to research the issues related to labor force participation and by the mid-sixties he explored the link with unemployment in a chapter he contributed to a volume edited by Robert A. Gordon and Margaret S. Gordon entitled *Prosperity and Unemployment* (1966). Mincer started by noting that despite several decades of research the short-run behavior of the labor force was still a puzzle for many economists. The difficulty had to do mainly with the fact that labor short-run behavior seemed to be the result of frequently contradictory trends and effects and it was not always easy to anticipate or identify which ones were stronger. Nevertheless, Mincer pointed out that there was some provisional consensus emerging around the idea that the labor force responded positively even to mild fluctuations in economic activity.

Overall, Mincer considered that the labor force presented growing responsiveness due to the combination of various long-term trends (1966: 105). These included the growth of the female labor force and the decreasing attachment to the labor force by young and older male workers, due to the increasing length of schooling and growing visibility of early retirement, respectively. These trends had contributed to an increase in discretionary labor force participation and a weakening of the income effect, that is, of incentives for added-worker behavior. Thus, different groups within the labor force seemed to react differently to the same economic problems.[5]

The discussion of Mincer's paper produced some interesting and mixed reactions. Richard Easterlin seemed to be very much convinced by Mincer's work, especially by the amount and strength of the empirical evidence produced. A more critical stance was adopted by William Bowen and Thomas Finegan and especially by Frank Pierson.

It is noteworthy that, in their comments, Bowen and Finegan's first remark was that Mincer tried to use too much price theory in labor analysis. Mincer was criticized not only for trying to provide explanations based on a reduced set of variables, but also for trying to fit labor force behavior mostly into a microeconomic neoclassical framework. This highlighted the strong resistance that persisted in labor analysis about a deductive and neoclassical approach to labor market problems. This resistance also explained the positive reaction to the fact that in his analysis Mincer paid attention to some institutional and legal factors that could affect labor participation rates.[6]

An even stronger skeptical tone was expressed by Frank Pierson, who had participated in the 1950's efforts to revise the micro theory of wage determination (Pierson 1957). Pierson shared the more eclectic view that a new approach should be built by placing more emphasis on legislative and institutional factors of price theory. He considered that those institutional factors played a very significant role in explaining labor force participation, not only in the long run, but even in the short run.[7]

Mincer's initial attempts were well received and some years later he had the opportunity to include an article on labor force participation in the *International Encyclopedia of the Social Sciences* (Mincer 1968a) in which he focused on the most important and novel aspects of this analysis. The publication of his article provided him with the opportunity to disseminate this approach to a wider public. In terms of the participation of the younger cohorts he pointed out the productive side of education activities that enhanced their market productivity, thus promoting education as a profitable investment.

5.4. Linking Market and Nonmarket Behavior through the Household

The other main contribution that Mincer made in his reassessment of market labor supply concerned the appropriate decision-making unit of analysis. As suggested in his AEA 1959 paper (Mincer 1960b), he considered that the decisions concerning consumption behavior, income pooling, and the choices about leisure and the production of goods and services at home to be family decisions. Hence, the family was the relevant unit of analysis when studying the labor force participation of married women. Mincer emphasized that the distribution of leisure, home, and market-based work within the family was not merely the result of cultural or biological differences, but also of economic factors. He also considered that the distribution was largely influenced by relative prices, which were specific to each family member, due to differences in the market earning power and marginal productivities (at home and in the market) of each individual member of the family (Mincer 1962b: 66).

The consideration of the family as the relevant unit of analysis helped in a better understanding of the issue of income and substitution factors contained in the labor market supply force. In particular, it highlighted the importance of the substitutability between the wife's time and other factors of production at home and between home-produced and market-produced goods. The weaker the substitutability, the weaker the expected negative income effect on the hours of work at home, and the stronger the income effect on hours of work in the market (Mincer 1962b: 67).

In analyzing the labor force participation of married women, Mincer noted that this was characterized by strong variation or turnover in the short run. This was due to the fact that women seemed to have more variation in the allocation of time between the market, leisure, and home. This mobility was influenced by cyclical and random variations in wage rates, employment opportunities, income, and employment of other family members, particularly the husband. Moreover, the fact that the timing of participation or interruption in the labor market was likely to differ among women magnified the picture of high turnover at the aggregate level.

Mincer considered it important to distinguish to what extent these variations were caused by transitory or more permanent variations of structural parameters, namely of family income. Hence, he started by specifying a labor market supply function of married women based on the potential permanent level of family income. Since most data available in family surveys reported the husband's income at the current level, it was necessary to adapt the analysis in order to distinguish which variations in the labor force behavior of married women were due to variations in the husband's long-run income position or to deviations of current income from its normal level. The separation is particularly relevant if one observes that labor force behavior is more responsive to transitory income than to permanent levels of income, especially since the effects of each component of income are likely to differ. Hence, Mincer adapted his equation to include transitory income in addition to permanent levels of income. The data confirmed the relevance of distinguishing between permanent and transitory income.[8]

Related to the analysis of labor supply, and especially to the participation of women in the labor market, was the analysis of the allocation of time between market and nonmarket activities. As Mincer had explained in his previous work (1960b), these interactions were not only complex but also very significant. Hence, he devoted some attention to certain price variables usually neglected in consumption studies (Mincer 1963). Neglect of these variables led to specification biases that affected the parameters of certain economic relations.[9] Mincer considered that there was a nonmarket opportunity cost component due to the opportunity cost of labor, time, or other goods, that was not completely accounted for by market prices. Among those opportunity costs, the one most likely to be overlooked was that of time, which was expected to be positively associated with income.[10]

Mincer noted that many of our daily activities were natural candidates for the analysis of this issue. The examples of 'economic relations in which the important price variables appear[ed] mainly or partly in the form of opportunity cost' (1963: 68) included transportation costs,[11] the supply of the labor force, the demand for domestic servants, the link between income and family size (which overlooked the opportunity cost of child care), and the informational dimension on prices and income.[12]

The relevance of taking into account opportunity costs for the analysis of demand (especially the cost of time) was, according to Mincer, vividly illustrated in the analysis of the allocation of time between market activity and the household. Based on his previous work on the labor force participation of women, Mincer (1963: 71) pointed out that 'an improper understanding of the nature of the price variable' led to several estimation biases and to 'spurious puzzles and paradoxes'. First, he noted that the choices to be faced were not only between leisure and money income, but should also include a third option of nonmarket activity that was not leisure. Secondly, he argued that in the analysis of the demand for leisure and home production the relevant income concept was total family income.

Closely related to the issue of labor force participation was the demand for domestic workers. Mincer stated that this should take into account not only the wage rate to be paid to the worker or to the income of the family, but also the market wage rate of the employer, especially the female spouse. Since there was some substitutability between family members and domestic workers, changes in the relative wage rates of these two sides would affect their relative employment in the household.

Also related to women's labor force participation was the relationship between income and family size. In this case Mincer noted that not only was the importance of the cost of child care often overlooked, but also that the cost of child care differed in cross-sectional data. Similar to what happened in the case of domestic workers, this cost could be obtained by the mother's foregone wage in the labor market. The analysis suggested that the choices regarding labor force participation and family size were not causally related, but rather simultaneously determined by the same economic variables (the female's wage rate and the husband's earning power).

5.5. Links between Human Capital and Labor Supply Analysis

Unsurprisingly, one of the aspects to which Mincer devoted particular attention in his studies of labor supply was the role of education. Indeed, the level of education seemed to play a significant role in explaining empirical differences in labor force behavior. The labor force rates of wives increased with the head of family level of education and with the level of permanent income, since these two were positively associated (Mincer 1962b: 78).[13] Moreover, the educational and occupational trends had not only contributed in bringing more young married women into the labor force (especially when their husbands were acquiring formal education or training that temporarily lowered their family income) but also contributed in changing the expectations regarding long-term participation in the labor force. This in turn would stimulate women to invest further in education which would strengthen their attachment to the labor force.

Mincer's reassessment of labor force supply emphasized several important elements resulting from human capital research. First, there was the investment dimension of education activities, which had a productive effect that should be singled out in the analysis of time allocation decisions and should not be diminished by a general leisure concept.[14]

Second, there was the consideration of family rather than the individual as the suitable decision-making unit of analysis in the decisions concerning leisure versus work (or home vs. market activities), which later would be largely explored in Becker's theory (1965) of allocation of time. Whereas for an understanding of men's participation Mincer emphasized the importance of the role played by on-the-job training in explaining the long-term behavior of firms and individuals (both in terms of employment and earnings). In the case of women he emphasized the family context of decisions concerning labor force behavior.

Third, the interaction between the earning capacities of the different individuals constituting the household was emphasized. Hence, it was important to consider not only the individual wage, but also factors such as total family income, the individual's productivity (at home and in the market), the substitutability between market and home activities, and tastes. Education played an important role, either directly or indirectly, in all of those variables.

Fourth, there was the significant influence of education on labor supply decisions, not the least through changes in tastes. In particular, Mincer's work tended to emphasize the importance of the relationship between education (of both spouses) and the existence of children.

Finally, his work called attention to the distinction between transitory and permanent levels of income, which was crucial in clarifying the apparent empirical contradiction between the different data-sets and for understanding women's labor force participation.[15]

In summary, Mincer's work tended to emphasize the importance of the relationship between education (of both spouses) and the existence of children, and the variations of permanent and transitory income for understanding women's behavior in terms of labor force participation. Accordingly, education played a significant role via the earning power of women in particular. On the other hand, the diverse concepts of income were particularly meaningful in explaining the behavior of (younger) groups with college education.

5.6. The Revised Human Capital Earnings Function

By bringing together labor supply and human capital, Mincer could develop cutting-edge work on lifetime earnings and gender differences. As would frequently become the case, part of this work was done through close collaboration with his students who would eventually become leading researchers in labor economics. Thus, in his research with Solomon Polachek, another of his former students, Mincer focused on the effect of human capital accumulation on market earnings and on market activities (Mincer and Polachek 1974). Some of the main ingredients of Mincer's approach to labor market analysis were readily identifiable. Foremost was the idea that the household or family was the consumption behavior unit of analysis, especially in what concerned the allocation of time between market and nonmarket activities (notably the division of labor within the family). This reflected the comparative advantages of each member of the family, as reflected by their skills and earning power. Therefore, it was important to consider human capital not only as an investment but also as a family investment.

The analysis of human capital from a family perspective revealed important complexities, but also posed interesting and relevant questions to labor researchers. One of these was the distributional mechanisms within the family, which were relevant at both the marital and intergenerational levels. The distributional bargain within the family was crucial in explaining patterns of investment of human capital and allocation of time between the market and the household, since these two were often complementary. This was notably the case of women's labor market participation and home human capital. In their work, Mincer and Polachek (1974: S77) concentrated on the former, that is, 'the relation within the family between time allocation and investments in human capital which give rise to the observed market earnings of women'.

Mincer and Polachek's main purpose was to identify and estimate the effect of the accumulation of human capital on women's market earnings and wage rates. Moreover, they attempted to understand the role of those lifetime investments over the expectations regarding family life. This was done by using the so-called human capital earnings function, at that time a recent development in labor market analysis, that had been basically the result of collaborative research between Mincer and Barry Chiswick.[16]

However, due to the specificity normally associated with women's participation in the labor market, Mincer and Polachek used a revised version of the human capital earnings function. This revised version had been initially developed by Solomon Polachek in his Ph.D. thesis (presented at Columbia University in 1973 and supervised by Mincer), namely to accommodate the shorter, more heterogeneous and more discontinuous participation of women in the labor force. The major implication of these patterns was that since women had more discontinuous and shorter expected and actual participation in the labor market, the incentive to invest in human capital, and especially in specific training, was clearly weaker. This was especially the case for married women.[17]

This led Mincer and Polachek (1974: S83) to analyze some differences in women's investment behavior in human capital. The anticipation of discontinuous participation of women in the labor market would tend to promote less investment in job training, even at premarital ages. The situation of interruption of participation in the labor force, especially prolonged ones, could lead to some depreciation of the skills acquired previously. This discontinuity more than likely would be reduced once the children reached school age. Altogether, this implied that the investment profile of women, especially married ones, was not monotonic. Hence, earning profiles of women were less concave and steep than men's and, in the case of married women, they tended to be double peaked due to the lengthy interruption relating to childbearing.

The empirical analysis provided some interesting and relevant results.[18] First, there were indications of skills' depreciation, which tended to be higher: the larger the accumulated stock of human capital, the earlier the age of interruption of activity, and the stronger market orientation of the human capital accumulated. Second, the role of children was qualitative rather than quantitative. Third, although job mobility was normally associated with wage gains, this is less the case for women due to the fact that this mobility, especially the geographic one, is normally exogenously led, an aspect that Mincer would pursue further in his work on migration (see Chapter 6). The issue of discontinuity and its obsolescent effects would be later developed in Mincer's collaboration with Haim Ofek (1979) (see below).

Mincer and Polachek (1974) considered that the revised human capital earnings function highlighted several important aspects of the labor market. One of the most important applications was to the analysis of the so-called wage gap, that is, the comparison of wage rates between male and female workers. They acknowledged that a proportion of the wage gap could be due to discrimination, though this should not be used to explain all the wage rate differences between male and female workers. Mincer and Polachek's preliminary results indicated that a significant proportion of the difference between the wage rates of men and women was due to differences in work histories, investments in on-the-job training, and depreciation of skills. This seemed to be particularly significant in explaining why the gender gap was far more significant in the comparison between married workers than between married men and single women. The other major contribution of the revised human capital earnings function was related to the cost of time and children. Accordingly, 'the loss or reduction of market earnings of mothers due to demands on their time in child rearing represent[s]ed a measure of family investments in the human capital of their children' (Mincer and Polachek 1974: S104). An important part of this cost, often forgotten, was due to the depreciation of skills associated with interrupted participation in the labor market.

However, Mincer and Polachek noted that the discrimination could exist not only in direct ways, but also in indirect ways. Direct discrimination existed when different rates were paid for the same unit of human capital owned by different people. Indirect discrimination happened through issues such as fewer opportunities for training that hindered the accumulation of human capital for certain workers. Moreover, the existence of market discrimination could discourage the market orientation of certain workers, both in their allocation of time and in the amount and types of human capital accumulated. These factors altogether depressed the earning power of certain groups of workers, notably women.

In his comments at the conference, Otis Duncan considered Mincer and Polachek's work as suggestive and interesting, though too much centered on an economic explanation of the interrelationship between women's labor market behavior and the household, thus overlooking other important (sociological) dimensions of the problem. He thought that the tone of the paper was nevertheless a bit conformist regarding the conditions of women in the labor market.[19]

5.7. Exploring the Possibilities of Longitudinal Data

These important developments on the application of human capital to the understanding of lifetime income remained initially at the theoretical level. One of the major limitations in analyzing the impact of human capital on lifetime patterns of income was due to the available data. The growing availability of longitudinal data from the 1970s provided new opportunities to explore the issue. Due to his persistent interest in empirically testable theories, Mincer would be at the forefront of the efforts to use the new possibilities in terms of data and in bringing together the theoretical developments and empirical analysis.

Mincer was at the forefront of the effort to explore longitudinal data and analyze the lessons that could be drawn in understanding earnings profiles. In his work with another one of his students, George Borjas, Mincer analyzed 'longitudinal data to explore individual variation in the parameters of individual earnings functions' (Borjas and Mincer 1976: 4). In their work they fitted an earnings function to each of the individual histories contained in the sample analyzed. Then, they attempted to assess to what extent the estimated variation in individual parameters contributed to an explanation of the cross-sectional variation in terms of earnings. They completed this analysis by investigating the relationship between individual parameters and a set of personal characteristics as well as looking into indirect (through variables and parameters) and direct effects of those characteristics on earnings.

The first important conclusion that Mincer and Borjas drew from their empirical work was that the concavity of the typical earnings profile, with regard to experience, normally observed in cross-sectional data, was also verified in longitudinal data. This concave shape was normally less apparent in the group with the highest educational qualifications, though it became more visible after some years of work experience. The shape of the earnings profiles was due to significant individual growth in the early years of activity. However, they also acknowledged that there was significant individual variation in the slopes and curvatures of the early phase (first third) of the earnings profile.

This individual variation was normally understood in human capital analysis as a consequence of different endowments at the beginning of the full-time working period. These endowments referred to schooling levels, rates of return to schooling, and capacity levels that were independent or preceded investments in schooling. On the other hand, the variation in the slopes and curvatures reflected differences in the volume, timing, and profitability of postschool investments in human capital. These three aspects were due to a variety of issues such as occupational choice, opportunities for on-the-job training, job mobility and career progression, job search, and other dimensions of acquisition of information related to the job market. Most of these elements were normally absent from cross-sectional data, thus the usefulness of analyzing longitudinal data was identified.

In their work, Borjas and Mincer (1976) attempted to quantify this individual variation and concluded that longitudinal data allowed a better explanation of the relative variance of (monthly or weekly) earnings than the one normally provided by cross-sectional data. Moreover, in their estimation of individual capacities, within schooling groups they found that those individuals with greater investment ratios in human capital grew more rapidly than others and that the former also had lower initial earnings, if holding capacity constant (35–6). Their analysis also indicated that the understanding and measurement of factors underlying postschool investments in human capital and their efficiency would contribute almost as much to an explanation of earning capacity as all the other factors amalgamated in the residual category (18).

Borjas and Mincer's analysis (1976) tried to assess to what extent personal and behavioral characteristics affected earnings. These effects were regarded as mostly indirect, that is, via their influence on the endowments and investments in human capital, and also their efficiency in using the stock of human capital. On the one hand, Borjas and Mincer considered a set of variables related to human capital investments, such as education, work experience before schooling completion, on-the-job training, and job mobility. On the other hand, they considered background characteristics such as parental education, number of siblings, and the presence of both parents in the household at the age of 14 (Borjas and Mincer 1976: 24). Other variables that were also considered but did not fit exactly into these categories included aspects such as age and marital status, as well as verbal ability.

Borjas and Mincer's results suggested that although background characteristics, especially family ones, seem to have a very strong influence in schooling behavior and attainment, they have little impact on postschool investments or on earnings, if investment variables and parameters are kept constant. Hence, the indirect effects of those personal characteristics operate almost essentially through schooling and very little through postschool investment behavior and efficiency (Borjas and Mincer 1976: 34). Borjas and Mincer concluded that personal and background characteristics are very weakly, if at all, related to earnings profiles (in terms of individual coefficients and parameters).

The availability of longitudinal data was also seized upon by Mincer to explore the issue of work careers, in particular the relevance and effects of interruptions in work careers, which linked to his main research interests in labor supply and investments in human capital. The issue of interrupted work careers was extremely relevant for two types of workers to which Mincer had devoted particular interest: married women and migrants. Both types of workers were far more likely than most to interrupt their full-time working activity. The general view was that real wages at reentry were on average lower than at the point of withdrawal from the labor market. Moreover, the decline in wages seemed to vary positively with the length of the interruption.

This posed several important questions for human capital analysis. If the wages at reentry were not only lower than those of other workers who remained in a full-time occupation, but also lower than for the same workers at the time of withdrawal, it meant that it was not only a matter of foregone earning capacity due to foregone opportunities for investments in human capital but also that the lower wages at reentry could be due to the loss in terms of specific investments in human capital. The interruption of working careers raised the issue of depreciation of skills and provided the opportunity to ascertain its real relevance. Although interruptions would be associated with significant declines in earning power, there were also indications of 'relatively rapid initial growth in wages after the return to work' (Mincer and Ofek 1982). This suggested that the reconstruction of human capital could be more efficient and less costly than the accumulation of new human capital. It was also important to investigate how far reconstruction costs would vary with the length of the interruption.[20]

Mincer and Ofek (1982) attempted to construct a typology of interruptions. This was necessarily complex since a robust analysis of the depreciation phenomenon became very demanding in terms of the quantity and quality of data available. Moreover, the analysis of the long interruptions also became very complicated. On the one hand, the lengthier the interruption period, the more likely these workers would stay outside the labor force, hence the lack of data on reentry points. On the other hand, lengthier interruptions increased the probability that those returning to the labor market would be workers with stocks of human capital that were particularly resilient to depreciation, either due to personal or environmental factors. This would tend to lead to an underestimation of the short- and long-run effects of depreciation and an overestimation of wage growth. The longitudinal data confirmed the view that not only were the reentry wages lower than the withdrawal ones, but also that the decline increased with the duration of the interruption of the working activity. This supported the view that the decline in earning power was due not only to the foregone experience, but also to the negative effect of the earning power of the individuals due to the deterioration of skills.

Another interesting aspect highlighted by the analysis of the data was the fact that workers who interrupted their activity for longer periods had, on average, lower preinterruption wages. This suggested that those workers who possibly anticipated the interruption reduced their investment in human capital prior to the interruption, since they anticipated that that investment would be less profitable due to the reduction of the payoff period. Moreover, it could also be expected that lower wage workers would tend to interrupt their work more frequently and for longer periods, because the foregone earnings were smaller.[21]

In the empirical analysis, Mincer and Ofek (1982: 12) also explored to what extent the effects were different according to the nature and length of the interruption period. They found that the interruptions associated with layoff, health problems, and migration were related to greater than average depreciation. In terms of length, the longer interruptions of labor market participation tended to be associated with childbearing, and the shorter ones with divorce, layoff, and unemployment. The factors associated with intermediate interruptions in terms of length were marriage, health problems, and migration. Mincer and Ofek (1982) also explored the links between education and interruptions of labor market activity. As expected, the duration of interruption was negatively related to level of education, since the opportunity cost of interruption was clearly higher and the depreciation rate seemed to increase with the level of education. These forces appeared to provide a strong deterrent for more educated workers to interrupt or to extend their interruption of labor force participation.

5.8. Concluding Remarks

When Mincer started his academic career he felt repelled by most labor research done at that time. He disliked what he considered to be a lack of a theoretical framework that could guide empirical labor research. He also disliked the fact that, underpinning the resistance to use more neoclassical economics to analyze labor research, there was a persistent skepticism among labor researchers that labor market agents were similar in their motivations and behavior to any other economic agent. Mincer considered that labor economics would only advance and strengthen its stance vis-à-vis the discipline if it stressed the role that rationality, incentives, and choices had for economic agents participating in the labor market.

Thus, with the support of some of the leading neoclassical labor economists of the postwar generation, Mincer devoted a significant part of his work in labor economics to the analysis of the long-term behavior of the labor force by using a neoclassical framework. Mincer's initial motivation was to analyze the behavior of labor supply, especially that of women. This work, which was strongly connected to his research on income distribution, was further developed by an analysis of labor careers and patterns of lifetime income. Overall, this work strengthened his belief of regarding human capital as a major determinant of life-cycle patterns of labor supply and income.

During his career Mincer favored a long-term approach to the analysis of human capital and the labor market. By bringing together labor supply and human capital, Mincer opened the way to the very important work on patterns of lifetime earnings, labor force participation, and investments in human capital. One of the most significant contributions in this respect was a better understanding of the so-called wage gap, suggesting that an important difference between the wage rates of men and women was due to differences in their work histories, training, and depreciation of skills. Another result of Mincer's analysis was a close association between wage growth and firm training, which conformed to his emphasis on the explanatory role of investments in training. This emphasis on the long-term analysis of the labor market also provided Mincer with strong ammunition to face some major criticisms that would emerge in the early seventies against human capital analysis.

6

Human Capital and Labor Market Dynamics

Jacob Mincer is well known for his work on income distribution and the labor supply phenomena, in which he was strongly stimulated by his pioneering interest in human capital analysis. Nonetheless, his intellectual activities led him to explore other topics of labor research. This chapter explores his efforts to better understand the dynamic nature of the labor market, especially with regard to workers' mobility and unemployment. With regard to workers' mobility, Mincer analyzed migration and its effect on the labor market and job turnover. In his research on unemployment, he analyzed the association between education and the duration and incidence of unemployment. Mincer also studied the impact of some labor market regulations and the way these could impair mobility and accumulation of human capital. More recently he devoted some attention to the employment effects of economic growth.

Mincer made a relevant contribution to various aspects of the labor market, though clearly his role was less influential than the one he played in research on income distribution and labor supply. The analysis of that part of his research nevertheless provides a better understanding of the main characteristics of Mincer's work and helps to fully grasp his influence on contemporary labor research. Moreover, the analysis of Mincer's work on those other topics will also reveal that underlying and unifying his research was a persistent aim at exploring the explanatory power of human capital analysis and its implications for the dynamics of the labor market.

6.1. Geographical Mobility and Migration

Until the 1960s, very limited attention was paid in labor economics to the economic dimension of migration. However, since its early days human capital research had focused on issues of migration, stimulated by the broader views on human capital, especially as stated in T. W. Schultz's initial work (1961a, 1963). Schultz was particularly interested in the role of human capital in terms of migration analysis, since the former would promote a better distribution of the labor force, one of his earliest concerns. Accordingly, in the classic 1962 issue of the *Journal of Political Economy* on 'Investment in Human Beings' (to which Mincer contributed his paper on the economic returns to on-the-job training), there was an article by Larry Sjaastad exploring the matter, based on his Ph.D. dissertation at Chicago (1961) on 'Income and Migration'. In his article, Sjaastad tried to analyze the influence of migration, as a balancing mechanism, by promoting a better allocation of resources (which echoed Schultz's concerns about the maldistribution of labor, especially in farm activities). For that matter, Sjaastad considered the decision to migrate as an investment, and attempted to identify the direct and indirect costs and returns to migration in a way that is analogous to Schultz's approach to human capital returns.

Under the mentoring of Schultz, several Chicago graduate students started exploring more systematically the economic motivations underlying migration, paying particular attention to the role of investment in human capital. Micha Gisser (1965) analyzed the role of schooling in terms of the so-called farm problem, that is, the surplus of workers on farms. In this context, schooling could have two effects: (*a*) to improve the productivity of labor, (*b*) and to increase the mobility of farm people. Gisser (1965) concluded that the second effect of schooling was clearly dominant, and that schooling could have a significant impact on reducing the supply of farm labor. This supported Schultz's view that better formal qualifications for farm workers would raise their awareness of other work opportunities and stimulate the transfer of the surplus labor force away from the farm sector. Aba Schwartz (1971, 1973, 1976) analyzed the decision to migrate in a wider context (not specifically in terms of farm labor) by trying to assess the influence that higher levels of education had in promoting more efficient migration behavior. His analysis suggested that more educated people seemed to be more responsive to better opportunities promised by a migration decision and they also seemed to have more opportunities to migrate because their search area increased with level of education.

By the mid-seventies, Mincer also became interested in issues of migration behavior and their underlying economic motivations. He regarded the study of migration behavior as an important contribution to the understanding of family economics and especially of labor supply and human capital formation (1977: 1). His study of migration is largely indebted to human capital analysis and to the idea that many economic individual decisions, and many related to the labor market in particular, should take into account the family context in order to be properly understood. Moreover, the advances in terms of data, with the increasing availability of large and detailed household data, made this not only a necessity but a real possibility.

Mincer's analysis of migration highlighted several interesting aspects. Paramount was the reduced mobility necessarily faced by married people and especially by those having children, notably since it was reasonable to expect that for those families the increase in the family returns from migration was less than costs. In fact, married people were perceived as less likely to migrate than singles, and especially divorced individuals. Whereas single individuals could still have other kinds of family attachments, such as parents and close relatives, divorced individuals saw their mobility enhanced by the change in marital status.[1]

As mentioned earlier, migration decisions were analyzed in the family context. However, this did not mean that one should lose sight of individual differences, namely regarding individual earnings and attachment to the labor force. These two factors suggested that, due to different situations in terms of earnings and labor force participation, the two spouses were likely to have different potential gains and losses from migration. The more unbalanced the situation, in terms of individual earnings, the more likely the family decision would tend to be dominated by the earnings potential of the higher income member of the family.

Due to the traditional patterns of participation in the labor force and the accumulation of human capital, the more likely situation would be that wives' decisions would be dominated by their husbands' (Mincer 1977: 9). Moreover, Mincer considered that these prospects were a potentially important explanation for the fact that women's choices regarding training and occupation had traditionally been inclined toward areas with lower geographical specificity and stronger potential geographical mobility (e.g. nursing, teaching, and secretarial work).

However, the acceleration of convergence between genders in terms of human capital accumulation, earnings, participation, and attachment to the labor force was changing this context. This was particularly important due to evidence showing that families where both partners worked had lower migration rates. On the one hand, this reduced the propensity for stable families to migrate. On the other hand, it created tensions within those families. Women were more likely to be trained and to take jobs which provided not only higher earnings but also strong incentives for geographical immobility. Moreover, the more unstable families became the weaker the incentive for women to make those training and occupational choices on the assumption that they would be passive movers in terms of geographical mobility (Mincer 1977: 13).

Educational variables also played a significant role. In his analysis, Mincer (1977) confirmed earlier views that educational attainment had a positive impact in terms of migration. The positive effect of education on the husband's migration reflected not only larger individual gains from migration but also an intrafamily substitution effect (1977: 30). The relative earning advantage of one of the spouses led to a weaker attachment of the other spouse to the labor market, or, in a Beckerian sense, a division of labor between spouses in terms of market and nonmarket activities. The situation of the latter spouse created less resistance to migration in this type of family. On the other hand, the more educated the lower earning spouse, the stronger the deterrent effect of their occupational status.[2]

Mincer concluded that these trade-offs within the family showed how significant it was to consider the household decision-making process for the economic analysis of migration. A case of mutual causality seemed to exist. The gains of the higher earning spouse brought about a reduction in labor supply and earnings losses of the tied spouse, while those losses reduced migration but increased the gains in the earnings of the higher earning spouse in families that eventually decided to migrate.

Mincer's interest in migration issues was also pursued in his analysis of work careers since these workers posed an obvious case of interruption in labor market participation. In his work with Haim Ofek, particular attention was paid to the case of interruption in the labor force participation due to migration since prior research suggested that these workers had strong upward mobility when they reentered the labor market at the country of destination, though this growth followed an initial decline from the exit point of the country of origin (Mincer and Ofek 1982). This was another example of what the authors considered to be a pattern among interrupted working careers, that is, that readaptation and renewal of skills are likely to be faster and/or more efficient than new investments in human capital, notably because the post-reentry wage growth remained after controlling for education, age, and work experience.

This work also highlights the strong sense of community and collaboration between many human capital researchers in the earlier years. In fact, Mincer and Ofek were pursuing further work that had started to be developed some years earlier by people such as Barry Chiswick.[3] Ofek himself had written his doctoral dissertation under the supervision of Gary Becker on the topic 'Allocation of Time and Goods in a Family Context' (1971). Once again we see the close interaction between Becker and Mincer in those years at Columbia and its impact for human capital research.

Mincer and Ofek (1982) considered that the drop in wages and rapid growth at least partly reflected the depreciation and restoration of human capital, both important issues when analyzing interrupted working careers. However, they also noted that the country of origin had some important effects on the post-reentry evolution of wages, with particular emphasis on the cost of adaptation in linguistic terms. The analysis of migrant workers posed specific problems. On the one hand, there was the issue of self-selection. Migrants can be expected to be different from the average worker at both the country of origin and destination, in terms of opportunities and effectiveness in human capital investments. On the other hand, there are the patterns of long-term investments in human capital in amounts and types. In particular, there is the expectation that workers with more intermittent participation in the labor market tend to invest less in human capital over their lifetime and therefore their wage profiles tend to be lower and flatter than those of more continuous workers. These aspects would be further developed in subsequent human capital research on migrants.

6.2. Human Capital and Mobility in the Labor Market

Since its outset, human capital theory has pointed out the implications of the acquisition of some types of skills specific to certain jobs or certain firms. Gary Becker's classical distinction (1964) between general and specific types of human capital suggested that workers would have to face difficulties (and some costs) in transferring some acquired skills when changing jobs. Moreover, the fact that workers differ in the absolute and relative amounts invested in specific human capital led to the emergence of different earnings profiles and to differences in mobility–firm attachment. Hence, whereas those workers with strong preferences for firm-specific human capital would present with low mobility and strong tenure effects, those with low levels of specific human capital, either due to their preferences or due to the opportunities available to them, would tend to have high mobility, independent of tenure.

At the beginning of the eighties, Mincer became more interested in the role that human capital could play in explaining job mobility. This was another aspect that benefited from recent improvements in the quantity and quality of data. The availability of longitudinal data had made it possible to explore 'the implications of human capital and search behavior for both the interpersonal and life-cycle structure of inter-firm labor mobility' (Mincer and Jovanovic 1979: 2).[4] In his work with Boyan Jovanovic, a recent graduate from Chicago, Mincer tested the hypothesis that individual differences in firm-specific human capital led, through wage effects, to heterogeneity in mobility behavior and to tenure effects in the attachment to the firm. Mincer and Jovanovic expected that complementarities and firm-specific skills acquisition would produce differences in mobility behavior and in relation to job tenure, wages, and mobility. Accordingly, individual differences in the acquisition of specific human capital would have major implications in differential tenure effects. These tenure effects on wages would equate with those due to general human capital accumulation.[5]

The empirical analysis suggested to Mincer and Jovanovic that the established view that mobility declined with age had to be qualified. In fact, mobility did not seem to decline with age at given tenure levels within each age cohort (1979: 4). The estimation with the inclusion of prior mobility variables confirmed the existence of heterogeneity in mobility behavior between workers. Moreover, people who moved more frequently prior to their current job were more likely to leave the job earlier than others (Mincer and Jovanovic 1979: 23). The effectiveness of these patterns as a predictor of future mobility seemed to be greater for older workers than for younger ones, since persistent mobility at older ages is more meaningful than at younger ages when it can be mixed with other factors.

Mincer and Jovanovic proposed that the significance of mobility should be interpreted differently according to the phase of the life cycle. Intensive earlier mobility should not be taken as an indication about patterns of investment in human capital or ability to find a good job match. Instead, it can be the result of greater search intensity or efficiency in wage gains associated with inter-firm mobility (Mincer and Jovanovic 1979: 32). Persistent mobility at an advanced phase of the life cycle suggested the existence of significant turnover and of reduced investment in specific human capital.[6] Hence, the empirical analysis confirms that those workers moving more frequently receive lower wages than those moving less, after controlling for levels of education, experience, and current tenure. Mincer and Jovanovic's estimates suggested that roughly half of the lifetime wage growth was due to general and transferable experience; the remaining half being divided equally between firm-specific experience and inter-firm mobility.

Mincer's interest in job mobility and human capital investments led him to carry out comparative work between American and Japanese labor markets (Mincer and Higuchi 1988). In their analysis, Mincer and Higuchi explored the extent of the differences between these two labor markets. Were the differences due to differences in the labor policies of firms in both countries (namely, in terms of training) or due to other factors such as cultural ones (loyalty, discipline, and tradition)? In particular, they were interested in testing the duality hypothesis, that is, that turnover was inversely related to tenure-wage growth.

In their analysis, Mincer and Higuchi (1988) emphasized the different training policies followed by firms in both countries, which were reflected in terms of wage profiles and labor turnover. The data indicated that larger volumes of human capital were accumulated in Japan than in the USA, which was particularly apparent at the firm level. Accordingly, on-the-job training seemed to be more continuous and more evenly distributed over the working age in Japan. In this country, the policies of training, retraining, and job rotation assumed larger significance than in the USA. These policies at the firm level could be understood as a response to the rapid technological change that characterized Japan's postwar economic evolution. The persistent high rates of return to education in Japan seemed also to be consistent with this view of strong skill-bias in the Japanese economic growth. Consequently, the issue of obsolescence gained increasing importance in this market, in comparison with the USA, making Japanese firms more attentive to the necessity of training workers for flexibility.

Further support for Mincer and Higuchi's conclusions (1988) was provided by the analysis of the practices of Japanese firms established in the USA. The training costs per worker were much higher in the Japanese plants, especially for new employees. The turnover rates were lower in Japanese plants than in American ones, despite the fact that the former were more recent and had a higher proportion of younger workers who are normally more mobile. The layoff and quitting rates were much lower in the Japanese plants. This led Mincer and Higuchi to conclude that roughly two-thirds of the differential between the US and Japanese wage and turnover behavior were due to the hiring and training practices of the Japanese firms. They nevertheless noted that their sample was a peculiar one and therefore their results should not be readily generalized.

6.3. Unemployment and Education

The other main area of attention in Mincer's analysis of the dynamics of the labor market was unemployment. This is another facet of his research as a labor economist that illustrates the pervasiveness of human capital theory. His first piece of work was his article on labor force participation and unemployment (see Chapter 5) in which he analyzed the response of the labor force during the postwar decades in the USA (1966: 95–9).[7] In that work, Mincer also paid attention to the issue of disguised unemployment, which seemed to be almost exclusively concentrated in the secondary labor force. Overall, Mincer concluded that employment seemed to be clearly sensitive to variations in economic activity.

During the following decade, Mincer was significantly occupied with his two main areas of research, lifetime earnings and labor supply, and devoted very little attention to issues of unemployment.

However, by the late seventies he started to work on youth unemployment (Leighton and Mincer 1982). The issue was timely since youth unemployment had been rising in the USA during the seventies. Leighton and Mincer considered that youth unemployment had grown due mainly to higher incidence, as the duration of unemployment tended to decrease with age. The high rates of unemployment also declined quite sharply beyond the first years of work experience, namely after the first half decade of the working life. Hence, the short tenure level of younger workers seemed to be the main reason for the age differences in the incidence of unemployment. While this was not peculiar to young people, the dynamics of job search in the labor market was largely independent of age but strongly associated with years of labor market experience. The higher visibility of this phenomenon by the late seventies was therefore largely due to the arrival of larger cohorts of young workers to the labor market. Leighton and Mincer also analyzed the impact of individual characteristics such as education and job training to see how they affected the probabilities of separation and unemployment, given tenure. Both issues were negatively related to education among young individuals. Of the three measures used to test the effects of training (training on the current job, training prior to the current job, and off-the-job training), only the first seemed to be statistically significant and as expected reduced both separation and unemployment incidence.[8]

The relevance that Mincer attached to human capital in the analysis of unemployment was illustrated by his two papers of the early nineties on the effects of education on the unemployment patterns among women and men (1991b, 1991c). In one study, he tried to explore the relationship between workers' education and their unemployment experience (Mincer 1991c). The analysis confirmed previous results indicating that the unemployment difference between more-educated workers and less-educated workers was mostly due to the incidence of unemployment and far less to the duration of the unemployment experience, though in both cases more educated workers had an advantage (1991c: 6). This result, in terms of incidence of unemployment, was largely due to their greater attachment to firms employing them and the lesser risk of these workers becoming unemployed when separated from the firm.

The analysis also confirmed the reduced job turnover of more educated workers. This was strongly linked to the fact that more educated workers have a greater investment in on-the-job training activities, either because of complementarities between types of human capital or due to the fact that firms provide more opportunities for more educated workers in terms of training. Since these training activities were likely to have a significant degree of firm-specificity, their costs would tend to be shared between employers and workers, and therefore both would lose with job turnover.

The reduced incidence and duration of unemployment for more educated workers seemed also to be associated with higher efficiency in search behavior. The costs of on-the-job searching relative to costs of searching while unemployed seemed to be lower for more educated workers, hence leading to less transitional unemployment. Moreover, more educated workers tended to be more efficient in acquiring and processing information about prospective alternative employment. Finally, both employers and workers seemed to search more intensively when it came to job vacancies requiring more skilled workers.

In his analysis of the impact of human capital on unemployment, Mincer developed a separate analysis for the female labor force due to his strong conviction of a different labor force attachment for women (Mincer 1991b). Despite major changes in recent decades, which had significantly contributed to growing levels of education, women's participation in the labor force was still well below that of men's and the attachment of the former to the labor force still presented significant variations during the life cycle.[9] Hence, in the case of women, it was relevant to analyze the impact of education not only on intralabor force turnover but also on movements out of the labor force associated with the unemployment phenomenon.

The analysis also confirmed the human capital prediction that women's attachment to the labor force tended to increase significantly with level of education (Mincer 1991b). However, given that women had on average shorter and more discontinuous participation in the labor force as well as lower market orientation in terms of time allocation, they were less likely than men to invest in schooling and training types of human capital. Moreover, women would also tend to favor more general types of training because interruption of labor force participation made it less likely that they would return to the same employer (thus leading to a loss in terms of firm-specific skills), and also because women would tend to have more job changes due to family decisions such as geographical and residential mobility.

Education was also found to reduce labor turnover in the case of women. This was mostly due to the general result that education increased attachment to the labor force and therefore reduced inter-labor force mobility. Whereas for men education had a strong negative effect on intralabor force turnover, it seemed to have a rather weak effect on women's labor mobility. More education seemed to be a consequence rather than a cause of reduced mobility in the case of women. Hence, the largest proportion of women's labor market mobility was due to interlabor force mobility, and especially due to quits.[10]

The incidence of unemployment seemed to decline with growing levels of education, as sharply for women as it did for men. Moreover, the probability of unemployment due to a job change also declined significantly with increased education. However, the fact that labor force withdrawal was more common among less-educated women, reduced significantly the duration of unemployment for groups with less-educated women. The withdrawal from the labor force of less-educated women compensated the higher duration of unemployment expected for those groups of women. Thus, the labor force withdrawal of less-educated women masked the positive effect that education had on the duration of unemployment.

The impact of human capital on the duration and incidence of unemployment developed therefore on three levels. First, through the complementarity between education and job training. Second, through the interaction between job training and labor turnover, since the development of firm-specific human capital created a loss for both sides in the case of interjob mobility. Finally, by the links between education and labor mobility, since firms with higher recruitment costs tended to reduce turnover, and, in an attempt to minimize these costs, they recruited a larger proportion of higher educated workers. Although there were other effects that contributed to an explanation of the pattern of less duration of unemployment, overall, Mincer (1991c) considered that the results gave robustness to the view that human capital had an impact on several dimensions of unemployment: incidence, duration, and job-search behavior (on and off the job).[11]

6.4. The Impact of Labor Market Regulations on Employment and Training

Throughout his career, Mincer devoted limited attention to labor policy topics. The few exceptions were motivated by his interest in the analysis of unemployment dynamics, through his work on minimum wages (see above) and on the role of unions in the labor market. In both cases, he was in general agreement with most standard neoclassical labor economics, criticizing the adverse effect these had on labor market adjustment and the creation of employment. Unsurprisingly, in his analysis Mincer also emphasized the negative impact these factors had on investment in human capital (1974*b*, 1983*b*).

In the early seventies, Mincer (1974*b*) analyzed the impact of minimum wages in terms of employment. He distinguished between the effects on employment from those on unemployment, which arose from the fact that only one part of the economy was covered by minimum wage legislation and/or the supply of labor to the market was not perfectly inelastic. Thus, Mincer aimed at addressing the interaction not only between the sectors covered and not covered by minimum wage legislation, but also between the market and non-market sectors. According to Mincer, the effects of the introduction or increase of the minimum wage were significant and not limited to the growth of unemployment. Mincer emphasized not only the importance of the reemployment of labor at lower wage rates, but also and more significantly the labor force withdrawals that reduced the size of the labor force in a substantial manner (1974*b*: 20). The latter was partly due to a perception of deteriorating wage prospects by workers in the sector not covered by minimum wage legislation.[12]

One of the most significant aspects of Mincer's discussion of minimum wages is that it demonstrates his insightful approach to price theory. In his analysis, Mincer points out that the disemployment effect will generally be greater than the effect on measured unemployment. This has to do with the definition of a supply curve and the mechanism used to allocate the jobs available at the minimum wage among the larger number of workers who would supply themselves if they could get that wage.[13]

Some years later, Mincer continued to explore the effects of minimum wages, though now he concentrated on human capital formation of schooling and on-the-job training types (Mincer and Leighton 1980). According to Mincer, minimum wages had a negative impact on training opportunities which created additional difficulties for younger workers. On the one hand, there was the loss of jobs whose equilibrium wages would be below the minimum wage levels. On the other hand, the reduced opportunities of training had a long-term impact on young workers' career prospects and wage profiles, namely by slowing down their wage growth. The potential negative impact on training prospects would tend to be higher in types of general job training than in more specific training, since in the latter case the firm was willing to bear part of the costs of training. This was also linked to work that Mincer developed on youth unemployment in the late seventies (Leighton and Mincer 1982) (see above).

Mincer's critical views toward wage regulation in the labor market were also expressed when he analyzed the effects of wage floors (Mincer 1984*a*). In a clear expression of how things had changed in labor research, he noted that the 'usefulness and richness of supply–demand analysis is never as apparent as when attempts are made to overrule market forces by decree' (1984*a*: 311). Hence, he tried to explore the consequences for the labor market when wages were imposed above the equilibrium level, either due to legislation or due to the pressure of labor unions.

One of the interesting effects Mincer identified in the (supply) responses to increases in the minimum wage concerned the profitability of human capital (1984*a*). Although one expected that increases in minimum wages would attract more youngsters to the labor market and increase the number of early school leavers, the observed movements out of the labor force suggested worsening employment prospects for those searching for jobs in both the sector covered by minimum wage legislation and the sector not covered. This scenario reduced the opportunity cost of schooling and therefore increased the profitability of investments in human capital. Mincer also devoted some attention to the impact of the effects of minimum wages on the nonwage components of jobs, namely the training component, which was often partially financed by employees, through lower initial wages.

Following human capital theory, Mincer concluded that the imposition or the increase of a minimum wage reduced the possibility of firms passing some of the training costs on to the workers, thus reducing the amount of training they were willing to provide. Thus, younger workers, who were disproportionally present in first-time job searchers, would therefore face a double difficulty in the labor market, due to the imposition of minimum wages (Mincer 1984*a*: 318). The reduced incentive for firms to provide training had caused other important long-term effects in the labor market since those entering the labor market at levels close or equal to the minimum wage should expect smaller wage growth due to the fewer opportunities of on-the-job training. Moreover, the reduced amount of training diminished the attachment of workers to a specific job that on-the-job training normally created and therefore the turnover would tend to be higher than if there were more training.

Mincer's critical views about the role of unions were made explicit when he analyzed the impact of the effects of unions on wages, fringe benefits, labor turnover, and wage training (1983b). Although most labor researchers believed that unions were successful in stimulating wage increases above competitive levels, Mincer nevertheless pointed out that some of the differences in wages could be due to differences in the quality of labor and to differences in human capital investments. The empirical results suggested the existence of some, statistically significant, wage gains for union joiners. The so-called union premium seemed to be especially significant at younger ages and smaller for older workers, if they joined a union and moved between industries. In terms of job mobility, those workers who joined unions experienced visible reductions in quit rates when compared to all other groups. This effect was more significant the larger the wage gain from joining a union, since job mobility became clearly less attractive for those workers since it could mean a greater loss in wages.

Mincer noted that unions advocated not only for higher wages but also for improvements in other components of the wage package. In fact, he believed that the evidence suggested that unions were more successful in obtaining an advantageous situation for their members, vis-à-vis non-union workers, in so-called fringe benefits. The empirical results indicated that average weekly hours were not less in the union sector, when compared to the nonunion one. In the union sector, overtime and temporary layoffs, which were normally favored by unions, were also more prominent. This led Mincer to conclude that rather than trading fringe benefits for wage increases, unions seemed to be able to increase both earnings and job security for their members (1983b).

Finally, Mincer explored the impact of the effects of unions on the amount of training their members received (1983b). The comparison of wage growth equations for union and nonunion workers indicated that the former presented flatter wage profiles mainly due to less worker investment in general training. This was supported by the fact that the experience coefficient was much smaller in the union case. Overall, total training seems to be less frequent in unionized firms, also confirmed by survey results. Mincer noted that union–non-union wage differentials seemed to diminish with age, according to cross-sectional data. Although this was often explained on the basis of union preference for equity that contributed to compress wage profiles, Mincer considered that this could also be due to union preference for progression based on seniority rules.[14] Thus, union behavior tended to reduce the stimulus for general training since this was not strongly rewarded within unionized firms, and unionized workers were not prone to job mobility which would benefit from investments in general training.

6.5. Economic Growth, Technology, and Employment

Mincer's work on economic growth emerged at a later stage in his career, especially from the eighties onward. His interest was mainly in its effects on the dynamics of the labor market, namely in assessing the impact of economic and technological progress on employment and to what extent the former favored more skilled vis-à-vis unskilled labor.

As the human capital research program started to take off in the early sixties, the visibility of education and training among economists and policy makers was rapidly becoming an important topic of debate fostered by growing expectations regarding the potential role of human capital investments in economic growth.

The debates on growth and development economics attracted attention within and outside the discipline, and the expansion of the government's role in the funding and management of education and science made it a focus of attention. Education was being integrated into growth models, and concentrated much attention in terms of empirical measurement of the sources of growth. It was also becoming a priority for the less-developed parts of the world, especially with the first signs of government withdrawal from direct economic intervention. Thus, the postwar surge of interest in economic growth and development topics played no minor role in the development of human capital theory.

However, in the early years of the development of human capital research there was far less work on growth topics than on labor analysis and income distribution. One of the pioneers of human capital analysis, T. W. Schultz, promoted some work, but mostly in the framework of developing countries and the modernization of the agricultural sector. The empirical support for the relevance of education to national economic performance came from work being done by others at the NBER and the Brookings Institution, which did not necessarily share the whole human capital approach (cf. Bowman 1970). In the seventies and early eighties, with the decline of interest in economics for growth and development, human capital research paid little attention to the macro perspective.

The revival of human capital within growth analysis gained nevertheless a strong impetus by the mid-eighties with the emergence of the so-called new growth models. As had happened in the fifties, human capital benefited from the revival of growth research. In both Lucas' (1988) and Romer's (1986) approaches, human capital featured again in a prominent way, and subsequent literature tended to emphasize its role (Aghion and Howitt 1998). Moreover, this new wave of research on growth and development emphasized the externalities associated with education and training, providing additional strength to government support for these activities (Bardhan 1993).

However, the role of human capital in this new generation of writings was more complex than in the previous one, following early criticisms of it in both economic growth (Arrow 1962; Nelson and Phelps 1966) and economic development (Carnoy 1977). In particular, some of the research started to explore the role of human capital in dealing with economic disequilibrium (as in Schultz 1975). This made the analysis more subtle, less automatic, and less confident, but more convincing for some of its critics. In fact, some of its fiercest critics more recently have come to accept that education makes people more productive through skills other than the ones considered by the production function by molding the behavioral response of workers through the application of employers' sanctions and incentives (see Bowles and Gintis 2000).

According to Mincer, human capital analysis could improve our understanding of the processes of economic growth and development through its interaction with population issues (Mincer 1984b). Mincer considered that human capital was a key element in understanding the process of demographic transition associated with economic growth and development and that what happened in the West was eventually being mirrored in less-developed areas of the world. Mincer thought that human capital helped to understand why the Malthusian view had been contradicted empirically, since economic growth had not been prevented by rapid population growth in either Western countries or developing ones.

The resilience of Malthusian views was due not only to the traditional overview of the quality dimension in population, but especially to the lack of awareness about the way human capital influenced individuals' economic motivations. Whereas in traditional agricultural systems, unlimited fertility could be an economically rational choice enhanced by the cultural and social context, the historical decline of mortality had inevitably led families to adopt mechanisms of birth control and to change their preferences in terms of quality versus quantity of children. Underpinning those decisions was an assessment by families in terms of psychic and monetary costs and benefits of having children. Given family budgetary limitations, Mincer believed that the process of economic development led families to invest more in the quality of their children, and therefore in their human capital, since the process of economic development made these investments increasingly attractive from a financial point of view. Accordingly, Mincer also suggested that education was a most effective instrument of birth control and pointed out some empirical evidence to support that claim (1984*b*).

Another major force associated with economic development that contributed to change fertility behavior was the rising cost of time. The rising cost of time meant that the opportunity cost of rearing children, a time-intensive activity, would increase. This aspect linked with Mincer's previous work (see Chapter 5) on the labor supply of women, since this rise in the opportunity cost was particularly important in the case of educated women whose foregone earnings increased with education. Moreover, more educated women were also more likely to have stronger participation in the labor force, which would also increase the opportunity cost of having children. This was another indirect way through which investment in human capital, especially in women, would contribute to reduce the average size of families in the process of economic development.

Despite the relevance of these reflections, Mincer's interest in economic growth was clearly concentrated in assessing the relevance of human capital for the analysis of the labor market, namely in testing the hypothesis that technological progress was skill-biased, that is, that the path of technological development was such that it would enhance the demand for more skilled labor. The relative increase in the demand for skilled labor would enhance the skill–wage differential, which, in turn, by exceeding the increase in opportunity cost, would make the acquisition of human capital more profitable and therefore create an expansion for further investment in human capital. According to Mincer, if that were the case it dismissed those critics of human capital who regarded education and training as basically having a filtering effect, since this microeconomic relationship would not carry over to the macroeconomic level.

Mincer (1989) considered that human capital played a dual role in the process of economic growth. On the one hand, human capital was a major production factor through the stock of skills that it created via education and training activities. On the other hand (and much in line with more recent developments in growth theory), human capital by being a stock of knowledge was a source of innovation and therefore an engine for economic growth. Hence, for Mincer, human capital was both a cause and a consequence of economic growth, due to the complementarity between physical capital and skilled labor:

The growth of human capital raises the marginal product of physical capital which induces further accumulation of physical capital, thus raising total output both directly and indirectly. Conversely and symmetrically, the growth of physical capital raises the marginal product of human capital. This produces an increased demand for human capital relative to unskilled labor, if human capital is more complementary with physical capital than is unskilled labor. (Mincer 1984*b*: 200–1).

Mincer believed that the secular growth in investment in human capital in the USA, and elsewhere, was consistent with this explanation of human capital supply responding to the growing demand for more skilled labor. He considered that the cyclical stability of skilled labor in terms of employment provided further corroboration of this hypothesis. Moreover, the fact that skilled labor would tend to have a greater proportion of specific human capital provided an additional reason for this stability in the employment relationship.

The skill-bias hypothesis had several important implications that Mincer considered needed empirical validation (Mincer 1989: 3). First, a faster pace of technological progress would make investments in human capital more profitable and therefore would promote increases in the accumulation of human capital. Second, since technological innovation was largely firm specific, the need for on-the-job investments and specific human capital would promote stronger attachment of workers to firms and thus reduce job mobility. Third, the time sequence in these human capital adjustments would differ between the hiring of workers with education needs and the training (or retraining) of other workers, since one would expect skills adjustments to be attempted first through recruitment and then by training. Fourth and finally, the question of technological unemployment would have to be investigated, namely by analyzing the impact of the job mobility phenomenon on the incidence of unemployment in the relevant sectors.

According to Mincer's view, the empirical evidence seemed to corroborate the claim that an acceleration of technological change increased the demand for more education and training activities. The shares of educated workers increased in industries where employment was expanding. Moreover, training activities were more common in faster growing industries, though they lagged behind educational utilization when productivity growth accelerated (Mincer 1989: 9).[15] With regard to the effects of productivity growth on labor turnover, rapid technological changes seemed to promote the hiring of younger and more educated workers in the short run, possibly due to the fact that the threat of partial obsolescence deterred older workers from investing in training. However, these studies used cross-sectional data that had some obvious limitations that clearly did not completely satisfy Mincer's empirical purposes.

Thus, Mincer continued to work on this topic and a few years later presented a subsequent analysis (using annual time-series data at the national aggregate level) in which he tried to identify the effects of changes in technology on changes in the demand for human capital (Mincer 1991a). This exercise aimed at understanding the sustained profitability of investment in human capital, especially of schooling types, despite the massive and sustained growth of educational enrollments, particularly college graduates.[16] The analysis indicated that short-term variations in the profitability of human capital, as pictured by wage differences associated with skill differences, seemed to induce reaction in terms of the supply of human capital through enrollments. This eventually shifted the labor market to another equilibrium through adjustments of supply. Moreover, the supply of human capital seemed to be responsive to changes in the profitability of human capital coming from either the benefit side returns or the cost side.

This combination of supply and demand forces explained the overall pattern in the evolution of the US wage structure (Mincer 1991a: 10–11). One of the main events was the stagnation of real wages since the seventies. Then, from the eighties onward, large and extended variations in wage differentials occurred among skilled groups in the workforce with a significant decline in real wages of less-skilled workers. Mincer noted that in the past decades whereas the wage differentials per age increased during most of the period, there was a narrowing of gender differences in terms of wages and a widening in black–white wage differentials, especially from the seventies onward.

In his analysis, Mincer pointed out some interesting and important patterns. First, that the yearly wage differentials between college-educated and high school-educated workers seemed to be closely monitored by relative supplies of graduates into the labor market during their first decade of experience. Also relevant, in an analysis of the evolution of the wage premium, seemed to be the changes in the relative demand for more educated workers supported by research and development expenditures per worker and by relative trends in service employment. Second, that the decline in average productivity growth and the almost stagnation of real wages that took place in the seventies have implied that the skill-biased changes in demand have translated to an increased demand for workers with postsecondary education and a decrease in the demand for workers with lower educational qualifications. Finally, that the cohort effects, that is, the changes in the age distribution of the labor force, seemed to account for a significant share of the steeper experience profiles of wages. This appears to be largely associated with the growing profitability of human capital, also in terms of on-the-job training.

In his analysis, of economic and technological progress, Mincer also devoted some attention to the effect of the impact of the latter on the creation of net employment. Once again, the link of this work with labor market analysis and the centrality of human capital for that matter became apparent. Mincer (1989) concluded that the empirical evidence suggested that all components of unemployment declined with productivity growth. The decline in the incidence of unemployment was small in the short run but became more prominent in the long run. The duration of unemployment was also reduced due to productivity growth. This effect was also more pronounced in the long run than in the short run. Unemployment also declined as a consequence of growth in capital intensity.

These findings suggested that technological change tended to reduce unemployment in more technologically progressive sectors. This was significant due to the widespread belief that technological change promoted large and persistent unemployment.[17]

This interest in the effects of technological change on unemployment has been one of the dominant features in Mincer's recent work. In this recent work, Mincer downplayed the relevance of technological unemployment, considering it a short-run problem or even 'a myth' (Danninger and Mincer 2000: 16). Using several alternative measures of technological progress, he observed that in the short run the acceleration of technological growth seemed to increase the demand for skilled labor, thus reducing their levels of unemployment, which also tended to be low in general. The unemployment of unskilled labor could increase, though this was not inevitable. Although the unemployment gap between both types of workers was likely to widen, aggregate unemployment would not necessarily increase. In the long run, with the growth of training also likely to expand to less-skilled workers, total unemployment was expected to decrease. Whereas technology seemed to reduce unemployment in both the short and long run, the most significant effects were really in the latter case.

At the sectoral level, Danninger and Mincer (2000) observed that the technology effect reduced the incidence of unemployment. This was not only consistent with the reduction in turnover and the reduction (or no effect) in conditional unemployment in the so-called high-tech sectors, but also due to the training response. Although rapid technological change could discourage workers to invest (due to the danger of rapid obsolescence), firms nevertheless needed to keep their workers technologically updated and therefore were willing to bear some of the training costs.

6.6. Concluding Remarks

The strength of human capital from the sixties onward was very much connected with its popularity within labor research, and the person who arguably most contributed to place human capital at the forefront of labor research was Jacob Mincer. In his extensive and prolific career, Mincer addressed the main issues emerging in the labor market and to each of them he was able to make a relevant and interesting contribution. Human capital emerged as the thread connecting the multifarious aspects of the labor market as discussed by Mincer.

In his quest to explore the implications of investments in human capital for labor market analysis, Mincer turned his attention to the issues of workers' mobility and unemployment. From the outset, human capital theory has suggested the implications of the acquisition of some specific skills and the potentially significant implications these could have when analyzing workers' geographical and job mobility. The improvements in data availability made it possible to explore in a much more systematic way these effects of human capital on labor mobility. In his work, Mincer explored the impact those individual differences in specific human capital had through their effects on wages, mobility, and tenure in the labor market. Mincer's interest in job mobility and human capital investments also led him to carry out comparative work between different national labor markets. The results of this work underlined the relevance of investments in human capital and especially of different training policies for the understanding of wage profiles, labor turnover, and the performance of migrant workers in the labor market.

Mincer's analysis of unemployment issues also contributed in giving a prominent role to human capital, and to training in particular. In his work, he confirmed his views that human capital had an impact on several dimensions of unemployment, namely in the incidence and duration of unemployment. In his work on unemployment, Mincer also explored the effects of restrictions on the conditions of the labor market and the way these impaired mobility and the accumulation of human capital. According to Mincer, minimum wages had an important negative effect on training opportunities available to workers, especially younger ones. The reduced incentive for the firms to provide training had important long-term effects on the labor market, which were negative for most workers. In his analysis of the effects of the role of unions, Mincer identified, as well, some negative effects of unionization on training opportunities, by pointing out that union workers presented flatter wage profiles (mainly due to less worker investment in general training) and that total training seemed to be less frequent in unionized firms.

The links between unemployment and human capital investments also underpinned Mincer's more recent interest in economic growth topics. In this work, he produced some support for the hypothesis of skill-biased technological development. In what concerned the hypothesis of technological unemployment, Mincer thought there was firm ground to reject that possibility, not only on a long-term basis, but even as a relevant short-term labor market issue.

This chapter has vividly illustrated that, in various instances of his research activity, Mincer used human capital as a basic framework to explain several issues of labor market analysis. In doing this, Mincer's work had three major effects. First, it made interesting and valuable contributions to the analysis of several important dimensions of the labor market such as job mobility, workers' migration, unemployment, and labor market regulations. Second, it strengthened the role of neoclassical economics as the basic analytical framework in labor economics. And last but not least, Mincer significantly promoted the centrality of human capital within labor research by pointing out the multiple applications that the human capital concept could have in explaining individual behavior in the labor market. Thus, human capital became a unifying principle that by providing coherence and consistency would develop into a central research program for contemporary labor economics.

7

The Influence of Jacob Mincer on Modern Labor Economics

Despite their intrinsic capacities, all prominent scientists, especially those pioneering in a field or a topic, know that in order for a certain topic of research to prosper and endure it needs to develop a community of researchers. Hence, researchers, especially those working in new areas, need to go through a process of identification and self-awareness in order to create a sociologically identified community that shares certain tenets providing methodological and theoretical coherence to the group (cf. Backhouse 2000). The creation of this social circle (see Crane 1972: 13–18) that can intellectually engage in this scientific quest is necessary and expresses the need this community has to organize itself and to create instruments of communication.

Mincer is certainly a good example of the capacity that many academics have to attract the attention of those around them and to interest them in pursuing similar lines of research. His ability to lure students and colleagues to human capital research was extremely relevant for the development of the human capital research program, especially in the early crucial years. Moreover, his persistent and methodic interest in the analysis of the implications of human capital for labor market analysis had a lasting influence on several generations of labor economists and contributed to the strengthening of the position human capital came to occupy in labor economics during the last forty years.

The aim of this chapter is to appraise the role played by Jacob Mincer in labor economics during his long and prolific career. A general picture of the influence of Mincer's work is provided through a brief citation analysis followed by a more detailed analysis of the role Mincer played as a teacher and especially as a mentor of several emerging leading labor economists, and the impact he had on the training of several generations of labor economists. Then, the impact that this relationship with his students had on the development of the human capital research agenda will be examined. Finally, the discussions promoted by some of Mincer's main contributions to economics and his provisional legacy emerging from those debates will be assessed.

7.1. Citation Analysis

One of the possible instruments to analyze the impact of a particular author is through the use of citation analysis. In applying this analysis to Mincer's economic research, namely in labor economics, it provides a general impression of the quantitative impact of Mincer's work. Data have been collected for the period between 1972, the year the Social Science Citation Index became available, and 1991, the year of Mincer's retirement (see Table 7.1). Although Mincer continued to work intensively after his retirement and his works continued to be cited in large numbers, the period selected covers the most significant time of his career and the years of consolidation of the human capital research program.

Table 7.1 indicates that Mincer's work has been very influential as measured by the number of citations. It is also noticeable that the number of citations has remained stable throughout the years, even when referring to research published many years earlier. This is normally regarded as a clear sign of influential research. During the period analyzed, Mincer's work received an average of more than 200 citations and each piece of research has been cited on average more than ten times per year. This is highly significant due to his prolific career. It is also noticeable that some of his work continues to be cited more than thirty years after its publication.

Mincer's most highly cited publication is by far his 1974 book *Schooling, Experience, and Earnings*. The number of citations for this book is remarkable, even more so as this is largely an empirical piece of economic research. It is also extremely significant that almost twenty years later the book continued to be cited, even more than

Table 7.1. Citations of the main publications of Jacob Mincer, 1972–91

	Total pY	Avg pY	Thesis 1957	JPE 1958	JPE-S 1962	AspLabEc 1962	MeasEc 1963	ProspUne 1966	SchExpEr 1974	JPE 1974	JPE-S 1976	JPE 1978	JHR 1978
Total	2236	203.3	3	90	132	284	148	139	815	353	111	103	58
Average	111.8	11.2	0.2	4.5	6.6	14.2	7.4	7.0	45.3	20.8	6.9	7.9	4.8
1972	25	4.2	0	3	6	4	6	6	—	—	—	—	—
1973	55	9.2	1	3	11	20	12	8	—	—	—	—	—
1974	69	9.9	0	6	16	15	7	11	14	—	—	—	—
1975	77	9.6	0	5	14	18	9	6	19	6	—	—	—
1976	132	14.7	0	9	13	18	9	15	45	20	3	—	—
1977	128	14.2	1	6	7	20	14	10	46	18	6	—	—
1978	107	11.9	0	9	6	12	9	9	38	21	3	—	—
1979	134	13.4	0	1	4	19	9	11	52	19	17	2	—
1980	145	13.2	0	4	6	23	7	11	57	18	11	7	1
1981	147	13.4	0	12	11	20	8	5	47	29	5	5	5
1982	158	14.4	0	4	6	11	7	9	56	29	18	9	9
1983	131	11.9	0	7	5	14	10	5	46	25	8	7	4
1984	119	10.8	0	4	5	10	4	5	49	25	4	5	8
1985	135	12.3	0	2	5	22	5	7	55	22	6	8	3
1986	102	9.3	0	2	2	9	4	4	42	20	2	12	5
1987	124	11.3	1	2	2	11	6	5	51	25	8	8	7
1988	116	10.5	0	5	1	10	6	1	47	19	6	14	5
1989	115	10.5	0	4	3	11	6	4	50	15	3	14	5
1990	102	9.3	0	1	2	7	6	2	49	22	3	6	4
1991	115	10.5	0	1	7	10	4	5	52	20	8	6	2

Source: SSCI-ISI.

in the years after its publication. These are clear indications of the enduring relevance of the book for labor economics.

However, the impact of Mincer's research cannot be fully appreciated through this simple quantitative analysis. A large part of his lasting influence has been through his role as a mentor for several generations of labor economists. We now turn our attention to that role in order to obtain a fuller picture of his impact in shaping contemporary labor economics.

7.2. Mincer's Influence as a Teacher

The obvious networks for attracting other researchers to work on the same topic are graduate teaching and research training. In the case of human capital, the teaching hubs were certainly Chicago and, later, Columbia. The early examples of teaching of human capital issues come arguably from T. W. Schultz's courses at Chicago in the second half of the fifties in growth topics and the economics of agriculture. Also in Chicago was Gregg Lewis (though teaching on labor topics), who had a close supervisory role in the doctoral work of people who played an important role in the development of human capital such as Gary Becker, Marvin Kosters, Morton Zeman, Walter Oi, Glen Cain, Sherwin Rosen, and Giora Hanoch. Becker moved to Columbia in 1957, making it a major center—with Chicago—of research on human capital at that time.

The visibility of human capital research at Columbia was intensified when Mincer went back to teach there in the early sixties. Throughout the sixties, Mincer and Becker joined forces to establish a community of human capital researchers based at the Labor Workshop and the NBER. During that period they attracted many of their students at Columbia to human capital topics, and guided them through the early phase of their research careers by supervising their Ph.D.s or making them their research assistants at the NBER which, during the early years of the human capital research program, had its offices located in mid-town Manhattan. The impact of this community was emphasized by the fact that several of them eventually became leading researchers in human capital, and in economics.

The recollections of former students are quite unanimous about the impact that both Mincer and Becker had on them in their first year of graduate education. The students normally had Becker for *Microeconomic Theory* and Mincer for *Statistics* (which included some econometrics) and, from the mid-sixties onward, *Labor Economics*. By the late sixties, Mincer concentrated his teaching activity on labor economics, since he felt increasingly attached to that field. Moreover, he regarded econometrics as more relevant than statistics for empirical economics. Mincer was praised for his clear, articulate, informed teaching. He taught the students basic elements about statistics especially its usefulness for economic analysis.

Mincer's approach to teaching labor economics was both seductive and somehow elusive to students. His deep commitment to price theory led him to tell students who enquired about the course that labor economics was simple, and basically consisted of supply and demand analysis. Many students only later understood that this apparent simplicity was not trivial. Underlying his effort to identify the essential traits of the labor market, there was a number of fundamental methodological and theoretical issues needing to be understood.[1] Mincer's aim at making labor analysis simple and concise was both sophisticated and demanding. The fact that so many of his students persisted in this effort is a tribute to his scientific and pedagogical skills.

The appeal that Mincer had for so many students is even more striking due to his well-known perfectionism and rigor which he applied firstly to his own work than to that of those who worked closely with him. As one of his former students recalled, 'He was reluctant to let a student finish until he was convinced no stone was left unturned to verify a thesis' assertions' (Polachek 2006b: 30). The students' task was even more complicated by the fact that Mincer did not seem to be terribly impressed by the use of sophisticated mathematical and statistical techniques. Instead, he expected them 'to apply a sound specification using a number of data-sets so one could assess robustness' (30). Thus, his sense of rigor required from students a solid grasp of theory and a rigorous testing through robust empirical work.[2]

The influence that Becker and Mincer had on their students meant that many of those who had gone to Columbia aiming to work with other professors in the department would change their minds and turn to them at the time of choosing their dissertation topic. Despite cooperating closely Becker and Mincer always had very different styles of research, which in this case proved to be effectively complementary. Whereas Becker explored matters on a theoretical basis, Mincer took a more empirically oriented approach, showing his students how human capital research could be applied in order to explain aspects of the actual labor market.

The success of human capital in creating a network of researchers was certainly linked to its ability in attracting graduate trainees and providing the area with new and able researchers, notably in the concerns of labor research. Several studies confirm that the years of doctoral training, and the period immediately after, are crucial in setting the pattern of research productivity of new (successful) researchers (see for instance Clemente 1973). The same studies also emphasize the importance of learning-by-doing in terms of scientific activity, both in graduate training and in early career research (postdoctoral fellowships, initial appointments, etc.).

In the postwar decades, doctoral training in economics was still very much concentrated in a handful of departments, which contributed to their dominance in research and publication activity. In the specific case of labor economists this pattern of concentration in a handful of departments was also very noticeable (Table 7.2). The field was dominated by four departments (Wisconsin, Columbia, Harvard, and Chicago), which remained the backbone of the field, though part of this dominance was eroded as the number of departments producing labor economists increased significantly during the postwar period. These four departments were joined by the increasing vitality of the MIT (since the fifties), the University of California (especially Berkeley), New York, and Cornell (during the fifties). Some departments, such as the MIT, Penn State, Stanford, Princeton, and Yale, that had traditionally overlooked labor research started to change their attitude from the fifties onward, producing in some cases an important number of graduates.

The content of the dissertations was also changing rapidly. Much more attention was given to training and manpower issues, supply and migration of labor, wage differentials, and employment/unemployment matters. Other aspects that used to be prominent, such as unionism, collective bargaining, industrial relations, and analysis of labor legislation retained some importance but lost ground in their relative importance for new generations of labor researchers. The approach was also different, with the increasing adoption of econometric techniques and the shift away from the

Table 7.2. Ph.D.s awarded by American universities in labor economics, 1940–68

Ph.D.s	Total	CHG	COL	HVD	WIS	MIT	CAL	CRN	NY	PRIN	PEN	NC	YAL	MCH	STA	Other
Total	917	67	86	72	102	51	55	43	36	21	28	16	12	24	10	280
1940–9	222	24	41	23	32	3	10	6	5	4	3	4	0	13	1	48
1950–9	319	30	26	25	41	19	19	27	14	10	11	5	8	5	0	77
1960–8	376	13	19	24	29	29	26	10	17	7	14	7	5	6	10	155

Source: American Economic Association (various years).

institutional study of specific markets (industry, region, and firm studies).

In terms of Ph.D.s related to human capital issues, until the early sixties human capital research was almost exclusively confined to Chicago (the exception was Mincer's 1957 Columbia dissertation). These Ph.D. students did their research work on occupational differentials (Morton Zeman and Becker in 1955, Mincer in 1957, Robert Polkinghorn in 1958, Paul Keat in 1959, and Henry Sanborn in 1960) and on the role of education in economic growth (Zvi Griliches in 1957). By the mid-sixties the situation started to change with the first Ph.D.s coming from other departments (Harvard and Washington in 1962; Yale and Virginia in 1963). Columbia became more evident with the work of students supervised by Becker and Mincer.

One of the major vehicles of Mincer's influence on labor research has been through the supervision of many doctoral dissertations. Although we do not have complete data on all the doctoral students whose dissertations Mincer acted as first or second sponsor, Table 7.3 provides an approximate idea of that role.

Accordingly, among his former students there are several subsequent prominent human capital and labor researchers. These include people such as Barry Chiswick, Dave O'Neill, Reuben Gronau, Robert Michael, Michael Grossman, June O'Neill, Arleen Leibowitz, George Borjas, Masanori Hahimoto, and Solomon Polachek. In their dissertations they developed several building blocks for the human capital research program and for contemporary labor economics. Many of Mincer's former students went on to become prominent academics and leading experts in their fields of research, and several of them confirmed the influence that Mincer's work and personality had not only on their research interests but also on their method of working.[3]

Mincer's role as a mentor to new generations of labor economists contributed to the fact that by the late sixties, doctoral research on human capital presented a significant expansion in terms of the number of graduates and departments from where they graduated. However, in order for this research potential to become effective and provide vitality to the area, it was essential that those newly trained professionals joined the academic profession and became successful academics. In the case of human capital there was not only high retention of these young researchers in the academic

Table 7.3. A selective list of doctoral students in economics supervised by Jacob Mincer at Columbia University, 1964–81

1964	Morris Silver—Birth, Marriages, and Business Cycles in the United States
	Gonan Smith—Occupational Pay Differentials for Military Technicians
1966	Dave O'Neill—Occupational Incidence of Unemployment
	Robert Rice—An Analysis of Private Wage Supplements
	William Landes—The Effect of State Fair Employment Legislation on the Economic Position of Nonwhite Males
1967	Barry Chiswick—Human Capital and Regional Inequality
	Reuben Gronau—The Effect of Traveling Time on the Demand for Transportation
1969	Robert Michael—The Effect of Education on Efficiency in Consumption
1970	Michael Grossman—The Demand for Health: A Theoretical and Empirical Investigation
	June O'Neill—The Effect of Income and Education on Interregional Migration
	Albert Zucker—Some Aspects of the Economic Effects of Minimum Wage Legislation: 1947–66
	Beth Niemi—Sex Differentials in Unemployment in the US and Canada 1947–66
1971	Linda Edwards—Investment in Human Capital: A Study of the Teenage Demand for Schooling in the USA
	Masanori Hashimoto—Factors Affecting State Differences in Unemployment
	Elizabeth F. Durbin—Family Instability, Labour Supply, and the Incidence of Aid to Families With Dependent Children
1972	Carmel Chiswick—Income Inequality in LDC's
	Arleen Leibowitz—Women's Allocation of Time to Market and Nonmarket Activities: Differences by Education
	Cynthia B. Lloyd—The Effects of Child Subsidies on Fertility: An International Study
	Fredericka P. Santos—Some Economic Determinants of Marital Status
1973	Solomon Polachek—Work Experience and the Difference Between Male and Female Wages
1975	George Borjas—Job Investment, Labor Mobility and the Earnings of Older Men
1976	Cordelia Reimers—Factors Affecting the Retirement Decisions of American Men
1978	Linda Leighton—Unemployment over the Work History: Structure, Determinants, and Consequences
1980	William Alpert—The Economic Determinants of Private Wage Supplements
	Margaret L. Hashimoto—The Effect of Industrial Composition Changes of the Relative Demand for Skilled Labor
	Gregory de Freitas—The Earnings of Immigrants in the American Labor Market
1981	Nancy A. Garvey—Job Investment, Actual and Expected Labor Supply, and the Earnings of Young Women

profession, but also high productivity. Moreover, many in this generation managed to get positions in some of the top departments in economics in the USA and abroad, as well as in major research institutions, helping to enhance the dissemination of research in this field.

The development of a field of research also requires institutional support. This is very important for the support and training of new research cohorts. In the case of human capital, the NBER was the research hub notably for large projects. In fact, the attraction of working at the NBER was one of the main reasons for Becker's decision to leave Chicago and move to Columbia in late 1957. This growing engagement of the NBER with human capital research was also a major factor in bringing Mincer to the institution in the early sixties (1961). He came primarily to develop his work on the role of on-the-job training in labor market earnings, and eventually in 1966 took charge of labor research, especially on labor participation and unemployment and its relation with skills differentials and investment in human capital. Many other young researchers came at that time to the NBER to start projects related to human capital. These included people like Albert Fishlow (economic history), Victor Fuchs (differentials in hourly earnings and eventually health economics), Paul Taubman and Terence Wales (returns to higher education and the potential screening effects), and Thomas Juster (who coordinated a series of studies on the relation between the stock of human capital and certain types of economic and social behavior).

The contribution of the NBER to the development of human capital research was also very important as a springboard for many of these new generation researchers. Many of the research assistants were Becker's and Mincer's doctoral students coming from Columbia and included people such as Barry Chiswick (regional income inequality), Dave O'Neill (black–white employment rate differentials), Robert Michael (consumption efficiency), Michael Grossman (health demand), and Gilbert Ghez (lifetime allocation of time and earnings within a human capital framework). The NBER played a very important role by providing an opportunity for these young researchers to interact and develop their work, mostly under the mentoring of Mincer and Becker. Several of these researchers continued to develop their research on human capital topics at the NBER after they finished their dissertations.

7.3. Creating Discipleship and Developing the Human Capital Research Program

The success in attracting, training, and supporting new groups of researchers had a major impact on the potential of human capital research. It allowed the exploration, empirically and theoretically, of many of the aspects identified in the initial contribution of the three pioneers. The fact that these young researchers worked in most cases closely with Schultz, Becker, and Mincer meant that the first installments of the human capital research agenda were very much shaped by their interests. The interaction with these new researchers also meant that human capital research explored other aspects that enriched its applicability.

In the case of Mincer, his influence was clearly felt in the analysis of the role of human capital for income distribution and labor market analysis. Several of the students and younger researchers with whom he interacted developed their careers, at least initially, around two large issues. On the one hand, a large group focused on analyzing the explanatory role of investments in human capital for income inequality, either in the overall population or between specific population groups, with particular attention paid to gender differences and migrant workers. On the other hand, another large group focused on exploring the contribution of human capital to understanding the interactions between market and nonmarket behavior, including issues such as labor force supply, nonmarket effects of human capital, and home investment in human capital. The analysis that follows is not an exhaustive list of those influenced by Mincer's work on human capital and labor economics, but rather a set of examples that aims at illustrating the breadth and depth of Mincer's legacy through his various collaborations with younger generations.

7.3.1. Income Inequalities

One of the areas that initially attracted most interest in human capital, following the pioneering work of Mincer's doctoral research, was income inequality. Barry Chiswick, one of Becker's and Mincer's earliest students at Columbia, analyzed in his dissertation the effect of education and training on (regional) inequality (finished in 1966, but only published in an extended version in 1974). Chiswick attempted to show that distribution of income was related to investments in human capital and that schooling and postschool training were important determinants not only of individual differences in income, but also of regional differences (1974). The preliminary results of his work with Gary Becker (on the role of human capital for a theory of income distribution) presented at the 1965 meeting of the AEA (Becker and Chiswick 1966) suggested that education had a reasonable explanatory power in terms of the distribution of earnings between and within US regions. Chiswick pursued this area further with Mincer some years later when they analyzed the role of human capital in US personal income distribution (Chiswick and Mincer 1972).

Important research developed on the role played by education in explaining differences in the economic performance of several specific population groups (especially in the USA). This attempted to explore the variability of the return to education between groups identified by Becker's pioneering work (Becker 1964).

One of the aspects that received significant attention was the possible role of human capital in explaining gender differences. The human capital explanation developed by Mincer and Solomon Polachek (1974) focused on the effect of human capital accumulation on market earnings and on market activities, but also took into consideration the elements of discontinuity in labor force participation and in human capital investments that characterized much of women's work behavior. This led them to adapt the so-called Mincerian earnings function in order to take account of discontinuous processes of human capital accumulation. The issue of discontinuity and its obsolescent effects was further developed in Mincer's collaboration with Haim Ofek (Mincer and Ofek 1982). Accordingly, they considered that the issue of depreciation and possible restoration of human capital became a central aspect of labor market analysis: the longer the interruption the greater the impact.

This view of the gender gap was strengthened throughout the eighties by several studies that frequently adopted the human capital framework as a major explanatory principle. Among these are the studies by June O'Neill (1985), a former student of Mincer's at Columbia, and James Smith (see Smith and Ward 1989), one of the first NBER postdoctoral fellows in human capital in the late sixties. These studies enhanced the emphasis on women's market skills, notably human capital, as the primary shaper of their (changing) economic status.

Another group that attracted particular attention was that of ethnic minorities. Both Mincer (1958) and Becker (1964) noted that although education was largely beneficial for all population groups, there were important variations between specific groups. Initial interest was concentrated on the Afro-American population; Dave O'Neill, one of Mincer's and Becker's first students at Columbia, used military test scores to analyze how far the differences in terms of earnings were due to discrimination. His results suggested that although some of the differences in earnings could be ascribed to current discrimination in the labor market, a significant, potentially bigger difference was the result of a poorer provision of schooling to certain groups. This idea was further developed by Finis Welch (1967), another of the earliest postdoctoral human capital researchers at the NBER, when studying income differences between white and black populations in the US rural south. Welch considered that the lower income was due not simply to labor market discrimination, but to the fact that the black community had less financial capacity to invest in education, which reduced their income potential. By the late seventies human capital researchers were suggesting that the vintage hypothesis seemed to get some support from this population group, and that human capital and experience seemed to be the most important characteristics in explaining the improving status of black Americans (see work by James Smith 1978). This work continued in the late eighties, suggesting that the evolution of the black–white wage gap was mainly explained via two types of human capital: education and migration opportunities (Smith and Welch 1987).

The analysis of ethnic groups in the USA was also expanded, notably to the Asian and Jewish communities. This allowed a better picture of the role of human capital in ethnic and racial minorities, enhancing differences in level of schooling and returns to schooling. Although it was recognized that discrimination played a role in access to schooling and in the labor markets, this seemed to be less relevant than expected. Based on the work of Barry Chiswick (since the late seventies), and later by James Heckman, it was suggested that the differences in the rate of return to education by ethnic group could be linked to complementarities between schooling and other family investments in human capital, notably home human capital, and had links with fertility behavior and labor force participation (Chiswick 1988; Heckman and Walker 1990).

The analysis of income inequality between different ethnic communities was also closely linked to the study of the labor market performance of immigrant workers. Most of the contributors to this latter topic in recent decades were Mincer's former students, such as Barry Chiswick, or research assistants, such as George Borjas. Their work and that of others on immigrants have contributed to a much better understanding of the determinants and impact of immigration emphasizing the role of human capital investments (Borjas 1999a and 1999b). This research indicated that the economic status of immigrants improved with duration of residence, although refugees experienced greater difficulty (Chiswick 1986). Although the same amount of years of schooling and labor market experience had a smaller effect on the economic status, if accumulated prior to immigration, the strong progression of earnings of economic migrants at the country of destination (Duleep and Regets 1997) could, *ceteris paribus*, eventually make them level with those native born workers. In contrast, research has downplayed both the importance of chance as a determinant of earnings and the possibility of selective return migration, that is, the return to the country of origin of the less successful immigrants. These results were found to be robust in both cross-sectional and longitudinal data.

The work on the economic effects of migration has provided empirical support to the human capital approach, namely to the idea that migration propensities are clearly associated with educational level (see Greenwood 1997). In many of these studies, nurtured by human capital analysis, the influence of Mincer's work can be found. First, human capital analysis has been used in the issue of transferability of skills between different labor markets and different jobs, especially concerning the now classic distinction between general and specific human capital. Second, the possible complementarities between different types of skills and their impact on the economic return to human capital have been pointed out, notably concerning linguistic skills in the case of migration. Third, Mincer's work with Polachek and Ofek on interrupted work careers and skills' obsolescence has been applied extensively in the case of migrant workers. Fourth, the analysis of migrant workers has highlighted the need for a long-term perspective of the identification of their income patterns, something that has been stimulated by Mincer's focus on a long-term view of the labor market. Finally, the study of migrant workers has enhanced the importance of the family as an essential unit of analysis for many important aspects of the labor market, a view to which Mincer has contributed significantly.

Mincer's approach to inequality was also influential in the development of the analysis of the role of human capital in a life-cycle framework. Some initial work had been developed by Yoram Ben-Porath in his doctoral dissertation at Harvard (1967) in which he attempted to integrate human capital into a lifetime framework, and analyze its interaction with earnings, notably by taking into account the role of foregone earnings.[4] Ben-Porath's model used human capital theory to explain the shape of the wage profile, its upward slope, deceleration, and eventual decline, by offering a productivity-based explanation of the growth of earnings with working age.[5]

At that time Becker was also increasingly interested in this view that broadened human capital's horizons for intergenerational aspects of education, as shown by his Woytinsky lecture (1967), where he developed a model of wealth maximization in order to explain the distribution of human capital investments, notably their concentration at earlier ages. This approach aimed as well to include the interaction between changes in wage rates over the life cycle resulting from the accumulation of human capital, the allocation of time between market and nonmarket sectors, and the impact of human capital on the productivity of household behavior (see Ghez and Becker 1975).

Becker's model was significantly strengthened empirically by Mincer's 1974 book, notably by emphasizing the role played by on-the-job training in the model's explanatory power. For Mincer, this wage growth was certainly related to firm training. He analyzed the issues by comparing indirect estimates of total worker investment costs derived from observed wage profiles with directly observed costs of job training investments. His initial estimates were based on the former method since at that time there were no direct estimates of training available (this only became possible in the mid-seventies for the US case). The direct estimates of job training investment costs require data on the time spent in training per period and the period opportunity cost of that training. The initial estimates were the ones initiated by Mincer's 1962 study and then became much more tractable empirically through his innovative use of the parametric wage function.

One important issue for the analysis of lifetime patterns of income was that of allocation of time. Ben-Porath's model assumed a two-way allocation of time between learning and earning, not taking into consideration the time spent in consumption or leisure or assuming it as fixed. Ghez and Becker (1975) had also considered a two-way option but between labor and leisure. This was due to the fact that considering three-way choices (between work, leisure, and human capital) was far more complicated. This was further developed in the mid-seventies by people such as James Heckman, Alan Blinder, and Andrew Weiss. Their results added complexity to the analysis of life-cycle patterns, notably in terms of the effects of production-function specifications and of consequences of differences in initial conditions, though they did not question Ben-Porath's main outcomes.

Although the analysis was focused on analyzing intertemporal differences in human capital investments over the life cycle, Mincer considered that it provided important insights into interpersonal differences. Accordingly, at any moment of the life cycle the marginal cost of producing human capital was lower for people with greater learning abilities. On the other hand, the marginal revenue was expected to be higher the easier the access to financing or the lower the interest rate. Altogether, these two conditions suggested that persons with greater ability to learn, lower funding costs, and lower time preference for the present would invest more in human capital in all periods. Since individuals with more schooling were more likely to be fast learners and to face lower discount rates, they were also more likely to invest more in job training. From this analysis, Mincer drew three major empirical implications in terms of lifetime patterns of investment in human capital (1997a: S41). First, persons with higher levels of schooling were expected to invest more in job training. Second, those who invested more in job training at earlier stages were also more likely to continue to do so at later stages of life. Finally, persons with greater learning ability or better schooling engaged in more job training activities, even when they had the same schooling attainment in quantitative terms.

7.3.2. *Linking Market and Nonmarket Behavior*

One of the most important developments brought about by human capital research was in drawing economists' attention to the interactions between market and nonmarket choices. Mincer's influence in this respect was very important due to his work on human capital and labor supply.

The impact of Mincer's work on labor supply has been acknowledged in various contexts. His influence was particularly felt in work dealing with family supply models and life-cycle profiles, though arguably the major effect was to greatly stimulate economists' interest in the topic (Gronau 2006). This interest has promoted important advances in the study of labor supply during the past decades, namely by recognizing and interpreting empirically the different labor supply functions (Heckman 1993). Other advances refer to the distinction between choices at the extensive margin (participation and employment) and at the intensive margin (about hours and weeks of work), and to the distinction between descriptive and structural labor supply functions. Although some of these advances questioned aspects of Mincer's pioneering work, it is hard to find a researcher working on this who has not been strongly influenced by his work (namely his 1962 paper). Moreover, several of these critical advances came from former students and close colleagues, illustrating the fact that intellectual admiration did not get in the way of analytical discernment.[6]

Some of Mincer's influence in linking market and nonmarket behavior was also felt through the analysis of the social and non-pecuniary benefits of education that was carried out in the late sixties and seventies at the NBER, namely by some of Becker's and Mincer's students. Particularly important at the time was Robert Michael's doctoral work which analyzed the impact of education on consumption behavior, notably on consumer efficiency. This would pursue in a more systematic and elaborate way one of the insights contained in Mincer's paper on opportunity costs and time (1963). According to Michael (1972) one should analyze the efficiency effect of education in terms of nonproductive activities, such as consumption, by using the new developments in consumer theory, developed by Becker and others. Michael's results suggested that expenditures changed with education (in particular, more educated individuals consumed more services) and that education enhanced people's capacity to produce useful commodities from a given level of factor inputs in the nonmarket sector (Michael 1972: 88).

Michael's work also followed in the footsteps of Becker who had been focused in reformulating consumer theory by adjusting it to household behavior (1965). Becker wanted to focus on the increasingly important nonworking time, especially given the scarce attention this part of human activity had received. This built on the contribution of people attached to the Columbia Labor Workshop, in which Mincer played a leading role, and on some significant developments in the economic analysis of education, in order to integrate production and consumption into the household. Hence, the traditional framework of choice between work and leisure would be adjusted to encompass the allocation of time and goods within the household.[7] Using this reformulation of consumer theory, which focused on household behavior, Becker moved increasingly into the analysis of individual behavior in a socially interactive context (1974). Becker has recently publicly acknowledged his profound (mutual) intellectual indebtedness to Mincer in what concerned their research activity during the sixties, namely by referring to his difficulty in disentangling their individual contributions from each other's.[8]

Another area stimulated by Mincer's work was research focusing on home human capital. This work was very much initiated by Arleen Leibowitz and Jacob Mincer at Columbia and the NBER at the beginning of the seventies. In her work, Leibowitz suggested that what was frequently regarded as the effect of natural ability could be in fact the result of preschooling human capital. Moreover, she challenged the view that women with higher levels of human capital and more attractive careers would invest less in their children's education (1974). In fact, these women were apparently reducing the time spent in other house activities (home production), but not the time spent with children and in particular doing activities that could have a significant positive effect on their cultural capital. Hence, there seemed to be a positive correlation between mothers' education and children's education, due to higher amounts invested in the children's (home) human capital.

The attention to home human capital led other researchers to explore better the factors underlying children's attainment, especially in terms of schooling, and the direct and indirect effects of family background on income, notably via educational achievement. Children's economic success was analyzed in terms of the impact of governmental policies (setting the environment), parents' behavior (work and earnings choices), and children's choices in using their talents and the resources made available to them (especially in terms of education, work, and family behavior) (cf. Haveman and

Wolfe 1995). The more persistent attention to the role of the family, education, and socioeconomic background led to several important empirical developments. Notably among these were the development of sibling studies, the improvement in the measurement of the role of education, and a better analysis of home investment in children. Altogether, these led to a more complex picture, in which factors such as the genetic endowment of ability, the family cultural background, and the family's endowment of physical and human capital converged. Moreover, it helped to consolidate the role of human capital both directly ascribed to the children and in inter-generational terms, especially through the mother's education (Hill and O'Neill 1994).

This work on the intergenerational effects of investment in human capital linked with developments in the economics of household production. Some of the pioneering work was developed by Reuben Gronau, who interacted closely with Mincer at the beginning of his career. The late seventies and early eighties were characterized by a loss of momentum in this area of research (Gronau 1980), which was ascribed to the dissolution of much of the network associated with the Columbia Workshop that followed the move of Becker from Columbia (Grossbard-Schechtman 2001). This area would acquire a renewed vitality at the start of the nineties (Gronau 1997).

7.4. Concluding Remarks

The development of human capital theory owes very much to the collective and articulated research efforts of a group of authors, of whom the pioneers were Theodore Schultz, Jacob Mincer, and Gary Becker. The importance of the three pioneers was not restricted to their individual contributions, since they played a crucial role in establishing a community of scholars that could extend, discuss, and substantiate their initial contribution. Mincer played no minor role in this respect, especially in what concerned labor economics.

Social science does not develop research groups as easily as most of the laboratory sciences do, and this makes even more prominent the need for any researcher, and especially those exploring new topics, to find colleagues with whom to discuss and improve their arguments. This capacity of Mincer, alongside the efforts of Schultz, Becker, and others, to convince their students that human capital analysis was an exciting project explained the rapid development and success of human capital theory. Mincer stimulated several important developments related to human capital research. Among these, his influence is clear in such areas as income distribution, the comparison of the economic returns between different population groups, home human capital, and the effects of human capital on long-term labor market performance.

Overall, Mincer was a mentor to many younger labor economists, attracting many of them to topics related to his research, notably topics associated with human capital research. The influence Mincer had on the early research careers of many of those labor economists was felt in the choice of topic for their dissertation, in the choice of their area of specialization, and in their methodological approach to labor research. However, it should be very clear that this mentoring did not mean that the work of these so-called disciples was a mere imitation. Although influenced by Mincer, each of these researchers developed their own career and made individual contributions to human capital and labor economics. Their autonomy is clearly illustrated by the fact that several of these former students and research assistants introduced new topics of research, in some cases quite apart from human capital analysis. The point is that Mincer's important contribution to the development of human capital research was not limited to his own work but to the work that fructified through his interaction with his students and other labor economists.

8

The Human Capital Labor Economist

Despite his importance for contemporary economics, especially labor economics, little research has been devoted to the analysis of Mincer's work. This has been the main motivation underpinning this book. Through a systematic analysis of his extensive published work, it has been shown to what extent Mincer's prolific career has influenced modern labor economics.

Jacob Mincer is responsible for what is arguably the first systematic contribution to the emergence of human capital theory. By focusing in his doctoral dissertation on the contribution of schooling and training to an explanation of the distribution of income he changed the course of research in this area and, more significantly, helped shape the development of one of the most popular research programs in contemporary economics. Thereafter, economists paid not only greater attention to the study of education in the context of inequality, but also regarded it increasingly as a productivity-enhancing activity that could magnify future and lifetime income.

Mincer's initial work in human capital was devoted to the analysis of inequality. This started with his doctoral dissertation in which he advocated human capital as a major explanation for income distribution. He pursued this view further in subsequent work on human capital, lifetime income, and wage patterns, namely in his book on *Schooling, Experience, and Earnings* (1974*a*). It was this framework within which he developed the well-known human capital earnings function, which would become one of the most widely used tools in labor analysis. In this context, he analyzed the impact of human capital on earnings through wage rates and employment time, namely by exploring the contribution of various types of human capital.

Despite Mincer's initial critical views about labor economics, it eventually became his natural disciplinary habitat. When he started his academic career, by the end of the fifties, labor economics was completing a significant process of change from a prior theoretical and methodological eclecticism to a growing attachment to the use of neoclassical price theory for analyzing labor markets. This evolution of labor research paved the way for important developments in contemporary labor economics, not the least for human capital theory. Mincer's discomfort faded as the field became increasingly attached to neoclassical economics, and he made an important contribution to the prominence of neoclassical economics in labor analysis in recent decades.

A very important part of his labor research, especially in the sixties and seventies, was devoted to the analysis of the long-term behavior of the labor force. Mincer's initial motivation was to analyze the behavior of labor supply, especially that of women. This work, which has strong connections to his research on income distribution, was further developed by the analysis of labor careers and patterns of lifetime income. This work strengthened his position of regarding human capital as a major determinant of life-cycle patterns of labor supply and income.

In recent decades, the future of human capital became more associated with its popularity in labor research and the person who most contributed to put human capital at the center of contemporary labor research was Jacob Mincer. His lifetime interest in exploring the multiple implications of human capital extended in recent decades to two major topics: worker's mobility in the labor market and employment. Stimulated by significant improvements in data availability, Mincer turned human capital research's attention to the implications of the acquisition of some specific skills for the analysis of workers' geographical and job mobility. Mincer's analysis of employment dynamics also gave human capital, and training in particular, a prominent role. These links between unemployment and human capital investments have also underpinned more recent interest in economic growth topics, in which he produced additional support for the hypothesis of skill-biased technological development.

Throughout this book it has been shown how Mincer used human capital as a basic framework to explain several issues of labor market analysis, thus providing human capital with a central and unifying role in explaining individual behavior in the labor market. Human capital theory performed the role of unifying a variety of issues and empirical phenomena under a common and simple set of principles.

Mincer's research is characterized by a broad concept of human capital. In the early years of human capital research, when most work was concentrated on the effects of schooling, Mincer insisted on the need to avoid placing all emphasis on formal schooling. Namely, his aim was to show the significance of postschool training in a broad perspective (including formal and informal training, and learning from experience). His pioneering estimates of the rates of return to some training activities showed similar results to those obtained for schooling activities, thus confirming that human capital research should pay increasing attention to training activities.

Mincer's work is well described as a preference for a long-term approach to the analysis of human capital and the labor market. By bringing together labor supply and human capital, Mincer opened the way for very important work to be carried out on patterns of lifetime earnings, labor force participation, and investments in human capital. One of the most significant contributions in this respect was a better understanding of the so-called wage gap, suggesting that an important part of the difference between the wage rates of men and women was due to differences in their work histories, training, and depreciation of skills. Another result from this analysis was a close association between wage growth and firm training, which fitted into his emphasis on the explanatory role of investments in training. Throughout his work the analytical and methodological prevalence of long-term trends and features of the labor market over short-term phenomena is clear.

In his approach to microeconomic analysis Mincer's work is characterized by a strong emphasis on bringing the household to the center of economic analysis. From a very early stage Mincer pointed out that family income formation, consumption, and labor force behavior were interrelated through simultaneous choices within the household. He took great care in demonstrating the relevance of the family perspective to the analysis of labor force participation, hence the need to consider the household as the appropriate decision-making unit of analysis in decisions concerning consumption behavior, income pooling, and the choices about leisure and the production of goods and services at home.

Mincer's analysis of human capital and labor supply issues also led him to a persistent emphasis on the interaction between market and nonmarket activities and the relevance of these interactions for an understanding of several important economic phenomena, especially concerning labor economics. This was based on a conceptual reevaluation of the work–leisure choices. He considered leisure not merely as a consumption activity, but also as including factors, such as education, that had productive elements. Moreover, he regarded it important to expand the concept of leisure by considering the hours of work at home, in nonmarket activities. This view would be shared and explored subsequently by several other human capital researchers.

Another theme that flows through Mincer's work has to do with the value (opportunity cost) of time. A significant part of his work on human capital, labor supply, unemployment, and even the minimum wage hinges on the concept of the value of time and the way this influences individual decisions. Moreover, his focus on long-term behavior allowed him to explore some important implications of the intertemporal analysis of the opportunity cost of time and the impact of its changing value throughout people's working life. This is apparent in the analysis of aspects such as lifetime investments in human capital and labor force participation.

The emphasis on the relevance of household decisions and nonmarket behavior is important for another reason. It illustrates Mincer's confidence in the explanatory power of economics, which is hardly surprising bearing in mind his close interaction with Gary Becker and their mutual intellectual influence (see Becker 2006). Although they had different research styles, and levels of aggressiveness in seminars and discussions—Becker being the more aggressive, Mincer the more courteous—the positive interaction between them was enormous. It was a mutually advantageous relationship that blossomed throughout the sixties fostered by their close interaction at Columbia and at the NBER. Both were interested in exploring crucial topics such as the implications of investments in human capital, family behavior, and time allocation.

This interaction was nurtured by a close friendship and a commonality of interests that outlived Becker's departure from Columbia in the late sixties. Nonetheless, whereas from the seventies onward Becker became increasingly involved in expanding the boundaries of the discipline by exploring the implications of economic analysis for nonmarket behavior, Mincer, though supportive of those efforts, remained very much within the traditional boundaries of economic analysis and remained focused on labor market phenomena.

Underpinning Mincer's work were other significant methodological options that influenced many labor economists. When Mincer started his career, he complained about the lack of emphasis on theoretical analysis and abstraction in labor economics. (Nowadays, he would suggest that the discipline has somehow moved too much to the other side.) In his early years of research, there was a clear methodological shift in labor research that placed the emphasis on general models of individual decision-making that should be assessed through their predictive power rather than by their realism. According to Mincer, the development of labor economics, and of human capital in particular, was carried out by maximizing the potential of price theory analysis in explaining economic behavior through models that should be kept simple and statistically tractable, in order to be useful and empirically testable (1969: 84). Mincer believed that empirical testing contributed to the progress of scientific knowledge by providing empirical robustness. This progress, by reflecting an improvement of (statistical) techniques, also improved the quality of the empirical tests, in a virtuous process of knowledge improvement.

In matters of method, Mincer is characterized by a peculiar blend between theory and empirical research that shaped the development of human capital research. Although many of the initial developments on human capital research remained at the theoretical level, the growing availability of longitudinal data from the 1970s provided new opportunities to explore the impact of human capital on actual lifetime patterns of income. Due to his persistent interest in empirically testable theories, Mincer pioneered efforts to combine theoretical and empirical analysis. According to Mincer, human capital development was intrinsically linked to the examination of available empirical evidence. For that reason Mincer was often at the forefront of exploring new types of data and in reassessing his own work when new possibilities opened (in terms of data).

Another feature that emerges from Mincer's work and from the recollections of those who studied and worked with him is his clarity of exposition, both in the classroom and in writing. This also played a major role in his ability to attract generations of students and colleagues to his research. Mincer's clear style of writing, unusual among many economists, also benefited from his attachment to the principle of Ockham's Razor. In his theoretical and empirical work, he always preferred, *ceteris paribus*, simple models and empirical techniques to complex ones.

Underlying this apparent simplicity was perfectionism and a rigorous handling of data. Testing for robustness was a cardinal rule for Mincer and he instilled in his students and colleagues the value of replication. Measurement and attention to detail in data were another core feature, with refinements of data being the objective. As his students and research assistants quickly learned, the idea of running one regression and considering a paper completed was just not his style. He did not rush to publish, preferring, instead, to rerun an entire set of equations or rewrite the full draft of a potential paper.

One aspect that is very close to Mincer's view about the development of economic ideas is the idea of continuity. This idea of continuity and cumulative knowledge is according to him one of the major reasons for the development of human capital analysis. Economists are supposed to establish a persistent dialogue with the past in order to systematically revise and improve the legacy of economic ideas. According to Mincer it was this continuity that led him to explore Adam Smith's principle of compensatory differences as an explanation for earning differences, or to generalize previous attempts by Milton Friedman to develop a causal explanation for the income of professionals. This idea of continuity would also be very much present in Mincer's own work, since he frequently returned to his previous work in order to extend it or reassess it in light of new data.

The idea of continuity is also present regarding future work and it is clear that Mincer regarded research as a collective and tentative project. Hence, a large part of his work was carried out through close collaboration with his students who would eventually become leading researchers in labor economics. In fact, his ability to engage with younger generations of labor economists magnified the impact of his approach to labor issues and suggests that through that influence his work will continue to shape the development of labor economics in the future. Moreover, Mincer was a partner in one of the most important and famous *unwritten* coauthorships with Gary Becker. Although they never published a joint article, they both acknowledged that much of their work during the sixties was so influenced by the other that it would be hard to identify each specific contribution.

Mincer's economic philosophy stresses the role of economic choice. This is particularly obvious in his work on income distribution, where he aimed to move the focus from exogenous forces to individual economic choices. However, the role of individual choices was also apparent in aspects such as labor supply and work careers. Mincer's work also displays a great confidence in the rationality of the economic agents and the role of individual choices in explaining labor market phenomena. This is often less explicit than in the work of other pioneers in human capital analysis, such as T. W. Schultz or Gary Becker, but it is still clearly there. This is surely perceptible in the rationale of investments in human capital and in the analysis of women's participation in the labor force. Thus, in Mincer's few forays into policymaking, there is a negative assessment of government's regulation and its potential effectiveness on the labor market, as can be seen in his work on unemployment, minimum wages, and unions.

Mincer's work has certainly suffered criticisms and it will continue to do so in the future. After intensive debate during recent decades, most economists believe that the role of human capital in understanding inequality and labor market phenomenon is very important, though possibly less explicit and straightforward than was initially thought in the early sixties. Nowadays, more attention is given to factors other than human capital, such as ability, and to differences in the role of human capital between population subgroups. The effects of human capital are also regarded as more complex due to the importance of issues such as the relative importance of on-the-job training vis-à-vis schooling, the differences in the patterns of accumulation of human capital, and the motivations and conditions underlying it (e.g. the role of the economic cycle and the short-term variations of the labor market).

Altogether, these debates and criticisms have produced a much more informed and robust view about the labor market and inequality phenomena. This is one of the major aspects of Mincer's legacy. His research influenced not only the way of thinking but also the interests of several generations of labor economists. Even when reaching different conclusions, these researchers were motivated to investigate those issues to which Mincer had drawn the discipline's attention.

The influence of Mincer's work shows the relevance of studying the development of applied fields if one aims at understanding what has happened in economics in recent decades. Despite some recent efforts (Backhouse and Biddle 2000), little is known about specialized fields and our knowledge of the evolution of economics is dominated by what happened in the core fields. However, that view ignores the fact that, in recent decades, economists have become increasingly specialized and that most practitioners develop their research in applied fields. Thus, what happens in those fields is a growing part of the intellectual activity of the economic discipline. Mincer's work has double significance for labor economics as an applied field. On the one hand, it has provided much vitality to this field and also stimulated some significant and heated intellectual debates. On the other hand, the impact of Mincer's work on the discipline as a whole has given prestige to labor economics.

It is always hard to appraise the contribution of any academic, especially when performing that task without significant temporal distance. This book confirms that Mincer will be remembered for his contribution to economics as a pioneer in human capital analysis, a mentor for many generations of labor economists, and a formidable labor researcher who seduced many of his readers with his originality, skill, and clarity. The significance of his work for (labor) economics has made his contribution an important chapter in the history of economic thought in the second half of the twentieth century.

Notes

Chapter 1

1. Mincer's lack of inclination for biographical or retrospective writing also did not help. The few sketches of a biography come from his prefaces to the two volumes of collected essays, and from the brief editorial introductions to special volumes in his honor. His influence was magnified by his role in the training of many labor economists, including several female ones (Bloom and Siow 1993).

2. This section is largely based on an interview with Jacob Mincer, conducted by the author at Jacob and Flora Mincer's residence on 16 July 2002, which has been subsequently revised (Teixeira 2006).

3. The following paragraphs are based on a personal memoir that Jacob Mincer wrote some years ago. I am grateful to Barry Chiswick who made me aware of it, to Flora Mincer for providing me with a copy of that moving testimony, and especially to the late Jacob Mincer for sharing his personal recollections with me.

4. I thank Barry Chiswick for sharing this with me.

5. This interest would not cease as illustrated by his activity in statistics, especially at the beginning of his career, both as a teacher and a researcher (see Mincer 1957b, 1969).

6. The innovative character of his work is curiously suggested by its classification in the *American Economic Review*'s list of doctoral dissertations under the item Statistical Methods, Econometrics, and Social Accounting.

7. Mincer's absences from Columbia were few and short, as visiting professor to the Hebrew University, Jerusalem (1964), the Stockholm School of Economics (1971), and the University of Chicago (1973–4).

Chapter 2

1. In fact, there was an important emphasis on policy consequences, which are linked with their emphasis on political economy as a science of the legislator. The classics were often focused on social reform, and in influencing the political power to change and adjust the institutional

framework. That was one of the main reasons why their approach was frequently much more prescriptive than most of the modern economists would accept. In fact, they regarded themselves as political economists (and not only as such), not as economists.

2. The exception was Jevons who despite giving some attention to education and to its impact on the heterogeneous nature of the labor factor was nonetheless ambiguous about the possibility of considering skilled labor as a type of capital.

3. This is apparent in the work of William Farr and of the Scottish J. S. Nicholson, professor of Political Economy at Edinburgh, both prominent advocates of this exercise of valuing 'the living capital'. Other authors also noted that the movements of population would also affect the economic value of a country's population (cf. Mears 1923).

4. Some of the most important works in this respect were written by Louis I. Dublin, a statistician working at the Metropolitan Life Insurance Company. Although he acknowledged, as did many others, that to place an economic value on human life was a tricky subject, he clarified that the purpose was to focus on a narrow aspect of life, more precisely the net value of earnings. This implied likening the raising of children to a (human) capital investment through an analysis of the maintenance costs (food, clothing, and education) and the potential productive value expressed in expected lifetime earnings. In Dublin's most famous book, *The Money Value of a Man* (1930), coauthored by Alfred J. Lotka a mathematician also working at the Metropolitan Life Insurance Co., the role of human capital was emphasized, meaning those expenditures that enhanced human capacities which could translate themselves into production and generate income.

5. In this respect Gorseline pioneered the use of samples of brothers to assess the economic contribution of education vis-à-vis other factors, a practice that would prove very successful from the 1970s onward.

6. In Harrod's work the dynamics of economic growth was devised as a disequilibrated one, difficult to reverse, and calling for a policy intervention that combined a long-term policy of low interest rate (encouraging capital accumulation) and a cyclical program of public works. Domar's growth model was not exactly the same as Harrod's, since he placed more emphasis on the role of capital accumulation in expanding employment, and his approach focused on the possibility of the rate of growth being below that necessary for full employment, more than on the idea of unbalanced dynamics.

7. Schultz's role was very prominent in the earlier stages and particularly in publicizing significant work that was being done by several lesser-known researchers in exploring human capital potential. He was also fundamental in coordinating and stimulating these efforts, especially

through his skilled research stewardship. His influence would eventually decline because he did not frame his ideas in a way that most of his younger fellow economists would expect. He had neither the training in mathematics that would allow him to develop it nor the interest in the development of models which was becoming so popular among the discipline.

8. The problems were not over, since publication of the study was delayed due to some of his very critical conclusions, in particular those referring to the restrictions affecting access to the medical profession. Finished in 1941, after some delay, the study was eventually published in 1945, with a very critical remark by one of the NBER's directors, G. Reinold Noyes, who downplayed the effect of education in explaining differences in incomes, and showed himself unconvinced by the arguments on social and legal obstacles. For him the differences were mostly the result of differences of ability.

9. Nonetheless, it should be noted that the study enhanced the role of education and training in income patterns through a compensatory principle. That is, the impact of educational differences on income differences was sustained on the basis of a compensation for its costly and lengthy nature and not so much by its enhancing-productivity character.

10. In his report Brunsman highlighted the fact that 'the amount of income received by persons tends to vary directly with the amount of training they have obtained' (1953: 5B–11). Moreover, it was noted that for college educated men the relationship was less clear since while studying they could only afford part-time employment that provided them with smaller earnings, though the data for subsequent ages confirmed the correlation between education and income.

11. The results suggested to Reid that nonwhites, even when more qualified in terms of formal education, had greater difficulties in finding a place in occupations requiring considerable educational levels. This lower effectiveness could also be due to the inferior quality of the educational institutions attended by nonwhites, or even because the average years of college were lower for nonwhites rather than for whites.

12. Two small articles preceded the publication of the study. In the first, Miller (1951a) examined the possible contribution of some factors to the apparent increased equality in the distribution of income. In the second paper, Miller (1951b) discussed the plausibility of a less unequal distribution of income, in the USA, between the mid-thirties and the late forties.

13. Some of the problems raised by this controversy were considered to be due to a deficient statistical approach, such as the inclusion of both men and women on the same income distribution curve. The author considered that it was recommendable to use separate distributions, since

it was the inclusion of women that explained most of the skewness of the distribution curve. On the other hand, in terms of women workers there were wide differences in work experience and length of working period. Separate analysis was also advisable between farmers and non-farmers, since the reasons for the skewness of the curve were somehow different.

14. Other factors related to education, such as occupation, geographical origin, and race, provided some additional support for the impact of education on income.

15. This reduction in terms of wage differentials was also confirmed by the work of another Chicago student, Robert Evans (1963).

Chapter 3

1. The assumption of a normal distribution of human abilities was inspired by Sir Francis Galton's work on heredity (see especially Galton 1978), and first applied to the distribution of personal income by Otto Ammon (1899). Based on probability doctrine, Ammon substantiated that the main characteristics crucial to determine people's occupational level would follow the normal distribution. This idea could be found in the work of several authors of the first half of the twentieth century (e.g. Moore 1911).

2. These causes were considered to be in two main groups: first, the characteristics of the environment of the income recipients which included items such as occupation, type of industry, age, sex, and color; second, the ebbs and flows of business activity.

3. Kuznets' work was aimed mainly at 'how income affects the recipient's use of its demands' (1953: 6), in order 'to find out what regularities prevail in the relation between size of income and the mode of its disposition as a basis for interpreting changing reality and for reasonable prognosis of the future' (1953: 7).

4. The innovative character of Mincer's work is curiously suggested by its classification in the *American Economic Review*'s list of doctoral dissertations under the item Statistical Methods, Econometrics, and Social Accounting.

5. In this respect Mincer reviewed the work of people like Woytinsky, Staehle, and Friedman and Kuznets (1945).

6. Mincer explicitly acknowledged Adam Smith as an important source of inspiration when he started working on his dissertation on personal income distribution. He thought that Smith's compensatory principle, notably the extension and cost of training, could be a major explanatory principle for the variability of lifetime income (Mincer 1957a: 4, 31).

7. It is present in the positive evaluation of the performance of his model, but also in the poor capacity of alternative models, in particular those based on the normal distribution of abilities and its significance for the distribution of income: 'the substance of this study is the formulation of a hypothesis and the exploration of its predictive power' (1957a: 5). Moreover, 'ultimately, it is the degree of conformity of empirical data to the conclusions suggested by the model which establishes the usefulness of the model' (1957a: 49).

8. In terms of compensatory returns, Mincer followed Friedman's approach of excluding indirect costs.

9. One could not rely completely on the information available from the employers since firms were expected to transfer part or all of those training costs to the worker through the payment of lower wages. On the other hand, one could not base the analysis completely on an analysis of workers' earnings, since it was likely that the firms would pay part of the training costs. Moreover, the assessment of foregone earnings would require extensive data on earnings that were not readily available. One would need extensive data on earnings for workers receiving training, during and after the period of training, and comparable data for those with similar schooling but without on-the-job training. Hence the values reported by either the firms or through earnings would provide a poor estimate of the real costs of training.

10. These estimates were supported by his analysis of some complementary evidence on foregone incomes of workers and some educated guesses about firms' costs and outlays (1962a: 60ff.).

11. Mincer noted that although, in general, investments in human capital should be located at earlier stages of life, there were exceptions. The tendency to locate them at earlier stages was due to their costly nature, namely in terms of foregone earnings, and because the period of repayment became necessarily shorter at later stages, thus some investments would become less profitable. However, there were cases where this rule did not apply, namely the periods of life when the productivity in learning grew as fast, or even faster, than the productivity in earnings (Mincer 1974a: 14).

12. This also underlined the role of individual preferences and differences with regard to nonpecuniary aspects of work and work–leisure preferences.

13. For reasons of simplicity, Mincer initially assumes that the direct costs are not significant, though he acknowledges that this is more credible for the case of on-the-job training than for other types of human capital. However, he notes that direct costs can be introduced into the model without great effort and without changing the essentials of the analysis.

14. Due to the lack of direct information on job experience, Mincer measured it by subtracting the age of completion of schooling from reported age. He also assumed that the rates of return to postschool investments were not much different from those of schooling investments and that those individuals without further investments, after completing schooling, would present largely flat earnings profiles for most of their working lives.

15. These included, as well, the effect of differences in the quality of schooling, initial earning capacity, and expenditures in time and money of students attending the same educational institutions.

16. The comparison between the updated and old estimates revealed that the latter were not that much off the mark. The main difference was at the lower levels of schooling, whose investments were probably underestimated.

17. This was based on the results of the tests made by Heckman and Polachek (1974). Based on the same tests, Mincer considered that a functional form using the log of years of schooling was not derived from the human capital model, and was an inferior specification that normally underestimated the returns to schooling and overstated the returns to experience.

18. The theory implies that the returns to on-the-job investments decline with age, because the remaining working period becomes shorter. At the same time, individuals face increasing costs of those investments, since their wages increase over their working life and the opportunity cost of time thus becomes higher.

19. For a recent assessment, see Lemieux (2006).

20. This perception was strengthened by previous analyses of differences in earnings within schooling groups that pointed out the relevance of factors such as quality of schooling, time supplied to the market and in unemployment, and, last but not least, investments in postschool activities.

21. Mincer noted, nevertheless, that these conclusions should be handled with care since they were largely based on cross-sectional data and that allocation of human capital investments over the life cycle could not be simply based on cross-sectional profiles, since these referred to different individuals at different ages (Mincer 1974*a*: 76ff.).

22. In her comment, Mary Jean Bowman, another pioneer in human capital analysis, stated the need to enlarge the analysis to groups other than that of white nonfarm males considered in the study (1972). She also pointed out that the informational asset provided by education should be taken into consideration.

23. Chiswick's dissertation (1967), supervised by Mincer and Becker, had explored the relevance of regional differences in the degree of inequality and skewness of the distribution of earnings. In subsequent publications Chiswick continued to explore this theme eventually leading to his 1974 book *Income Inequality* for the NBER.

24. The estimation of the contribution of investments in human capital to understand earnings inequality was made on the assumption that the residuals were homoscedastic. Mincer tested this hypothesis due to strong indications of the existence of significant intraschooling group variability of earnings.

25. This was apparently explained by the stronger incidence of employment instability at lower levels of schooling. Thus, the marginal distributions skewness would tend to increase with age and schooling, not only because skewness within each schooling group was larger in groups with higher levels of schooling and older ages, but also because, in the aggregation process, the positive correlation between group variances and group means, normally observed empirically, increased skewness (Mincer 1974a: 111).

26. This was already clearly perceptible in his survey on personal income distribution for the *Journal of Economic Literature* (Mincer 1970). The importance of this text resided not so much in its novelty, but in its significance. First, Mincer regarded human capital theory as one of the main explanations for the phenomena of personal income distribution, alongside much more established hypothesis of noncompeting groups, ability/genetic factors, or mathematical models based on chance. Second, being a survey and commissioned by one of the most prestigious research publications in the discipline, it was a sign of recognition by the discipline of the coming of age of this theory. Finally, it provided a major vehicle for the dissemination of a state-of-the-art assessment of human capital theoretical and empirical achievements to the wider community of economists, not only to specialists in the field of inequality and income distribution.

27. Even if Mincer acknowledges the possible existence of a random component, he considers that it does not need to have the stochastic properties attributed by random shock models.

28. The empirical evidence confirmed the existence of a positive relation between schooling or age and the mean number of weeks worked in a group, and a negative relation between schooling or age and the standard deviation of weeks worked in a group (Mincer 1974a: 120).

29. Other groups that were largely left aside by Mincer's study included groups of nonwhite male workers, and also farm workers, self-employed, and over 65-year olds (Mincer 1974a: 125). Mincer noted that although these workers were characterized by earnings that were more dispersed, fluctuating, and intermittent than those of white, urban, male workers, human capital analysis could also provide important insights into the analysis of these groups. However, and since those workers presented a much more intermittent participation in the labor force, it was necessary to give much more extensive and systematic attention to the effects of

employment on the earnings of those groups, something that was only cursorily analyzed in the main group considered in his study. Mincer noted nevertheless that an exploratory analysis of these groups indicated that the overall picture painted by the human capital model for the under-65 white, urban, male workers still holds its explanatory power well.

30. Mincer also considered that, among other factors that contributed to explain within-group variation in earnings, there were differences in the quality of schooling and individual differences in the rates of return to schooling and to postschool investments, besides a variety of other factors that he labeled as unexplained or unmeasured (Mincer 1974a: 115).

31. Among the factors considered by Smith, Mincer pointed out nonpecuniary aspects of wages, instability of employment, uncertainty of success, and problems of trust (Mincer 1976: 137).

32. Mincer pointed out some elements of convergence with both the ability and the noncompeting hypotheses. The former could be integrated into a human capital framework, though playing a minor role. The latter emphasized a pragmatic statistical approach that stimulated the analysis of several demographic and institutional variables.

Chapter 4

1. This was one of the main outcomes of a vivid debate on the Equality of Educational Opportunity Survey, which had attracted the attention of many important social scientists in the late sixties and early seventies such as James Coleman, Otis Dudley Duncan, Herbert Gintis, and Daniel P. Moynihan.

2. One of the leading authors in this group, Samuel Bowles, argued that the evidence on intergenerational transmission of economic status was consistent with a view of education and work as reflecting a broader social structure (Bowles 1972a, 1972b). Bowles considered that this picture was overlooked by human capital explanations because of its emphasis on a cognitive role of education, instead of a socialization one, and due to empirical problems in terms of previous analysis (Bowles 1972a).

3. In particular, Taubman emphasized the family environment, which affected income though various channels: acquisition of items that increased skills, child-rearing techniques that instilled differences in skills and tastes toward nonpecuniary rewards and risks, type of school attended, and access to good jobs through nepotism (1975: 37–46).

4. For a recent assessment of the role of education on intergenerational mobility, see Solon (1999).

5. A few years later in a paper with Nigel Tomes, Becker focused on the determinants of unequal opportunity and their impact on intergenerational

mobility (Becker and Tomes 1986). The model built on Becker's work of altruism toward children, investment in human capital, assortative mating, and demand for children, in order to provide a more complete and realistic model of family behavior.

6. However, some have questioned the widespread conviction that the impact of technology on the wage structure has accelerated in recent years (Mishel and Bernstein 1998).

7. This was apparently inspired by George Akerlof's now revered paper 'Market for Lemons' (1970) that has recently been published (cf. Spence 2002). It is fitting that both men, together with Joseph Stiglitz, were awarded the Nobel Memorial Prize in Economics at the same time in 2001.

8. Though in recent years Spence (2002) clearly admitted that he viewed education as productive human capital.

9. See, for instance, Layard and Psacharopoulos (1974).

10. However, an important caveat was placed on the evidence of sheep-skin effects and the interpretation that these supported the screening theory. According to Barry Chiswick (1973), the dropout group could be mainly composed of inefficient learners who left school when they realized how little their productivity was being increased by education. In contrast, graduates mainly consist of efficient learners whose productivity is strongly increased by education.

11. This type of test was first used by George Psacharopoulos (1979) in a two-step strategy. The first step indicated that earnings ratios increased with the level of education and that this pattern was more pronounced in the competitive sector (considered here as the distributive trades sector) than in the noncompetitive one (public administration). The second step indicated that the human capital earnings functions had a stronger explanatory power for the competitive sector than for the public one, and that the returns to schooling were higher in the former than in the latter. This was understood by the author as contradicting the (strong) screening theory, since the educational factor was (more) important in a sector where productivity was supposed to play a determinant role in the wage process. A similar test was developed by Tucker (1986) for American data (1980 PSID data), and for testing the strong and weak versions of the screening hypothesis (the results indicated a rejection of both versions).

12. The importance of this aspect has been enhanced by some evidence revealing a selectivity bias and an ability bias in the composition of samples of workers employed in the public and private sectors (see Oosterbeek 1993).

13. The studies on siblings made some assumptions about family behavior and genetic influences which had significant impact on the results and their analyses. As far as the former is concerned there is mixed evidence on whether the parents tend to invest more on the more able children, or

whether they have a preference for equality (see Behrman and Taubman 1989). The genetic aspect is rather problematic and is not expected to be solved easily. In fact some of the assumptions about the transmission of genetic effects had no theoretical or empirical supporting evidence, but were merely based on the necessities of estimation, since without them the models would be indeterminate (cf. Goldberger 1979).

14. However, Taubman recognized that his approach had some serious limitations, namely that it required 'strong assumptions to separate the contributions of genetics and family environment' (1976: 859). Other shortcomings were possible bias in the sample of respondents, and the lack of comparative studies.

15. However, it should be noted that the independent variables did not explain more than one-third of the observed variance in the logarithm of income (Griliches and Mason 1972: S90). Moreover, in the comment to this paper, Paul Taubman emphasized the fragility of these conclusions due to the shortcomings of the sample and the variables used (both acknowledged by the authors).

Chapter 5

1. These researchers disdained most of the general economic theorists' work, which was considered to be based on a set of unreal assumptions leading necessarily to an incorrect understanding of labor phenomena and misguided policy advice. The Wisconsins attempted to provide an alternative institutional theoretical framework that addressed the existence of conflict in labor relations. For Commons it was also important to introduce some government regulation that promoted full employment, through an arbitration role on collective bargaining disputes.

2. Later in his life, Hicks seemed to become very critical of this book. He thought that it had a too critical view of the role of trade unions and a naive belief in the neoclassical/perfect competition framework and its effectiveness for the analysis of the labor market (see Klamer 1989).

3. This lack of a clean-cut theoretical and methodological affiliation of many authors is not exclusive either to this period or to labor economics (see Rutherford 1997; Samuels 1998). The economics discipline as a whole was also still in the process of defining its modern identity, with the emergence of a clear dominance of the neoclassical school, and the marginalization in the American context of institutionalism (see, e.g. Yonay 1998). The postwar period is widely recognized as a crucial period during which the main characteristics of modern economics coalesced: the particular emphasis on measurement and quantification, the prevalence of deductive reasoning, the strong belief in the explanatory power of a

self-contained economic theory, and the centrality of the competitive market as the locus for analyzing and benchmarking economic reality.

4. Marc Nerlove saw this as the main contribution of Mincer's paper, among many other important features (Mincer 1960*b*).

5. This point would stimulate an exchange between Mincer and Glen Cain (1969) and Joseph Mooney (1967). Mooney argued that there was an inverse relationship between unemployment rates in urban areas and the labor force participation of poor population groups (both white and non-white) in the same areas. Mincer and Cain (1969) argued that Mooney's results were due to a misspecification of the statistical model and that other empirical research did not support his conclusions. Mooney (1969) replied stating that Mincer and Cain relied too much on a rationality assumption and that many poor and nonwhite workers were not in a condition to assess job opportunities in terms of their monetary and nonmonetary characteristics, let alone make a choice between work and leisure. Again, the disagreement impinged on the role and relevance of neoclassical assumptions for labor market analysis.

6. Nonetheless, Bowen and Finegan (1969) acknowledged that on a substantive basis, Mincer made a very significant contribution to the understanding of labor force behavior, especially by emphasizing the relevance of migration to explain interarea differences in labor force participation rates (1969: 115).

7. Hence, Pierson considered that Mincer's claim of short-term insensitiveness to cyclical variations was weakly supported and generally unconvincing.

8. Notably, a change in weeks worked by heads, with total earnings constant, produced labor force responses in all groups but the younger one without small children. This exception was not very surprising, since this group referred to a period normally short in which most married women were employed (Mincer 1962*b*: 82).

9. This was problematic mostly to cross-sectional studies, since in time series both income and price coefficients were biased.

10. Although the concept of opportunity costs was normally overlooked in consumption and demand studies, Mincer considered nevertheless that many consumption activities involved 'some specific costs to consumers over and above the money price paid to the seller of the consumption goods' (1963: 67). Hence, the specification of a demand function and budget constraint should take into account those costs whose analysis was complex since these were specific to the consumers and likely to be linked to their income.

11. In the case of transportation costs, Mincer noted that a basic dimension of the evolution of this activity was greater speed and this was economically relevant precisely because time had an economic value. Thus, those

changes were expected to have an impact on prices once the opportunity cost of time was taken into account. Due to the relationship between income and the opportunity cost of time, the demand for faster means of transportation would change with any changes in income, regardless of additional changes in technology or in the relative prices of different means of transport.

12. In this latter aspect the influence of Stigler's work (1962) was felt on the economics of information.

13. On the contrary, the responses to permanent income were weaker the higher the educational level, for heads of income older than 35 years (Mincer 1962b: 83). The weaker response in these groups to changes in transitory income was predictable due to the likelihood that available assets would reduce the need for temporary income through wives' labor force participation.

14. This was already harbinged in Mincer's paper 'Employment and Consumption', presented at the annual meeting of the Econometric Society in 1958 and published in the *Review of Economics and Statistics* in 1960, in which he explored 'the effects of variations in employment on family and aggregate consumption' (1960a: 20). On that occasion he noted that, based on cross-sectional and time-series data, the effects depended on the source of income variation.

15. On the importance of the link between human capital and labor supply to modern labor research, see Blinder and Weiss (1976).

16. In their study, Mincer and Polachek used data from the 1967 National Longitudinal Survey, since this provided detailed data that allowed them to relate women's family and work histories to their market earning power. Since they could face a simultaneity problem, in the second part of the article they decided to use a 2SLS (Two-step Least Squares) estimation approach. This nevertheless did not significantly affect the results obtained with OLS (Ordinary Least Squares) and in both cases a good predictive power was found, though the power of the test was weak. The use of the 2SLS procedure stimulated an exchange between the authors and Sandell and Shapiro (1978). The latter considered that the simultaneity problem and discontinuity led to some econometric incorrections. Mincer and Polachek (1978) replied that they left unchallenged the substantive and methodological interests of their contribution.

17. The discontinuity pattern also made the optimization assumption of continuous decline of the amount of human capital investments over the life cycle more dubious.

18. Mincer and Polachek (1974) did a separate analysis for the case of black women who invested less in on-the-job training despite spending more time than white women in the labor market. Rates of return to schooling seemed to be higher for black women.

19. Duncan (1974) considered that this picture could be challenged once several conceptual and technical improvements were addressed. According to his view the main weak points in the analysis had to do with the poor treatment of other family members, the lack of a fertility function, and the lack of attention to the quality of schooling and work experience.

20. This work had been somehow stimulated by a comment published by Mincer and Ofek in 1979, in which they rejected corner solutions for women's labor supply on long-run analysis, based on supporting empirical evidence from longitudinal data. In the same comment they rejected as well homogeneity in the labor supply. In their later study, Mincer and Ofek (1982) used both retrospective and panel data. They also applied this framework to the case of migrant workers, which normally presented strong social mobility. These results suggested a higher rate of readaptation when compared to the initial accumulation of human capital (an analogous phenomenon to that observed with returnees to the labor market).

21. The longitudinal data also allowed several aspects of the interrupted earnings profile to be parameterized and estimated. This provided estimates of the short- and long-run effects of nonparticipation and the short- and long-run effects of experience. The statistical analysis indicated that the long-run effects of market experience and nonexperience were both statistically significant and in the expected direction. Moreover, 'experience and nonexperience have not only lagged effects on wages, but also... these effects persist throughout and last beyond spells of labor force withdrawal, which typically involve new jobs and new employers' (Mincer and Ofek 1982: 9). The short-run effects of nonparticipation seemed to be substantially higher in the short run.

Chapter 6

1. The effectiveness of children as a deterrent to migration was particularly associated with schooling, rather than with the number of children. On the other hand, this factor would tend to enhance migration decisions in those families considering that option when children were a preschool age. Moreover, very young children were strongly associated with a weaker participation of the mother in the labor market, which also reduced the resistance to migration in those families.

2. Mincer also explored the relationship between migration behavior and unemployment. As expected, individuals who migrated tended to have higher unemployment rates than nonmigrants. Family issues were also relevant in this respect. Strong family ties seemed to contribute

to lengthen the unemployment of the main earner spouse prior to migration and to create unemployment among the tied spouse after migration (1977: 35). For these spouses, migration contributed to increase the relevance of temporary interruptions of participation in the labor force, and also to increase the long-term withdrawals from work, by making it harder for these individuals to reenter the labor force.

3. Research on human capital implications for migrant workers led to a greater emphasis on the importance of issues such as transferability of skills, which has implications in various areas as well, such as transferability of skills across occupations. Although some work was carried out on internal migration, little attention was paid to the relevance of human capital to international migration until the late seventies. In his work, Barry Chiswick explored the determinants of investment in human capital and the consequences of this investment, both for the individual and for a broader, aggregate, macroeconomic framework. He devoted particular attention to the impact of human capital investment on the labor market and income trajectories of American Jewish workers. Later, he also focused on the complementarity between traditional forms of human capital and language, which he considered another type of human capital, and tested the robustness of that complementarity for several countries (USA, Canada, Australia, and Israel) and for various data-sets (illegal aliens, census data, survey data, and longitudinal data).

4. Labor mobility was defined as 'change of employer, whether or not unemployment intervenes' (Mincer and Jovanovic 1979: 3) and excluded exits from and entries into the labor force. The latter exclusion was not very significant since the sample included only male workers who presented almost continuous participation in the labor force. Hence, for this analysis, labor mobility was identical to job mobility, which could be due to geographical, industrial, or occupational mobility.

5. This led Mincer to some reformulations on the earnings function to integrate a tenure term. The inclusion of the tenure variable attempted to capture returns to specific human capital, so that the experience term would measure returns to general human capital.

6. The education variable seemed to predict some reductions in mobility at given levels of initial mobility, but it does not appear to have much predictive power in the case of older workers.

7. This analysis showed that, first, the cyclical conformity of the disaggregated groups was not as clear as in the aggregate group of secondary workers. Second, the additional worker was more likely to be a low-income individual than the discouraged worker. This was particularly apparent in the group of nonwhite female workers. Third, the pattern of labor force

participation of older men seemed to be dominated by secular declines in participation. Fourth, the groups of teenagers and youngsters continued to present their secular decline in the labor force participation. A large part of this behavior was correlated to increases in school enrolment. Fifth, the primary labor force, namely male workers aged 25–54, seemed to be quite insensitive to demand fluctuations.

8. The analysis of specific ethnic differences confirmed the relevance of training for labor market performance. African-American workers received not only less training but also less specific training in relative terms. They also had less education which was associated with a pattern of less tenure and more intermittent participation in the labor market. This contributed to an overall picture of greater job instability and greater difficulties in job finding that was consistent with longer duration of unemployment, inhibition of quits, and augmentation of layoffs. Nevertheless, it remained to be explained how much these effects were due to discrimination in the labor market, though Mincer seemed to somehow downplay that factor.

9. This was essentially explained by the different allocation of time between market and family nonmarket activities within the household that still placed a major responsibility on women.

10. This reflected two important aspects. On the one hand, it pointed out the importance of family issues in women's labor force participation. On the other hand, it highlighted the fact that women tended to work more in industries where layoffs were less likely to occur, such as the services industries.

11. Among those other factors are the opportunity costs, the discount rate, and the expected length of the payoff period. These seemed to have symmetrical effects. The opportunity costs seemed to be higher for more educated workers and therefore to have a negative effect in terms of unemployment. The other two seemed to have a positive effect. The discount rate was expected to be lower, as suggested by the fact that these individuals decided to engage in lengthier processes of training. The payoff period was expected to be longer since more educated workers tend to enjoy longer working lives. However, greater intensity and efficiency in job search by the more educated workers seemed to be the dominant aspects in explaining the difference in unemployment incidence and duration among groups with differential educational levels. Educated workers tended to invest more on training and they expected to continue to do so in the future even if they moved to another firm. This would tend to increase their attachment to firms and therefore their expected association with a firm. Since they expected to stay longer, they would also search more thoroughly. On the other hand, a more informed search would improve the probability of a successful job match, thus the

probability would be high that these newly recruited workers would stay longer in their new jobs.

12. Moreover, Mincer concluded that the main results hold regardless of the size of the labor market covered by minimum wage legislation and of the degree of responsiveness of the total labor force to wage changes. He also performed the analysis using single period and multiple period frameworks without significant changes appearing in the main conclusions.

13. I thank Barry Chiswick for drawing my attention to this.

14. In those cases where job promotion required additional training, unions usually placed pressure on the firm to provide training opportunities for senior workers, which reduced both the supply of trained workers from the outside and the benefits of transferable training.

15. Mincer then analyzed the effects of sectoral productivity on the wage structure, distinguishing between the effects on the demand for labor, given the level of human capital, and the effects on the demand for human capital. The results indicated that, in the short run, higher productivity growth reduced wages in that sector relative to wages in other sectors, but in the long run this effect was reversed. Sectors with faster productivity growth presented higher rates of return to education, for both younger and older workers, and these effects did not decline in the long run. Since training increased in the long run in the sectors with faster long-run productivity growth, these sectors also presented steeper wage growth, especially for younger workers.

16. The analysis of the effects of technology over the educational premium faced significant complexities, notably due to the impact of exogenous shocks likely to have changed the demand and supply curves of the labor market during the last decades (Mincer 1991a: 5–6). On the supply side, there were important aspects such as the arrival of the baby boomer cohorts to the labor market during the seventies, and especially of the college graduates. There were also important events on the demand side, namely the evolution of patterns of productivity and the growth of world trade with the acceleration of globalization. Finally, there were important institutional changes in the labor market, with increasing deregulation and especially a decline in union membership.

17. Mincer conceded that the analysis had some limitations. First, the short run considered was a decade, meaning that there could be some shorter run effects that supported popular beliefs about the unemployment effects of technological change. Second, he did not distinguish between technological changes resulting in cost-cutting production of new products and the introduction of new products, though the latter was more likely to have positive employment effects, even in the short run. Finally, the statistical analysis performed was basically cross sectional.

Notes

Chapter 7

1. Mincer's kind but extremely rigorous approach toward students is corroborated by one of his closest friends and colleagues, Gary Becker (2006).
2. Polachek also recalls that this sense of rigor and perfectionism was deeply embedded in Mincer's way of doing economics. In their joint work, Polachek experienced how Mincer took it seriously, even to the point of completely rewriting an entire draft and rerunning the entire set of regressions. Thus, differently from many others, Mincer actually practiced what he preached.
3. It is also interesting to note that someone who devoted so much interest to the labor supply of women has had such an important role in training so many women labor economists (Bloom and Siow 1993).
4. According to Mincer (1997*a*: S27):

   The lifetime accumulation of human capital is the process on which Ben-Porath concentrated by modeling it as an optimal path of human capital investments over the individual's life-cycle ... his approach points out that human capital is a double-edged response to puzzling findings in growth accounting and in income distribution statistics, i.e., whereas aggregate accumulation of human capital is a major factor in generating aggregate economic growth, individual accumulation is the process that generates individual economic growth. The latter has become a fundamental building block of modern labor economics.

   Although the ideas expressed in the model were shared by others, this model provided possibly 'the most succinct, rigorous and fruitful formulation' (Mincer 1997*a*: S44).

5. Accordingly, investments in human capital were done rationally, and therefore most investments occurred at younger ages since later investments faced a shorter payoff period. Moreover, if investments in human capital were profitable, their postponement meant a reduction in their net present value. Postponement of these investments could also be costlier since as earnings increased with lifetime, their opportunity cost would increase. Ben-Porath's model assumed neutrality for matters of simplification. Mincer's empirical testing during the seventies suggested that the decline of investments in human capital was faster than predicted, and with stronger investments in human capital at early ages.
6. As in the case of Gregg Lewis (1967), Ben-Porath (1973), and work by James Heckman.
7. This model was extended in 1967 (published later as an addendum to the second edition of *Human Capital*) to a framework of decisions over time and to investment in human capital. Along these lines was also Becker's work

with one of their graduate students, Gilbert Ghez (1975), on the allocation of resources by families over the lifetime of their members, where they analyzed the acquisition of skills, and why the investment tended to fall with age.

8. This was done at Mincer's 80th anniversary conference that took place at Columbia in July 2002.

References

1. List of Works by Jacob Mincer

Borjas, George and Mincer, Jacob (1976). 'The Distribution of Earnings Profiles in Longitudinal Data', NBER Working Paper 143, Cambridge, MA: National Bureau of Economic Research.

Chiswick, Barry and Mincer, Jacob (1972). 'Time-Series Changes in Personal Income Inequality in the United States from 1939, with Projection to 1985', *Journal of Political Economy*, 80/3 Pt 2: S34–S66.

Danninger, Stephan and Mincer, Jacob (2000). 'Technology, Unemployment, and Inflation', in S. Polachek (ed.), *Worker Well-Being*. Research in Labor Economics Series. 19, Amsterdam: Elsevier, pp. 1–28. (Previously NBER Working Paper 7817.)

Leighton, Linda and Mincer, Jacob (1982). 'Labor Turnover and Youth Unemployment', NBER Working Paper 378, Cambridge, MA: National Bureau of Economic Research.

Mincer, Jacob (1957a). 'A Study on Personal Income Distribution', Ph.D. Dissertation, Columbia University.

____ (1957b). 'Applications of a New Graphic Method in Statistical Measurement', *Journal of the American Statistical Association*, 52/280: 472–8.

____ (1958). 'Investment in Human Capital and Personal Income Distribution', *Journal of Political Economy*, 66/4: 281–302.

____ (1960a). 'Employment and Consumption', *Review of Economics and Statistics*, 42/1: 20–6.

____ (1960b). 'Labor Supply, Family Income, and Consumption', *American Economic Review*, 50/2: 574–583. Papers and Proceedings of the Seventy-second Annual Meeting of the American Economic Association.

____ (1962a). 'On the Job Training: Costs, Returns, and Some Implications', *Journal of Political Economy*, 70/5: 550–79.

____ (1962b). 'Labor Force Participation of Married Women: A Study of Labor Supply', in H. G. Lewis (ed.), *Aspects of Labor Economics*. Princeton, NJ: Princeton University Press, pp. 63–105.

____ (1963). 'Market Prices, Opportunity Costs, and Income Effects', in C. Christ, M. Friedman, L. A. Goldman, Z. Griliches, A. C. Harberger, N.

Liviatan, J. Mincer, Y. Mundlak, M. Nerlove, D. Patinkin, L. G. Telser, and H. Theil (eds.), *Measurement in Economics: Studies in Mathematical Economics and Econometrics in Honor of Yehuda Grunfeld*. Stanford, CA: Stanford University Press, pp. 67–82.

_____ (1966). 'Labor Force Participation and Unemployment', in Robert A. Gordon and Margaret S. Gordon (eds.), *Prosperity and Unemployment*. New York: John Wiley and Sons, pp. 73–134.

_____ (1968a). 'Economic Factors in Labor Force Participation', in D. L. Sills (ed.), *International Encyclopedia of the Social Sciences*, vol. 8. New York: Macmillan and Free Press, pp. 474–81.

_____ (1968b). 'Urban Poverty and Labor Force Participation: Comment', *American Economic Review*, 59/1: 185–93.

_____ (ed.) (1969). *Economic Forecasts and Expectations*. New York: Columbia University Press.

_____ (1970). 'The Distribution of Labor Incomes: A Survey', *Journal of Economic Literature*, 8/1: 1–26.

_____ (1974a). *Schooling, Experience, and Earnings*. New York: Columbia University Press.

_____ (1974b). 'Unemployment Effects of Minimum Wages', NBER Working Paper 39, Cambridge, MA: National Bureau of Economic Research. Published (1976). *Journal of Political Economy*, 84: S87–S104.

_____ (1976). 'Progress in Human Capital Analysis of the Distribution of Earnings', in A. B. Atkinson (ed.), *The Personal Distribution of Incomes*. London: George Allen & Unwin, pp. 136–92. (Previously NBER Working Paper 53.)

_____ (1977). 'Family Migration Decisions', NBER Working Paper 199, Cambridge, MA: National Bureau of Economic Research. Published (1978). *Journal of Political Economy*, 86: 749–73.

_____ (1979). 'Human Capital and Earnings', in D. M. Windham (ed.), *Economic Dimensions of Education*. Washington, DC: National Academy of Education, pp. 1–31. Reprinted in Jacob Mincer (1993a). *Studies in Human Capital*. Cheltenham, UK: Edward Elgar.

_____ (1983a). 'George Stigler's Contributions to Economics', *Scandinavian Journal of Economics*, 85/1: 65–75.

_____ (1983b). 'Union Effects: Wages, Turnover, and Job Training', in Ronald G. Ehrenberg (ed.), *Research in Labor Economics*, vol. 5. Greenwich, CT: JAI Press, pp. 217–52.

_____ (1984a). 'The Economics of Wage Floors', in Ronald G. Ehrenberg (ed.), *Research in Labor Economics*, vol. 6. Greenwich, CT: JAI Press, pp. 311–33.

_____ (1984b). 'Human Capital and Economic Growth', *Economics of Education Review*, 3/3: 195–205. (Previously NBER Working Paper 803.)

_____ (1986). 'Wage Changes in Job Changes', in Ronald G. Ehrenberg (ed.), *Research in Labor Economics*, vol. 8. Pt A. Greenwich, CT: JAI Press, pp. 171–97. Reprinted in Jacob Mincer (1993*a*). *Studies in Human Capital*. Cheltenham, UK: Edward Elgar.

____ (1989). 'Human Capital Responses to Technological Change in the Labor Market', NBER Working Paper 3207, Cambridge, MA: National Bureau of Economic Research. Reprinted in Jacob Mincer (1993*a*). *Studies in Human Capital*. Cheltenham, UK: Edward Elgar.

____ (1991*a*). 'Human Capital, Technology, and the Wage Structure: What Do Time Series Show?', NBER Working Paper 3581, Cambridge, MA: National Bureau of Economic Research. Reprinted in Jacob Mincer (1993*a*). *Studies in Human Capital*. Cheltenham, UK: Edward Elgar.

____ (1991*b*). 'Education and Unemployment of Women', NBER Working Paper 3837, Cambridge, MA: National Bureau of Economic Research. Reprinted in Jacob Mincer (1993*b*). *Studies in Labour Supply*. Cheltenham, UK: Edward Elgar.

____ (1991*c*). 'Education and Unemployment', NBER Working Paper 3838, Cambridge, MA: National Bureau of Economic Research.

____ (1991*d*). 'Job Training: Costs, Returns, and Wage Profiles', in D. Stern and J. M. M. Ritzen (eds.), *Market Failure in Training?* Berlin: Springer-Verlag, pp. 15–39. (Previously NBER Working Paper 3208.)

____ (1993*a*). *Studies in Human Capital*. Cheltenham, UK: Edward Elgar.

____ (1993*b*). *Studies in Labour Supply*. Cheltenham, UK: Edward Elgar.

____ (1994). 'Human Capital: A Review', in Clark Kerr and Paul D. Staudohar (eds.), *Labor Economics and Industrial Relations—Markets and Institutions*. Cambridge, MA: Harvard University Press, pp. 109–41.

____ (1997*a*). 'The Production of Human Capital and the Lifecycle of Earnings: Variations on a Theme', *Journal of Labor Economics*, 15/1: S26–S47. (Previously NBER Working Paper 4838.)

____ (1997*b*). 'Changes in Wage Inequality, 1970–1990', in S. Polachek (ed.), *Research in Labor Economics*, vol. 16. Greenwich, CT: JAI Press, pp. 1–18. (Previously NBER Working Paper 5823.)

____ (1998). 'Investment in US Education and Training', in S. Polachek (ed.), *Research in Labor Economics*, vol. 17. Greenwich, CT: JAI Press, pp. 277–304. (Previously NBER Working Paper 4844.)

____ (2006). 'Technology and the Labor Market', in Shoshana Grossbard (ed.), *Jacob Mincer: A Pioneer of Modern Labor Economics*. New York: Springer-Verlag, pp. 53–77.

____ and Cain, Glen (1969). 'Urban Poverty and Labor Force Participation: Comment', *American Economic Review*, 59/1: 185–94.

____ and Higuchi, Y. (1988). 'Wage Structures and Labor Turnover in the United States and Japan', *Journal of the Japanese and International Economics*, 2: 97–133. Reprinted in Jacob Mincer (1993*a*). *Studies in Human Capital*. Cheltenham, UK: Edward Elgar.

___ and Jovanovic, Boyan (1979). 'Labor Mobility and Wages', NBER Working Paper 357, Cambridge, MA: National Bureau of Economic Research. Reprinted in Sherwin Rosen (ed.) (1981). *Studies in Labor Markets*. Chicago, IL: Chicago University Press, pp. 21–63.

___ and Leighton, Linda (1980). 'Effect of Minimum Wages on Human Capital Formation', NBER Working Paper 441, Cambridge, MA: National Bureau of Economic Research.

___ and Ofek, Haim (1979). 'The Distribution of Lifetime Labor Force Participation of Married Women: Comment', *Journal of Political Economy*, 87/1:197–201.

___ ___ (1982). 'Interrupted Work Careers: Depreciation and Restoration of Human Capital', *Journal of Human Resources*, 17/1: 3–24. (Previously NBER Working Paper 479.)

___ and Polachek, Solomon (1974). 'Family Investments in Human Capital: Earnings of Women', *Journal of Political Economy*, 82/2 Pt 2: S76–S108.

___ and Polachek, Solomon (1978). 'Women's Earnings Reexamined', *Journal of Human Resources*, 13/1: 118–34.

2. List of Works by Other Authors on Jacob Mincer and his Work

Becker, Gary S. (2006). 'Working with Jacob Mincer: Reminiscences of Columbia's Labor Workshop', in Shoshana Grossbard (ed.), *Jacob Mincer: A Pioneer of Modern Labor Economics*. New York: Springer-Verlag, pp. 23–7.

Bloom, David and Siow, Aloysius (1993). 'Some Reflections on Jacob Mincer', *Journal of Labor Economics*, 11/1 Pt 1: v–viii.

Chiswick, Barry (2006). 'Jacob Mincer, Experience and the Distribution of Earnings', in Shoshana Grossbard (ed.), *Jacob Mincer: A Pioneer of Modern Labor Economics*. New York: Springer-Verlag, pp. 109–26.

Gronau, Reuben (2006). 'Jacob Mincer and Labor Supply—Before and Aftermath', in Shoshana Grossbard (ed.), *Jacob Mincer: A Pioneer of Modern Labor Economics*. New York: Springer-Verlag, pp. 149–59.

Grossbard, Shoshana (ed.) (2006). *Jacob Mincer: A Pioneer of Modern Labor Economics*. New York: Springer-Verlag.

Grossman, Michael (2006). 'Household Production and Health', in Shoshana Grossbard (ed.), *Jacob Mincer: A Pioneer of Modern Labor Economics*. New York: Springer-Verlag, pp. 161–72.

Hall, Robert (1975). 'Review of *Schooling, Experience, and Earnings* by Jacob Mincer', *Journal of Political Economy*, 83/2: 444–6.

Heckman, James (2006). 'Some Brief Remarks on the Life and Works of Jacob Mincer', in Shoshana Grossbard (ed.), *Jacob Mincer: A Pioneer of Modern Labor Economics*. New York: Springer-Verlag, pp. 3–5.

References

Heckman, James, Lochner, Lance, and Todd, Petra (2003). 'Fifty Years of Mincer Earnings Regressions', IZA Discussion Paper 775, Bonn, Germany.

Leibowitz, Arleen (2006). 'Household Production and Children', in Shoshana Grossbard (ed.), *Jacob Mincer: A Pioneer of Modern Labor Economics*. New York: Springer-Verlag, pp. 173–85.

Lemieux, Thomas (2006). 'The "Mincer Equation" Thirty Years After *Schooling, Experience, and Earnings*', in Shoshana Grossbard (ed.), *Jacob Mincer: A Pioneer of Modern Labor Economics*. New York: Springer-Verlag, pp. 127–45.

McMahon, Walter (1975). 'Review of *Schooling, Experience, and Earnings*', *Journal of Economic Literature*, 13/2: 544–5.

Polachek, Solomon W. (2006*a*). 'Proving Mincer Right: Mincer's "Overtaking Point" and the Lifecycle Earnings Distribution', in Shoshana Grossbard (ed.), *Jacob Mincer: A Pioneer of Modern Labor Economics*. New York: Springer-Verlag, 81–108.

—— (2006*b*). 'Labor Economics Mincer-Style: A Personal Reflection', in Shoshana Grossbard (ed.), *Jacob Mincer: A Pioneer of Modern Labor Economics*. New York: Springer-Verlag, pp. 29–33.

Rosen, Sherwin (1992). 'Mincering Labour Economics', *Journal of Economic Perspectives*, 6/2: 157–70.

Teixeira, Pedro (2006). 'An Interview with Jacob Mincer', in Shoshana Grossbard (ed.), *Jacob Mincer: A Pioneer of Modern Labor Economics*. New York: Springer-Verlag, pp. 7–18.

Weiss, Yoram (1971). 'Ability and the Investment in Schooling: A Theoretical Note on J. Mincer's "Distribution of Labor Income"', *Journal of Economic Literature*, 9/2: 459–61.

3. Bibliography

Abramowitz, Moses (1956). 'Resource and Output Trends in the United States Since 1870', *American Economic Review*, 46/2: 5–23.

Acemoglu, Daron (1998). 'Why Do New Technologies Complement Skills? Directed Technical Change and Wage Inequality', *Quarterly Journal of Economics*, 113/4: 1055–89.

Aghion, Philippe and Howitt, Peter (1998). *Endogenous Growth Theory*. Cambridge, MA: MIT Press.

Akerlof, George A. (1970). 'The Market for "Lemons": Quality Uncertainty and the Market Mechanism', *Quarterly Journal of Economics*, 84/3: 488–500.

Alderfer, Evan Benner (1935). *Earnings of Skilled Workers in a Manufacturing Enterprise, 1878–1930*. Philadelphia, PA: University of Philadelphia Press.

Altonji, Joseph G. and Blank, Rebecca M. (1999). 'Race and Gender in the Labor Market', in Orley Ashenfelter and David Card (eds.), *Handbook of Labor Economics*, vol. 3C. Amsterdam: Elsevier, pp. 3143–259.

American Economic Association (1956–1983). *Index of Economic Articles*. Homewood, IL: Richard D. Irwin.

American Economic Association (various years). *Annual List of Doctoral Dissertations*. AER, December issues.

Ammon, Otto (1899). 'Some Social Applications of the Doctrine of Probability', *Journal of Political Economy*, VII/2: 204–37.

Angrist, Joshua D. and Krueger, Alan B. (1991). 'Does Compulsory School Attendance Affect Schooling and Earnings?', *Quarterly Journal of Economics*, 106/4: 979–1014.

Arndt, H. W. (1987). *Economic Development—The History of an Idea*. Chicago: University of Chicago Press.

Arrow, Kenneth (1962). 'The Economic Implications of Learning by Doing', *Review of Economic Studies*, 29/3: 155–73.

—— (1973). 'Higher Education as a Filter', *Journal of Public Economics*, 2/3: 193–216.

—— (1993). 'Excellence and Equity in Higher Education', *Education Economics*, 1/1: 5–12.

Ascher, William (1997). 'The Evolution of Postwar Doctrines in Development Economics', *History of Political Economy*, 28/Supp.: 312–56.

Ashenfelter, Orley (1979). 'Estimating the Effect of Training Programs on Earnings with Longitudinal Data', in Ronald G. Ehrenberg (ed.), *Research in Labor Economics*, vol. 1. Greenwich, CT: JAI Press, pp. 97–117.

—— and Ham, John (1979). 'Education, Unemployment and Earnings', *Journal of Political Economy*, 87/5 Pt 2: S99–S116.

—— and Krueger, Alan (1994). 'Estimates of the Economic Return to Schooling from a New Sample of Twins', *American Economic Review*, 84/5: 1157–73.

—— and Mooney, Joseph (1968). 'Graduate Education, Ability, and Earnings', *Review of Economics and Statistics*, 50/1: 78–86.

—— and Rouse, Cecilia (1998). 'Income, Schooling, and Ability: Evidence from a New Sample of Identical Twins', *Quarterly Journal of Economics*, 113/1: 253–84.

—— and Zimmerman, David (1997). 'Estimates of the Returns to Schooling from Sibling Data: Fathers, Sons, and Brothers', *Review of Economics and Statistics*, 79/1: 1–9.

Atkinson, A. B. (1976). *The Personal Distribution of Incomes*. London: George Allen & Unwin.

Autor, David H., Katz, Lawrence, and Krueger, Alan (1998). 'Computing Inequality: Have Computers Changed the Labour Market?', *Quarterly Journal of Economics*, 113/4: 1169–213.

Backhouse, Roger (1997). *Truth and Progress in Economic Knowledge*. Cheltenham, UK: Edward Elgar.

—— (2000). 'Progress in Heterodox Economics', *Journal of the History of Economic Thought*, 22/2: 149–55.

References

Backhouse, Roger (2002). *The Penguin History of Economics*. London: Penguin.

—— and Biddle, Jeff (2000). 'The Concept of Applied Economics: A History of Ambiguity and Multiple Meanings', *History of Political Economy*, 32/Supp.: 1–24.

Backman, Jules and Gainsbrugh, M. R. (1949). 'Productivity and Living Standards (in Productivity)', *Industrial and Labor Relations Review*, 2/2: 163–94.

Bairam, Erkin (1994). 'Institutional Affiliation of Contributors to Top Economic Journals, 1985–1990', *Journal of Economic Literature*, XXXII/2: 674–9.

Barbash, Jack (1994). 'Americanizing the Labor Problem: The Wisconsin School', in Clark Kerr and Paul D. Staudohar (eds.), *Labor Economics and Industrial Relations: Markets and Institutions*. Cambridge, MA: Harvard University Press, pp. 41–65.

Bardhan, Pranab (1993). 'Economics of Development and the Development of Economics', *Journal of Economic Perspectives*, 7/2: 129–42.

Baron, James and Hannan, Michael (1994). 'The Impact of Economics on Contemporary Sociology', *Journal of Economic Literature*, 32/3: 1111–46.

Barton, Glen T. and Cooper, Martin R. (1948). 'Relation of Agricultural Production to Inputs', *Review of Economics and Statistics*, 30/2: 117–26.

Becker, Gary (1955). 'An Economic Analysis of Discrimination', Ph.D. Dissertation, University of Chicago, IL.

—— (1957). *The Economics of Discrimination*. Chicago, IL: University of Chicago Press.

—— (1960). 'An Economic Analysis of Fertility', in *Demographic and Economic Change in Developed Countries*. A Conference of the Universities–National Bureau Committee for Economic Research. Princeton, NJ: Princeton University Press for NBER, pp. 209–31.

—— (1962a). 'Irrational Behavior and Economic Theory', *Journal of Political Economy*, LXX/1: 1–13.

—— (1962b). 'Investment in Human Capital: A Theoretical Analysis', *Journal of Political Economy*, LXX/5 Pt 2: 9–49.

—— (1964). *Human Capital: A Theoretical and Empirical Analysis, With Special Reference to Education*. New York: Columbia University Press.

—— (1965). 'A Theory of the Allocation of Time', *Economic Journal*, LXXV/299: 493–517.

—— (1967). 'Human Capital and the Personal Distribution of Income: An Analytical Approach', Woytinsky Lecture 1. Ann Arbor, MI: University of Michigan, Institute of Public Administration.

—— (1974). 'A Theory of Social Interactions', *Journal of Political Economy*, 82/6: 1063–93.

—— (1976). *The Economic Approach to Human Behavior*. Chicago, IL: University of Chicago Press.

____ (1981). *A Treatise on the Family*. Cambridge, MA: Harvard University Press.

____ (1996). *Accounting for Tastes*. Cambridge, MA: Harvard University Press.

____ and Chiswick, Barry (1966). 'Education and the Distribution of Earnings', *American Economic Review*, LVI/1–2: 358–69.

____ and Tomes, Nigel (1986). 'Human Capital and the Rise and Fall of Families', *Journal of Labor Economics*, 4/3 Pt 2: S1–S39.

Behrman, Jere and Taubman, Paul (1989). 'Is Schooling Mostly in the Genes? Nature-Nurture Decomposition Using Data on Relatives', *Journal of Political Economy*, 97/6: 1425–43.

Ben-Porath, Yoram (1967). 'The Production of Human Capital and the Life Cycle of Earnings', *Journal of Political Economy*, 75/4 Pt 1: 352–65.

____ (1973). 'Labor-Force Participation Rates and the Supply of Labor', *Journal of Political Economy*, 81/2 Pt 2: 697–704.

Berg, Ivar (1970). *Education and the Jobs: The Great Training Robbery*. New York: Praeger.

Blackburn, McKinley and Neumark, David (1993). 'Omitted-Ability Bias and the Increase in the Returns to Schooling', *Journal of Labor Economics*, 11/3: 521–44.

____ and Neumark, David (1995). 'Are OLS Estimates of the Returns to Schooling Biased Downward? Another Look', *Review of Economics and Statistics*, 77/2: 217–30.

Blaug, Mark (1970a). *An Introduction to the Economics of Education*. London: Penguin.

____ (ed.) (1970b). *Economics of Education*. London: Penguin.

____ (1975). 'The Economics of Education in English Classical Political Economy: A Re-Examination', in A. S. Skinner and T. Wilson (eds.), *Essays on Adam Smith*. Oxford, UK: Clarendon Press, pp. 568–99.

____ (1976a). 'The Empirical Status of Human Capital Theory: A Slightly Jaundiced Survey', *Journal of Economic Literature*, 14/3: 827–55.

____ (1976b). *The Economics of Education: An Annotated Bibliography*, 3rd edn. Oxford, UK: Pergamon Press.

____ (1999). *Who's Who in Economics*, 3rd edn. Cheltenham, UK: Edward Elgar.

Blinder, Alan (1974). *Towards an Economic Theory of Income Distribution*. Cambridge, MA: MIT Press.

____ and Weiss, Yoram (1976). 'Human Capital and Labour Supply: A Synthesis', *Journal of Political Economy*, 84/3: 449–72.

Boissiere, M., Knight, J. B., and Sabot, R. H. (1985). 'Earnings, Schooling, Ability, and Cognitive Skills', *American Economic Review*, 75/5: 1016–30.

Borjas, George (1991). 'Immigrants in the US Labor Market: 1940–80', *American Economic Review*, 81/2: 287–91.

____ (1999a). *Heaven's Door, Immigration Policy and the American Economy*. Princeton, NJ: Princeton University Press.

Borjas, George (1999b). 'The Economic Analysis of Immigration', in Orley Ashenfelter and David Card (eds.), *Handbook of Labor Economics*, vol. 3A. Amsterdam: Elsevier, pp. 1697–760.

Bosanquet, Nicholas and Doeringer, Peter (1973). 'Is There a Dual Labor Market in Great Britain?', *Economic Journal*, 83/330: 421–35.

Bowen, William G. and Finegan T. A. (1969). *The Economics of Labor Force Participation*. Princeton, NJ: Princeton University Press.

Bowles, Samuel (1970). 'Migration as Investment: Empirical Tests of the Human Investment Approach to Geographical Mobility', *Review of Economics and Statistics*, 52/4: 356–62.

—— (1972a). 'Schooling and Inequality from Generation to Generation', *Journal of Political Economy*, 80/3 Pt 2: S219–S51 (followed by Becker, Gary S. 'Comment', S252–5).

—— (1972b). 'Understanding Unequal Economic Opportunity', *American Economic Review*, 63/2: 346–56.

—— and Gintis, Herbert (1975). 'The Problem with Human Capital Theory—A Marxian Critique', *American Economic Review*, 65/2: 74–82.

—— and Gintis, Herbert (2000). 'Does Schooling Raise Earnings by Making People Smarter?', in Kenneth Arrow, Samuel Bowles, and Steven Durlauf (eds.), *Meritocracy and Economic Inequality*. Princeton, NJ: Princeton University Press, pp. 118–36.

Bowman, Mary Jean (1970). 'Economics of Education', *Review of Educational Research*, 39/5: 641–70.

—— (1972). 'Time-Series Changes in Personal Income Inequality in the United States from 1939, with Projections to 1985: Comment', *Journal of Political Economy*, 80/3 Pt 2: S67–S71.

Brady, Dorothy (1951). 'Research on the Size Distribution of Income', in *Studies in Income and Wealth*, vol. 13. New York: National Bureau of Economic Research, pp. 3–55.

Bresciani-Turroni, C. (1937). 'On Pareto's Law', *Journal of the Royal Statistical Society*, 100/3: 421–32.

Brown, Emily, Douglas, Paul, Harbison, Frederick, Lazaroff, Louis, Leiserson, William, and Leland, Simeon (1949). 'Harry Alvin Millis, 1873–1948', *American Economic Review*, 39/3: 742–50.

Brown, Sarah and Sessions, John G. (2004). 'Signalling and Screening', in Geraint Johnes and Jill Johnes (eds.), *International Handbook on the Economics of Education*. Cheltenham, UK: Edward Elgar, pp. 58–100.

Brunsman, Howard G. (1953). *Special Reports—Education, 17th Decennial U.S. Census of Population 1950*. Washington, DC: US Department of Commerce, Bureau of Census.

Cain, Glen (1976). 'The Challenge of Segmented Labor Market Theories to Orthodox Theory: A Survey', *Journal of Economic Literature*, 14/4: 1215–57.

Cannan, Edwin (1905). 'The Division of Income', *Quarterly Journal of Economics*, 19/3: 341–69.

Card, David (1999). 'The Causal Effect of Education on Earnings', in Orley Ashenfelter and David Card (eds.), *Handbook of Labor Economics*, vol. 3A. Amsterdam: Elsevier, pp. 1801–63.

——— (2001). 'Estimating the Returns to Schooling: Progress on Some Persistent Econometric Problems', *Econometrica*, 69/5: 1127–60.

——— and Krueger, Alan (1992a). 'Does School Quality Matter? Returns to Education and the Characteristics of Public Schools in the United States', *Journal of Political Economy*, 100/1: 1–40.

——— and Krueger, Alan (1992b). 'School Quality and Black–White Relative Earnings: A Direct Assessment', *Quarterly Journal of Economics*, 107/1: 151–200.

——— and Krueger, Alan (1993). 'Trends in the Relative Black–White Earnings Revisited', *American Economic Review*, 83/2: 85–91.

Carnoy, Martin (1974). *Education as Cultural Imperialism*. New York: Longman.

——— (1977). 'Education and Economic Development: The First Generation', *Economic Development and Cultural Change*, 25/Supp.: S428–S48.

Cawley, John, Conneely, Karen, Heckman, James, and Vytlacil, Edward (1996). 'Cognitive Ability, Wages, and Meritocracy', NBER Working Paper 5645, Cambridge, MA: National Bureau of Economic Research.

Chamberlain, Neil W. (1967). 'Some Second Thoughts on the Concept of Human Capital', Reprinted in Ronald Wysktra (1971). *Human Capital Formation and Manpower Development*. New York: Free Press, pp. 205–15.

Chiswick, Barry (1972). 'Schooling and Earnings of Low Achievers: Comment', *American Economic Review*, 62/4: 752–4.

——— (1973). 'Schooling, Screening, and Income', in Lewis Solmon and Paul Taubman (eds.), *Does College Matter? Some Evidence on the Impact of Higher Education*. New York: Academic Press, pp. 151–8.

——— (1974). *Income Inequality: Regional Analyses Within a Human Capital Framework*. New York: National Bureau of Economic Research.

——— (1978a). 'Generating Inequality: Absolute or Relative Schooling Inequality?', *Journal of Human Resources*, 13/1: 135–7.

——— (1978b). 'The Effect of Americanization on the Earnings of Foreign-born Men', *Journal of Political Economy*, 86/5: 897–921.

——— (1986). 'Human Capital and the Labor Market Adjustment of Immigrants: Testing Alternative Hypotheses', in Oded Stark (ed.), *Research in Human Capital and Development*, vol. 4. Greenwich, CT: JAI Press, pp. 1–26.

Chiswick, Barry (1988). 'Differences in Education and Earnings Across Racial and Ethnic Groups: Tastes, Discrimination, and Investments in Child Quality', *Quarterly Journal of Economics*, 103/3: 571–97.

——— and Miller, Paul (1995). 'The Endogeneity between Language and Earnings: International Analyses', *Journal of Labor Economics*, 13/2: 246–87.

References

Cirillo, Renato (1979). *The Economics of Vilfredo Pareto*. London: Frank Cass.

Clemente, Frank (1973). 'Early Career Determinants of Research Productivity', *American Journal of Sociology*, 79/2: 409–19.

Coats, A. W. (1971). 'The Role of Scholarly Journals in the History of Economics: An Essay', *Journal of Economic Literature*, 9/1: 29–44.

Corcoran, Mary, Jencks, Christopher, and Olneck, Michael (1976). 'The Effects of Family Background on Earnings', *American Economic Review*, 66/2: 430–5.

Crane, Diane (1972). *Invisible Colleges: Diffusion of Knowledge in Scientific Communities*. Chicago, IL: University of Chicago Press.

Dalton, Hugh (1920). *Some Aspects of the Inequality of Incomes in Modern Communities*. London: George Routledge and Sons.

Denison, Edward F. (1962). *The Sources of Economic Growth in the United States and the Alternatives Before Us*. New York: Committee for Economic Development.

Domar, Evsey (1946). 'Capital Expansion, Rate of Growth, and Employment', *Econometrica*, 14/2: 137–47.

Douglas, Paul (1930). *Real Wages in the United States*. Boston, MA: Houghton Mifflin Company.

—— (1934). *The Theory of Wages*. New York: Macmillan.

Dublin, Louis and Lotka, Alfred (1930). *The Money Value of a Man*. New York: Ronald Press.

Duleep, Harriet O. and Regets, Mark C. (1997). 'Immigrant Entry Earnings and Human Capital Growth: Evidence from the 1960–1980 Censuses', in S. Polachek (ed.), *Research in Labor Economics*, vol. 16. Greenwich, CT: JAI Press, pp. 297–317.

Duncan, Otis Dudley (1974). 'Family Investments in Human Capital: Earnings of Women: Comment', *Journal of Political Economy*, 82/2 Pt 2: S109–S10.

Dunlop, John (1944). *Wage Determination Under Trade Unions*, 1st edn. Oxford, UK: Basil Blackwell.

—— (ed.) (1957). *The Theory of Wage Determination*. London: Macmillan.

Eckhaus, Richard (1962). 'Investment in Human Capital: A Comment', *Journal of Political Economy*, 70/5: 501–4.

Eckstein, Zvi and Wolpin, Kenneth (1999). 'Why Youths Drop Out of High School: The Impact of Preferences, Opportunities, and Abilities', *Econometrica*, 67/6: 1295–1339.

Evans, Robert (1963). 'Wage Differentials, Excess Demand for Labor, and Inflation: A Note', *Review of Economics and Statistics*, 45/1: 95–8.

Fisher, Irving (1896). 'What is Capital?', *Economic Journal*, 6/24: 509–34.

—— (1897). 'Senses of "Capital"', *Economic Journal*, 7/26: 199–213.

Frängsmyr, Tore (ed.) (1993). 'Gary S. Becker, Autobiography', *The Nobel Prizes 1992*, Stockholm: Nobel Foundation. http://nobelprize.org/nobel_prizes/economics/laureates/1992/becker-autobio.html

Freeman, Richard B. (1976). *The Over-educated American.* New York: Academic Press.

—— (1987). 'Demand for Education', in Orley Ashenfelter and Richard Layard (eds.), *Handbook of Labor Economics*, vol. 1. Amsterdam: Elsevier, pp. 357–86.

Friedman, Milton (1953). 'Choice, Chance, and the Personal Distribution of Income', *Journal of Political Economy*, LXI/4: 277–90.

—— and Kuznets, Simon (1945). *Income from Independent Professional Practice.* New York: NBER.

Galton, Francis ([1869] 1978). *Hereditary Genius: An Inquiry Into its Laws and Consequences.* London: J. Friedmann.

Ghez, Gilbert and Becker, Gary S. (1975). *The Allocation of Time and Goods Over the Life Cycle.* New York: Columbia University Press.

Gintis, Herbert (1971). 'Education, Technology, and the Characteristics of Worker Productivity', *American Economic Review*, 61/2: 266–79.

Gisser, Micha (1965). 'Schooling and the Farm Problem', *Econometrica*, 33/3:582–92.

Glasser, Carrie (1940). *Wage Differentials.* New York: Columbia University Press.

Goldberger, Arthur S. (1979). 'Heritability', *Economica*, 46/184: 327–47.

Goldin, Claudia and Katz, Lawrence (1998). 'The Origins of Technology-Skill Complementarity', *Quarterly Journal of Economics*, 113/3: 693–732.

—— and Polachek, Solomon (1987). 'Residual Differences by Sex: Perspectives on the Gender Gap in Earnings', *American Economic Review*, 77/2: 143–51.

Goldner, William (1955). 'Spatial and Locational Aspects of Metropolitan Labor Markets', *American Economic Review*, 45/1: 112–28.

Gorseline, Donald Eugene (1932). 'The Effect of Schooling Upon Income', Ph.D. Dissertation, Graduate Council of Indiana University.

Greenwood, Michael (1997). 'Internal Migration in Developed Countries', in Mark Rosenzweig and Oded Stark (eds.), *Handbook of Population and Family Economics.* Amsterdam: Elsevier, pp. 647–720.

Griliches, Zvi (1957). 'Hybrid Corn: An Exploration in the Economics of Technological Change', Ph.D. Dissertation, University of Chicago. Published (1957). *Econometrica*, 25/4: 501–22.

—— (1977). 'Estimating the Returns to Schooling: Some Econometric Problems', *Econometrica*, 45/1: 1–22.

—— (1979). 'Sibling Models and Data in Economics: Beginnings of a Survey', *Journal of Political Economy*, 87/5 Pt 2: S37–S64.

—— and Mason, William (1972). 'Education, Income, and Ability', *Journal of Political Economy*, 80/3 Pt 2: S74–S103.

Gronau, Reuben (1980). 'Home Production—A Forgotten Industry', *Review of Economics and Statistics*, 62/3: 408–16.

—— (1997). 'The Theory of Home Production: The Past Ten Years', *Journal of Law and Economics*, 15/2: 197–205.

Groot, Wim and Oosterbeek, Hessel (1994). 'Earnings Effects of Different Components of Schooling; Human Capital Versus Screening', *Review of Economics and Statistics*, 76/2: 317–21.

Grossbard-Schechtman, Shoshana (2001). 'The New Home Economics at Columbia and Chicago', *Feminist Economics*, 7/3: 103–30.

Grossman, Michael (1972). 'On the Concept of Health Capital and the Demand for Health', *Journal of Political Economy*, 80/2: 223–55.

—— (2000). 'The Human Capital Model', in Anthony Culyer and Joseph Newhouse (eds.), *Handbook of Health Economics*. Amsterdam: Elsevier, pp. 308–408.

Grubb, W. Norton (1993). 'Further Tests of Screening on Education and Observed Ability', *Economics of Education Review*, 12/2: 125–36.

Hanoch, Giora (1967). 'An Economic Analysis of Earnings and Schooling', *Journal of Human Resources*, 2/3: 310–29.

Hanushek, Eric A. (1986). 'The Economics of Schooling: Production and Efficiency in Public Schools', *Journal of Economic Literature*, 24/3: 1141–77.

Harbison, Frederick (1940). 'Seniority in Mass-production Industries', *Journal of Political Economy*, 48/6: 851–64.

Harrod, Roy (1939). 'An Essay in Dynamic Theory', *Economic Journal*, 49/193: 14–33.

Hartog, Joop (1983). 'To Graduate or Not—Does it Matter?', *Economic Letters*, 12/2: 193–9.

Hause, John (1971). 'Ability and Schooling as Determinants of Lifetime Earnings or If You're So Smart Why Aren't You Rich?', *American Economic Review*, 61/2: 289–98.

—— (1975). 'Ability and Schooling as Determinants of Lifetime Earnings, or If You're So Smart, Why Aren't You Rich', in Thomas Juster (ed.), *Education, Income, and Human Behavior*. New York: McGraw-Hill, pp. 123–45.

Haveman, Robert and Wolfe, Barbara (1995). 'The Determinants of Children's Attainment: A Review of Methods and Findings', *Journal of Economic Literature*, 33/4: 1829–78.

Heckman, James (1990). 'The Central Role of the South in Accounting for the Economic Progress of Black Americans', *American Economic Review*, 80/2: 242–6.

—— (1993). 'What Has Been Learned About Labour Supply in the Past Twenty Years?', *American Economic Review*, 83/2: 116–21.

—— and Payner, Brook (1989). 'Determining the Impact of Federal Antidiscrimination Policy on the Economic Status of Blacks: A Study of South Carolina', *American Economic Review*, 79/1: 138–77.

—— and Polachek, Solomon (1974). 'Empirical Evidence on the Functional Form of the Earnings-Schooling Relationship', *Journal of the American Statistical Association*, 69/346: 350–4.

_____ and Vytlacil, Edward (2000). 'Identifying the Role of Cognitive Ability in Explaining the Level of Change in the Return to Schooling', NBER Working Paper 7820, Cambridge, MA: National Bureau of Economic Research.

_____ and Walker, James R. (1990). 'The Relationship Between Wages and Income and the Timing and Spacing of Births: Evidence from Swedish Longitudinal Data', *Econometrica*, 58/6: 1411–41.

Hicks, J. R. (1932). *The Theory of Wages*. London: Macmillan.

Hill, M. Anne and O'Neill, June (1994). 'Family Endowments and the Achievement of Young Children with Special Reference to the Underclass', *Journal of Human Resources*, 29/4: 1064–1100.

Hirsch, Abraham and de Marchi, Neil (1990). *Milton Friedman—Economics in Theory and Practice*. Ann Arbor, MI: University of Michigan Press.

Hungerford, Thomas and Solon, Gary (1987). 'Sheepskin Effects in the Returns to Education', *Review of Economics and Statistics*, LXIX/1: 175–7.

Jaeger, David and Page, Marianne (1996). 'Degrees Matter: New Evidence on Sheepskin Effects in the Returns to Education', *Review of Economics and Statistics*, 78/4: 733–40.

Jencks, Christopher, Bartlett, Susan, Corcoran, Mary, Gouse, James, Eaglesfield, David, Jackson, Gregory, McClelland, Kent, Meuser, Peter, Olneck, Michael, Schwartz, Joseph, Ward, Sherry, and Williams, Jill (1979). *Who Gets Ahead?: The Determinants of Economic Success in America*. New York: Basic Books.

_____ Smith, Marshall, Acland, Henry, Bane, Mary Jo, Cohen, David, Gintis, Herbert, Heyns, Barbara, and Michelson, Stephen (1972). *Inequality: A Reassessment of the Effect of Family and Schooling in America*. New York: Basic Books.

Kane, Thomas J. and Rouse, Cecilia E. (1995). 'Labor-Market Returns to Two- and Four-Year College', *American Economic Review*, 85/3: 600–14.

Katona, George and Fisher, Janet (1951). 'Postwar Changes in the Income of Identical Consumer Units', in *Studies in Income and Wealth*, vol. 13. New York: National Bureau of Economic Research, pp. 62–119.

Katz, Lawrence and Autor, David (1999). 'Changes in the Wage Structure and Earnings Inequality', in Orley Ashenfelter and David Card (eds.), *Handbook of Labor Economics*, vol. 3A. Amsterdam: Elsevier, pp. 1463–555.

Kaufman, Bruce E. (ed.) (1988). *How Labor Markets Work*. Lexington, MA: Lexington Books.

_____ (1993). *The Origins and Evolution of the Field of Industrial Relations in the United States*. Ithaca, NY: Cornell University Press.

Keane, Michael P. and Wolpin, Kenneth (1997). 'The Career Decisions of Young Men', *Journal of Political Economy*, 105/3: 473–522.

Keat, Paul G. (1959). 'Changes in Occupational Wage Structure, 1900–1956', Ph.D. Dissertation, University of Chicago.

Kendrick, John (1961). *Productivity Trends in the United States*. Princeton, NJ: NBER and Princeton University Press.

Kerr, Clark (1954). 'The Balkanization of Labor Markets', in E. Wight Bakke (ed.), *Labor Mobility and Economic Opportunity*, Cambridge, MA: MIT Press, pp. 92–110.

—— and Staudohar, Paul D. (eds.) (1994). *Labor Economics and Industrial Relations—Markets and Institutions*. Cambridge, MA: Harvard University Press.

Kiker, B. F. (1968). *Human Capital in Retrospect*. Columbia, SC: University of South Carolina.

Klamer, Aro (1989). 'An Accountant Among Economists: Conversations with Sir John R. Hicks', *Journal of Economic Perspectives*, 3/4: 167–80.

Krueger, Alan B. and Lindhal, Mikale (2001). 'Education for Growth: Why and for Whom?', *Journal of Economic Literature*, 39/4: 1101–36.

Kuznets, Simon (1953). *Shares of Upper Income Groups in Income and Savings*. New York: NBER.

Lalonde, Robert and Topel, Robert (1991). 'Immigrants in the American Labor Market: Quality, Assimilation, and Distribution Effects', *American Economic Review*, 81/2: 297–302.

Layard, P. R. and Psacharopoulos, G. (1974). 'The Screening Hypothesis and the Returns to Education', *Journal of Political Economy*, 82/5: 985–8.

Leibowitz, Arleen (1974). 'Education and Home Production', *American Economic Review*, 64/2: 243–50.

—— (1976). 'Years and Intensity of Schooling Investment', *American Economic Review*, 66/3: 321–34.

—— (1977). 'Parental Inputs and Children's Achievement', *Journal of Human Resources*, 12/2: 242–51.

Lester, Richard (1941). *Economics of Labor*, 1st edn. New York: Macmillan.

—— (1946). 'Shortcomings of Marginal Analysis for Wage-Employment Problems', *American Economic Review*, 36/1: 63–82.

—— (1947*a*). 'Marginalism, Minimum Wages, and Labor Markets', *American Economic Review*, 37/1: 135–48.

—— (1947*b*). 'Reflections on the "Labor Monopoly" Issue', *Journal of Political Economy*, 55/6: 513–36.

—— (1949). 'Equilibrium of the Firm', *American Economic Review*, 39/2: 478–84.

Leven, Maurice (1938). *The Income Structure of the United States*. Washington, DC: Brookings Institution.

Levy, Frank and Murnane, Richard (1992). 'U.S. Earnings Levels and Earnings Inequality: A Review of Recent Trends and Proposed Explanations', *Journal of Economic Literature*, 30/3: 1333–81.

Lewis, H. Gregg (1963). *Unionism and Relative Wages in the United States*. Chicago, IL: University of Chicago Press.

—— (1967). 'On Income and Substitution Effects in Labor Force Participation', Unpublished Paper, University of Chicago.

Lindbeck, Assar (ed.) (1992). 'Theodore W. Schultz, Autobiography', in *Nobel Lectures, Economics, 1969–1980*. Singapore: World Scientific Publishing Co. http://nobelprize.org/nobel_prizes/economics/laureates/1979/schultz-autobio.html

Long, Clarence (1958). *The Labor Force Under Changing Income and Employment*. Princeton, NJ: Princeton University Press for the NBER.

Lucas, R. (1988). 'On the Mechanics of Economic Development', *Journal of Monetary Economics*, 22/1: 3–42.

Lydall, H. F. (1976). 'Theories of the Distribution of Earnings', in A. B. Atkinson (ed.), *The Personal Distribution of Incomes*. London: George Allen & Unwin, pp. 15–46.

Machin, Stephen (2004). 'Skill-biased Technical Change and Educational Outcomes', in Geraint Johnes and Jill Johnes (eds.), *International Handbook on the Economics of Education*. Cheltenham, UK: Edward Elgar, pp. 189–210.

Machlup, Fritz (1946). 'Marginal Analysis and Empirical Research', *American Economic Review*, 36/4: 519–46.

—— (1947). 'Rejoinder to an Antimarginalist', *American Economic Review*, 37/1: 148–54.

Marshall, Alfred ([1920] 1961). *Principles of Economics*, 9th variorum edn. with annotations by C. W. Guillebaud. 2 vols, London: Macmillan and Co.

Mathios, Alan D. (1989). 'Education, Variation in Earnings, and Nonmonetary Compensation', *Journal of Human Resources*, 24/3: 456–68.

McClaurin, W. Rupert and Myers, Charles (1942). 'Wages and the Movement of Factory Labor', *Quarterly Journal of Economics*, 57/2: 241–64.

McNulty, Paul J. (1966). 'Labor Market Analysis and the Development of Labor Economics', *Industrial and Labor Relations Review*, 19/4: 538–48.

—— (1986). *The Origins and Development of Labor Economics*. Cambridge, MA: MIT Press.

Mears, Eliot G. (1923). 'Financial Aspects of American Immigration', *Economic Journal*, 33/131: 332–42.

Michael, Robert (1972). *The Effect of Education on Efficiency in Consumption*. New York: NBER.

Miller, Herman (1951a). 'Changes in Income Distribution in the United States', *Journal of the American Statistical Association*, 46/256: 438–41.

—— (1951b). 'Factors Related to Recent Changes in Income Distribution in the United States', *Review of Economics and Statistics*, 33/3: 214–18.

—— (1955). *Income of the American People*. New York: John Wiley and Sons.

Mishel, Lawrence and Bernstein, Jared (1998). 'Technology and the Wage Structure: Has Technology's Impact Accelerated since the 1970s?', in S. Polachek (ed.), *Research in Labor Economics*, vol. 17. Greenwich, CT: JAI Press, pp. 305–55.

Mitchell, Wesley C., King, Wilford, Macaulay, Frederick, and Knauth, Oswald (1921). *Income in the United States, Its Amount and Distribution, 1909–1919*. 2 vols. New York: Harcourt, Brace and Company.

Mongin, Philippe (1992). 'The "Full-Cost" Controversy of the 1940s and 1950s: A Methodological Assessment', *History of Political Economy*, 24/2: 311–56.

Mooney, Joseph (1967). 'Urban Poverty and Labor Force Participation', *American Economic Review*, 57/1: 104–19.

―― (1969). Urban Poverty and Labor Force Participation: Reply', *American Economic Review*, 59/1: 194–8.

Moore, Henry (1911). *The Laws of Wages*. London: Macmillan.

Morgan, Mary and Rutherford, Malcolm (eds.) (1998). *From Interwar Pluralism to Postwar Neoclassicism*. Supplement to *History of Political Economy*, vol. 30. Durham NC: Duke University Press.

Murphy, Kevin and Welch, Finis (1993). 'Occupational Change and the Demand for Skill, 1940–1990', *American Economic Review*, 83/2: 122–6.

Nelson, Richard R. and Phelps, Edmund S. (1966). 'Investment in Humans, Technological Diffusion, and Economic Growth', *American Economic Review*, 56/1–2: 69–75.

Neumark, David and Taubman, Paul (1995). 'Why do Wage Profiles Slope Upwards? Tests of the General Human Capital Model', *Journal of Labor Economics*, 13/4: 736–61.

Nickell, Stephen (1979). 'Education and Lifetime Patterns of Unemployment', *Journal of Political Economy*, 87/5 Pt 2: S117–S31.

Olneck, Michael (1979). 'The Effects of Education', in Christopher Jencks, Susan Bartlett, Mary Corcoran, James Crouse, David Eaglesfield, Gregory Jackson, Kent McClelland, Peter Mueser, Michael Olneck, Joseph Schwartz, Sherry Ward, and Jill Williams (eds.), *Who Gets Ahead? The Determinants of Economic Success in America*. New York: Basic Books, pp. 159–90.

O'Neill, Dave (1970). 'The Effect of Discrimination on Earnings: Evidence from Military Test Score Results', *Journal of Human Resources*, 5/4: 475–86.

O'Neill, June (1985). 'The Trend in the Male–Female Wage Gap in the United States', *Journal of Labor Economics*, 3/1 Pt 2: S91–S116.

Oosterbeek, Hessel (1993). 'Evidence on Screening: A Comment', *Economics of Education Review*, 12/1: 89–90.

Pierson, Frank C. (1957). 'An Evaluation of Wage Theory', in George W. Taylor and Frank C. Pierson (eds.), *New Concepts in Wage Determination*. New York: McGraw-Hill, pp. 3–31.

Polachek, Solomon (1995). 'Earnings Over the Life Cycle: What Do Human Capital Models Explain?', *Scottish Journal of Political Economy*, 42/3: 267–89.

Polkinghorn, Robert (1958). 'Regional Wage Differentials', Ph.D. Dissertation, University of Chicago.

Psacharopoulos, George (1979). 'On the Weak Versus the Strong Version of the Screening Hypothesis', *Economic Letters*, 4/2: 181–5.

Ramstad, Yngve (1981). 'The Analytical and Methodological Orientations of Institutional Economists: Inferences from the Case of Labor Economics', Ph.D. Dissertation, UC-Berkeley.

Reder, Melvin (1954). 'Age and Income', *American Economic Review*, 44/2: 661–70.

—— (1955). 'The Theory of Occupational Wage Differentials', *American Economic Review*, 45/5: 833–52.

Rees, Albert (1950). 'Labor Unions and the Price System', *Journal of Political Economy*, 58/3: 254–63.

Reich, Michael, Gordon, David, and Edwards, Richard (1973). 'A Theory of Labor Market Segmentation', *American Economic Review*, 63/2: 359–65.

Reid, Margaret (1954). 'Distribution of Income and Consumption', in Elisabeth Hoyt, Margaret Reid, Joseph McConnell, and Janet Hooks (eds.), *American Income and Its Use*. New York: Harper and Bros, pp. 81–214.

Reynolds, Lloyd (1951). *The Structure of Labor Markets*. Westport, CT: Greenwood Press.

Robbins, Lionel (1934). 'Remarks Upon Certain Aspects of the Theory of Costs', *Economic Journal*, XLIV/173: 1–18. Reprinted in James M. Buchanan and George F. Thirlby (eds.) (1973), *L.S.E. Essays on Cost*. London: Weidenfeld & Nicolson, pp. 19–42.

Rodgers, Daniel (1969). 'Private Rates of Return to Education in the United States: A Case Study', *Yale Economic Essays*, 9/1: 89–134.

Romer, Paul (1986). 'Increasing Returns and Long-Run Growth', *Journal of Political Economy*, 94/5: 1002–37.

Rosen, Sherwin (1977). 'Human Capital: A Survey of Empirical Research', in Ronald G. Ehrenberg (ed.), *Research in Labor Economics*, vol. 1. Greenwich, CT: JAI Press, pp. 3–39.

Rosenzweig, Mark (1995). 'Why Are There Returns to Schooling?', *American Economic Review*, 85/2: 153–8.

Ross, Arthur (1948). *Trade Union Wage Policy*. Berkeley and Los Angeles: University of California Press.

Rostow, W. W. (1990). *Theorists of Economic Growth from David Hume to the Present*. New York and Oxford: Oxford University Press.

Rutherford, Malcolm (1997). 'American Institutionalism and the History of Economic Thought', *Journal of the History of Economic Thought*, 19/2: 178–95.

Samuels, Warren J. (1998). 'The Transformation of American Economics', *Research in the History of Economic Thought and Methodology*, 16: 179–223.

Sanborn, Henry (1960). 'Income Differences Between Men and Women in the United States', Ph.D. Dissertation, University of Chicago.

Sandell, Steven and Shapiro, David (1978). 'An Exchange: The Theory of Human Capital and the Earnings of Women: A Reexamination of the Evidence', *Journal of Human Resources*, 13/1: 103–17.

Schultz, Theodore (1959). 'Investment in Man: An Economist's View', *Social Service Review*, XXXIII/2: 109–17.

—— (1960). 'Capital Formation by Education', *Journal of Political Economy*, 68/6: 571–83.

—— (1961a). 'Investment in Human Capital', *American Economic Review*, LI/1: 1–17.

—— (1961b). 'Investment in Human Capital : Reply', *American Economic Review*, LI/5: 1035–9.

—— (1963). *The Economic Value of Education*. New York: Columbia University Press.

—— (1964). *Transforming Traditional Agriculture*. New Haven, CT: Yale University Press.

—— (1971). *Investment in Human Capital: The Role of Education and of Research*. New York: Free Press.

—— (ed.) (1974). *Economics of the Family: Marriage, Children and Human Capital*. Chicago, IL: University of Chicago Press for NBER.

—— (1975). 'The Value of the Ability to Deal with Disequilibria', *Journal of Economic Literature*, 13/3: 827–46.

Schumpeter, Joseph (1949). 'Vilfredo Pareto (1848–1923)', *Quarterly Journal of Economics*, 63/2: 147–73.

Schwartz, Aba (1971). 'On Efficiency of Migration', *Journal of Human Resources*, 6/2: 193–205.

—— (1973). 'Interpreting the Effects of Distance on Migration', *Journal of Political Economy*, 84/5: 1153–69.

—— (1976). 'Migration, Age, and Education', *Journal of Political Economy*, 84/4 Pt 1: 701–20.

Shister, Joseph (1946). 'The Locus of Union Control in Collective Bargaining', *Quarterly Journal of Economics*, 60/4: 513–45.

Sjaastad, Larry (1962). 'The Costs and Returns of Human Migration', *Journal of Political Economy*, 70/5 Pt 2: 80–93.

Slichter, Sumner (1939). 'The Changing Character of American Industrial Relations', Reprinted in John T. Dunlop (ed.) (1961). *Potentials of the American Economy: Selected Essays of Sumner H. Slichter*. Cambridge, MA: Harvard University Press.

—— (1941). *Union Policies and Industrial Management*. Washington, DC: Brookings Institution.

Smith, James (1978). 'The Improving Economic Status of Black Americans', *American Economic Review*, 68/2: 171–8.

—— and Ward, Michael (1989). 'Women in the Labor Market and in the Family', *Journal of Economic Perspectives*, 3/1: 9–23.

_____ and Welch, Finis (1987). 'Race and Poverty: A Forty-Year Record', *American Economic Review*, 77/2: 152–8.

Solon, Gary (1999). 'Intergenerational Mobility in the Labor Market', in Orley Ashenfelter and David Card (eds.), *Handbook of Labor Economics*, vol. 3A. Amsterdam: Elsevier, pp. 1761–1800.

Solow, Robert (1956). 'A Contribution to the Theory of Economic Growth', *Quarterly Journal of Economics*, 65/1: 65–94.

_____ (1957). 'Technical Change and the Aggregate Production Function', *Review of Economics and Statistics*, 39/3: 312–20.

Spence, Michael (1973). 'Job Market Signaling', *Quarterly Journal of Economics*, 87/3: 355–74.

_____ (1974). *Market Signalling*. Cambridge, MA: Harvard University Press.

_____ (2002). 'Signalling in Retrospect and the Informational Structure of Markets', *American Economic Review*, 92/3: 434–59.

Stevens, Philip and Weale, Martin (2004). 'Education and Economic Growth', in Geraint Johnes and Jill Johnes (eds.), *International Handbook on the Economics of Education*. Cheltenham, UK: Edward Elgar, pp. 164–88.

Stigler, George (1962). 'Information in the Labor Market', *Journal of Political Economy*, 70/5 Pt 2: 94–105.

Stiglitz, Joseph (1975). 'The Theory of "Screening", Education, and the Distribution of Income', *American Economic Review*, 65/3: 283–300.

Swan, T. W. (1956). 'Economic Growth and Capital Accumulation', *Economic Record*, 32/Nov.: 334–61.

Tachibanaki, Toshiaki (ed.) (1998). *Wage Differentials: An International Comparison*. London: Macmillan.

Taubman, Paul (1975). *Sources of Inequality in Earnings*. Amsterdam: North-Holland.

_____ (1976). 'The Determinants of Earnings: Genetics, Family, and Other Environments; A Study of White Male Twins', *American Economic Review*, 66/5: 858–70.

_____ and Wales, Terence (1972). 'Mental Ability and Higher Educational Attainment in the 20th Century', Occasional Paper 118, New York: NBER.

_____ and Wales, Terence (1973). *Higher Education and Earnings. College as an Investment and as a Screening Device*. New York: McGraw-Hill.

Teixeira, Pedro (2000). 'A Portrait of the Economics of Education, 1960–1997', *History of Political Economy*, 32/Supp.: 257–87.

_____ (2003). The Human Capital Revolution in Economic Thought, PhD Dissertation, University of Exeter.

_____ (2005). 'The "Human Capital Revolution" in Economics', *History of Economic Ideas*, 13/2: 129–48.

Thurow, Lester (1970a). 'Analyzing the American Income Distribution', *American Economic Review*, 60/2: 261–9.

_____ (1970b). *Investment in Human Capital*. Belmont, CA: Wadsworth.

Thurow, Lester (1975). *Generating Inequality*. London: Macmillan.

Topel, Robert (1999). 'Labor Markets and Economic Growth', in Orley Ashenfelter and David Card (eds.), *Handbook of Labor Economics*, vol. 3A. Amsterdam: Elsevier, pp. 2943–84.

Tucker, Irvin B. III (1986). 'Evidence on the Weak and the Strong Versions of the Screening Hypothesis in the United States', *Economic Letters*, 21/4: 391–4.

Ulman, Lloyd (1951). 'Union Wage Policy and the Supply of Labor', *Quarterly Journal of Economics*, LXV/2: 237–51.

Walsh, John R. (1935). 'Capital Concept Applied to Man', *Quarterly Journal of Economics*, XLIX/2: 255–85.

Weiss, Andrew (1995). 'Human Capital vs. Signalling Explanations of Wages', *Journal of Economic Perspectives*, 9/4: 133–54.

Welch, Finis (1967). 'Labor-Market Discrimination: An Interpretation of Income Differences in the Rural South', *Journal of Political Economy*, 75/3: 225–40.

West, E. G. (1964). 'The Role of Education in Nineteenth-Century Doctrines of Political Economy', *British Journal of Educational Studies*, 12/2: 161–72.

Willis, Robert (1986). 'Wage Determinants: A Survey and Reinterpretation of Human Capital Earnings Functions', in Orley Ashenfelter and Richard Layard (eds.), *Handbook of Labor Economics*, vol. 1. Amsterdam: Elsevier, pp. 525–602.

Yonay, Yuval (1998). *The Struggle Over the Soul of Economics—Institutionalism and Neoclassical Economists in America between the Wars*. Princeton, NJ: Princeton University Press.

Zeman, Morton (1955). 'A Quantitative Analysis of White-Nonwhite Income Differentials in the United States', Ph.D. Dissertation, University of Chicago.

Index

Index

Burns, Arthur 8
business cycles 7

Cain, Glen 135
Cannan, E. 35, 39
capital:
fixed relationship between labor
and 22
physical 23, 24, 126
capital formation 22
capital intensity 128
capital investment 20
capital scarcity 24
Card, D. 67, 76, 81
Carnoy, Martin 64, 124
causal analysis 38
Cawley, J. 20
chance 39, 40, 42, 50, 66
child care cost 97, 98
Chiswick, Barry 11, 55, 66, 101, 113, 139,
141, 142–3, 144, 145
choice 23, 43–4, 158
children's 149
endogeneity of 79
occupational 41, 42, 60, 104
political 24
women, regarding training and
occupation 112
work-leisure 93
Cirillo, R. 34
City College of New York 7, 10
Clemente, F. 137
cognitive skills 78–9
collective bargaining 88
Columbia University 7–8, 9, 12, 26, 82,
101, 113, 135, 136, 137, 139, 141,
142, 143, 144, 155
Workshop on Labor Economics 10, 11,
149, 150
Commons, John R. 83
community colleges 80
compensation 26, 28, 29, 75
inevitable 42
compensatory principle 18, 40–1,
60
competition 42
supply-demand 84
complementarity 22, 51, 118, 119
physical capital and skilled labor
126
technological change and skills 68
unplanned 44
concentration camps 4

consumption 90, 93, 96, 97, 100, 147,
148, 154
continuity 41
Corcoran, M. 65
Cornell 137
counterintelligence 5
Crane, D. 132
credentials 52, 70, 71, 75, 81
cross-sectional data 92–3, 98, 104, 123,
127
cumulative knowledge 41
Czechoslovakia 3–4, 5–6

Dalton, H. 35, 39
Danninger, S. 129
Danzig (Gdansk) 4
decision-making 96
demand 68, 97, 121
combination of supply and 128
educated workers 128
educational 64
labor 86
noncompetitive practices 29
skilled labor 125, 128, 129
De Marchi, N. 26, 40
demographic transition 124–5
Denison, Edward 45
Denmark 3
deportations 4
detention camps 5
developing countries 78, 124
need to reformulate economic role of
government in 23–4
development economics 23
discontinuity 102
discrimination 144
class 30
effectiveness of 67
labor market 47, 66, 69
proportion of wage gap due to
102
social 30, 65
disemployment effect 120
disequilibria 26, 124
division of labor 112
Doeringer, Peter 69
Domar, Evsey 21–2
Douglas, Paul 84, 92
dropouts 72, 73, 80
Duleep, H. O. 145
Duncan, Otis 103
Dunlop, John 85, 88
Dutch working population 72–3

Index

Index

Index

substitutability 94, 96, 98, 99
Sudeten 4
supply 68, 120, 121
  combination of demand and 128
  noncompetitive practices 29
  see also labor supply
surplus workers 110
Survey of Consumer Expenditures
  (1950) 91, 93
Swan, T. W. 22
Swanson, Ernst 7
Sweden 78

Tachibanaki, T. 76
Tanzania 78
tastes 64, 99
Taubman, Paul 65, 75, 141
Taussig, F. W. 39
technical advances 25
technological change:
  effects on unemployment 129
  rapid 116, 127, 129
  skill-biased 67, 68
technological innovation 126
technological progress 7
  alternative measures of 129
  impact on employment 123
  JM's analysis of 128
technology 7, 123–9
Teixeira, P. N. 90, 92
Thurow, Lester 50, 63
time allocation 97, 99–100, 118, 146–7
time-series data 92–3
Tomaszow 2
trade unions, *see* unionism
training 8, 23, 25, 35
  better-educated workers receive
    more 75
  choices in terms of 43–4
  cost of 27–8, 42, 45–6, 72, 116, 121,
    129
  decisions concerning 38
  externalities associated with 124
  formal 11, 30, 45
  general 30, 47, 53, 76, 118, 121, 122,
    123
  higher remuneration for occupations
    requiring 42
  impact of differences in 41
  informal 11, 45
  interaction between labor turnover
    and 119
  JM's emphasis on 76

labor market regulations impact
  on 119–23
older workers deterred from investing
  in 127
opportunities for 27, 43, 69, 120–1
postschool 11, 12, 43, 45
prior to current job 117
professional 20, 27
rate of return to 46–7
role of length of 26
specific 30, 47, 53, 76, 101, 121
underinvestment of 27
unequal access/opportunities 26, 75
visibility of 24
women's choices regarding 112
see also on-the-job training
transportation costs 97
trends 22, 56, 67–8
  educational and occupational 99
  service employment 128
turnover 53, 69, 109, 116, 122
  effects of productivity growth on 127
  interaction between job training
    and 119
  intralabor force 119
  migration and its impact on 16
  probability of 58
  reduction in 129
  significant 115
  strong variation in the short run 96
  women 47, 118
twin studies 75

Ukraine 3
Ulman, L. 88
unemployment:
  conditional 129
  decline in incidence of 128
  disguised 116
  education and 77, 116–19
  measured 120
  probability of 47
  technological 127, 129
  unskilled labor 129
  youth 117, 121
unionism/unionization 8, 68, 83, 84, 88,
  120, 121
  JM's critical views about the role of 122
  wage differentials 123
United States:
  Bureau of Census 27, 28, 31, 48
  Bureau of Labor Statistics 91, 93
  Department of Commerce 26, 28